I0709685

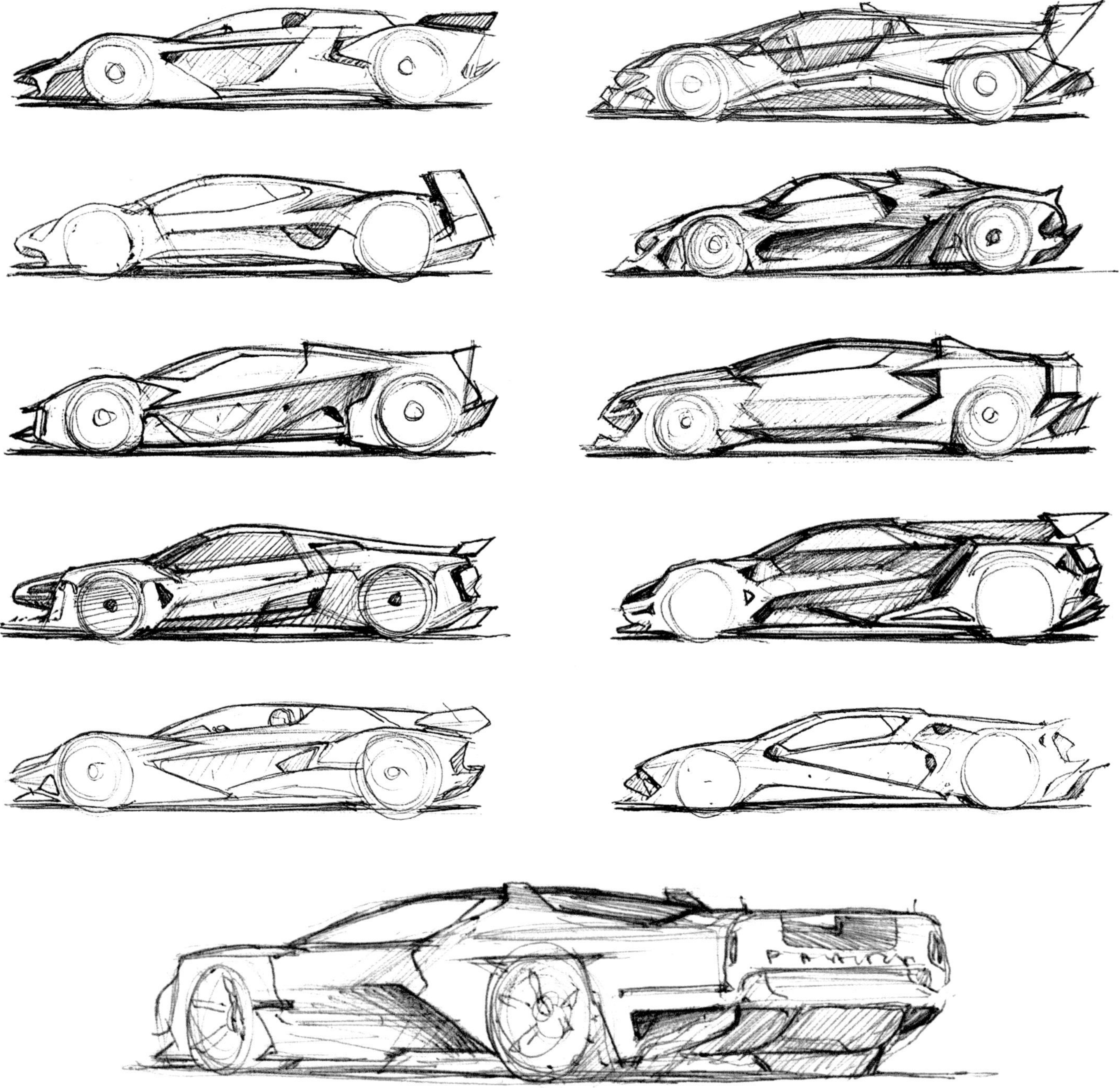
PANTER

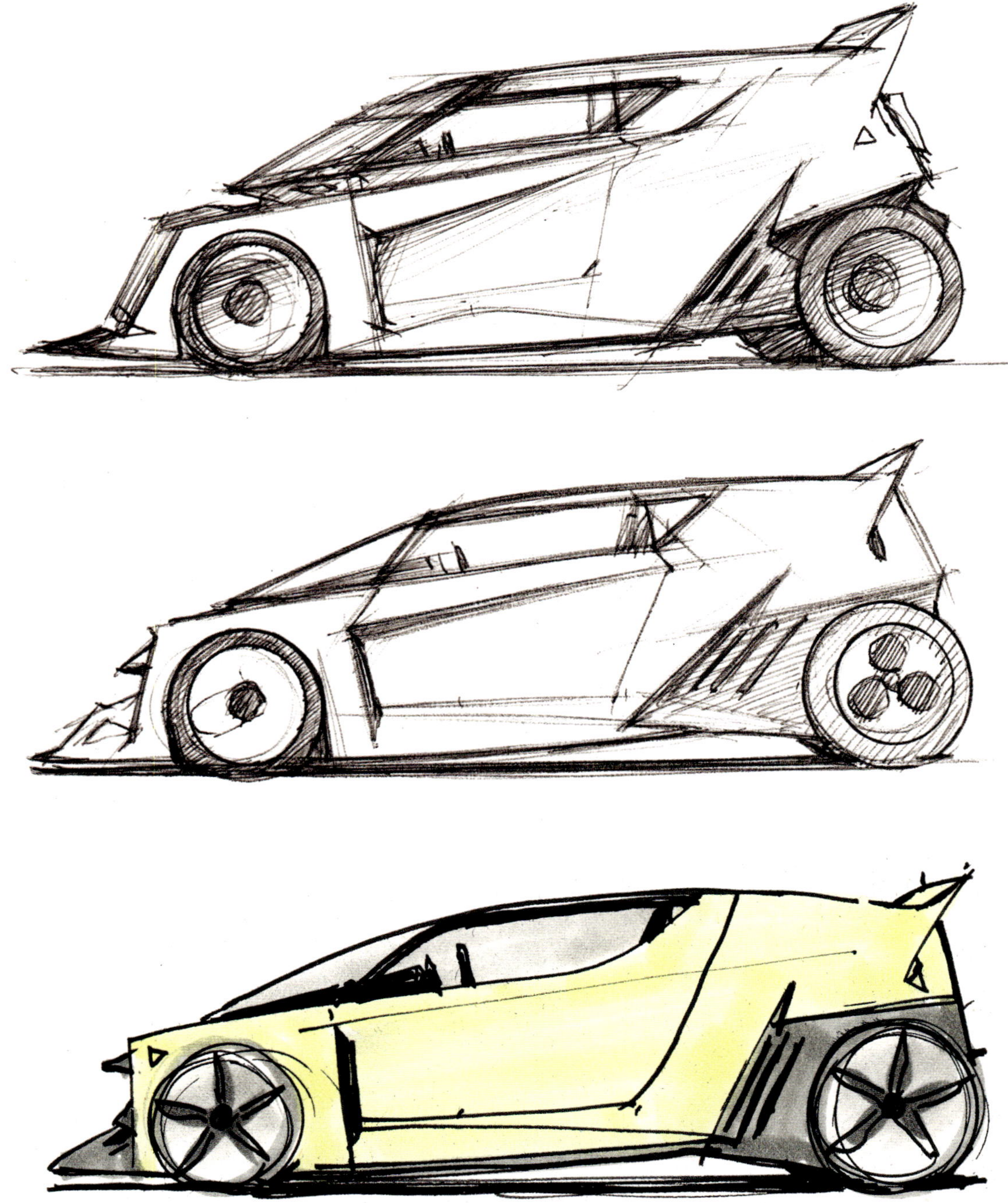

# ///SKETCH COLLECTION

## VOL. 03:

### SCOTT ROBERTSON

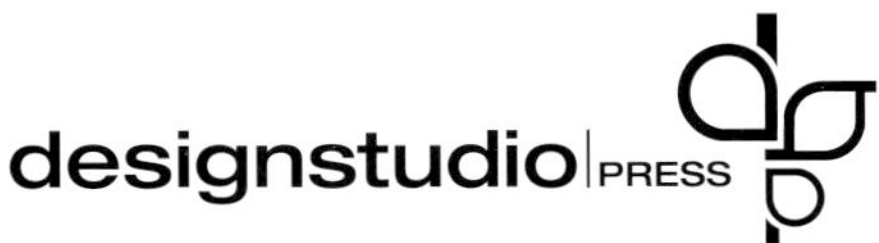

designstudio|PRESS

# introduction

Wow! I can't believe it's been six years since I released my last book into the world. Time seems to be accelerating for me—what is going on? And how did six years fly by? The time warp seems to have begun at the end of 2017 when I accepted a job at Apple. Just prior to this, I'd had a pretty productive 2017 Inktober effort, drawing mostly marine vehicles now included in this sketchbook. Upon entering the secret world of Apple, I made that job my primary focus along with the continued effort to build my 1934 Fordtruss hot rod pickup truck (see my @scoro5 Instagram account if you are curious about the build). Neither of these activities involved time for sketching, unfortunately, hence the long absence from the drawing table. In today's world of 3D modeling tools, both on a flat screen and in VR environments, our time is becoming ever more fractured, with evolving pipeline demands pulling us away from the wonderful solitude of thinking on paper. Let me first introduce the content of this sketchbook before I ramble on too much about the future of creativity and the myriad tools now available to us.

This is the third installment of the SRD Sketch Collection series, containing roughly double the number of sketches of the previous editions. I guess the six-year span between publishing was a plus in this regard. Many subjects are my usual favorites: wheeled vehicles, spaceships, and mechs, with a few environments. A large section, though, features marine machines new to my sketchbook collection. These were mostly done using traditional media, but the color images near the end were created by modeling in VR using Gravity Sketch and then rendering the models in Modo/Octane. This block of marine work represents the beginnings of a larger marine-focused book that might be published in the future.

Like the previous sketchbooks in the series, this one contains my Inktober efforts from 2017–2023. I left Apple in May of 2021, at which point I was fully engaged in VR modeling in Gravity Sketch and starting my research into how AI tools might boost creativity and productivity within my own design pipeline. The last ten pages of this book show some examples of trying to use Dream by WOMBO, Artbreeder, and Canvas by Nvidia to enhance my sketches and increase my productivity. The sketches on pages 91–97 were created by running my traditional media sketches through the Dream app on my iPhone. Page 98 displays two images initially created in Artbreeder by mashing together some of my hand sketches along with landscape paintings done by my father; both images were then refined in Photoshop. The last three pages in the book were created first by drawing color-keyed shapes in perspective in the Canvas app and then painting back into them in Photoshop. I chose only these examples to share here, as they best represent using the early AI tools that still heavily relied on my own sketches and drawing abilities and were pre-Midjourney/Stable Diffusion/Dall•E "type text-to-image" AI.

Things have changed quickly in the world of image creation since these early experiments in the spring of 2021. I think we can all feel the existential threat of AI to people's livelihoods, while at the same time witnessing the awesome abilities the tools unlock when paired with our own creativity and guidance. It is no longer a question of "if" these tools are going to be folded into all of our futures but how we as a species best cope with the integration of the tools into our chosen professions and day-to-day lives. Hopefully, through a competent legal system, along with some insightful governance, the obvious copyright-violation questions surrounding most of the AI-generation tools will be resolved sooner rather than later.

In my mind there is no question that these tools can give industrial designers a big bump in creative discovery and development in the visualizing of our ideas. As it became clear that AI tools would be a big part of the future of our design-visualization process, and having authored two books on this subject, How to Draw and How to Render, I felt compelled to figure out how best to help guide the ethical use of these new AI tools into the field of industrial design.

It was during the summer of 2021, after exiting Apple, that I did a deep dive into most of the creativity tools, both AR/VR and AI-focused, that were available. Pretty quickly some favorites rose to the top of the list. Working on the iPad, using Nomad for sculpting on a flat screen was my favorite, and Medium (now Substance 3D Modeler) and Gravity Sketch were my preferred VR 3D-modeling apps. Gravity Sketch has become an integral part of my 3D-modeling pipeline, and the renderings of the boats in this book were all modeled in VR using that app. While investigating many of the AI image-creation apps, Vizcom.ai became the one that interested me the most. Their approach to the much more responsible way that an AI tool can support a designer's creativity and boost productivity was and is very compelling. Since that summer of '21, I stayed in touch with the

Vizcom creators and occasionally helped out as an early product tester. In the fall of '23, they released the current version of their app, and I could quickly see that this would become a very valuable asset to design teams around the world. In January of 2024, I officially joined their team as a part-time product advisor, testing and helping to guide the development of the tools that will help designers retain authorship of their work and more quickly visualize their ideas to share with a design team. I am saving the results of those experiments to share in a future book on how to work with VR-modeling tools and AI image enhancement as it pertains to advancing design and communication skills of industrial designers.

I get asked a lot about whether I think AI will do away with the future need for designers to know how to draw and render, and so far, my experience has been the opposite. Working with Vizcom.ai is the one app that inspires me to draw more, and the better the drawing that I import into their tool to render, the better my output results. As the days of bespoke image datasets used for AI model training are finally upon us, I feel better and better about how these AI tools will greatly assist and empower us to share our ideas with others. In my own future, I look forward to more sketching time and staying engaged and curious in new technologies, always doing what I can to help be a positive part of the development of those tools and techniques well into the future.

*Scott Robertson*

March 31, 2024
Los Angeles, California

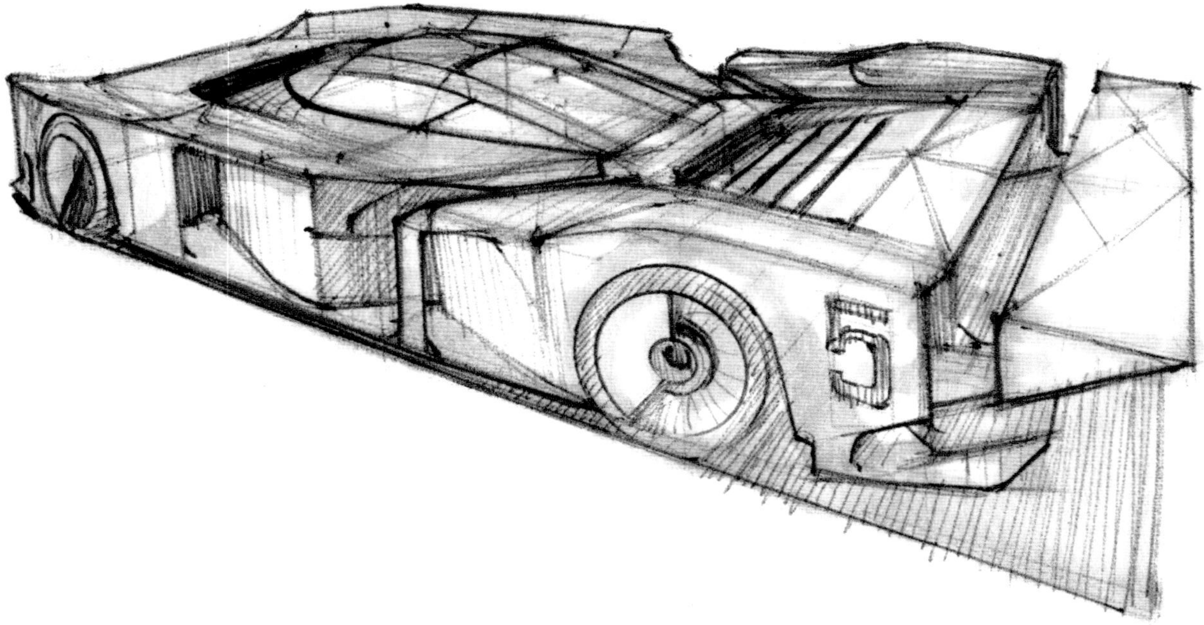

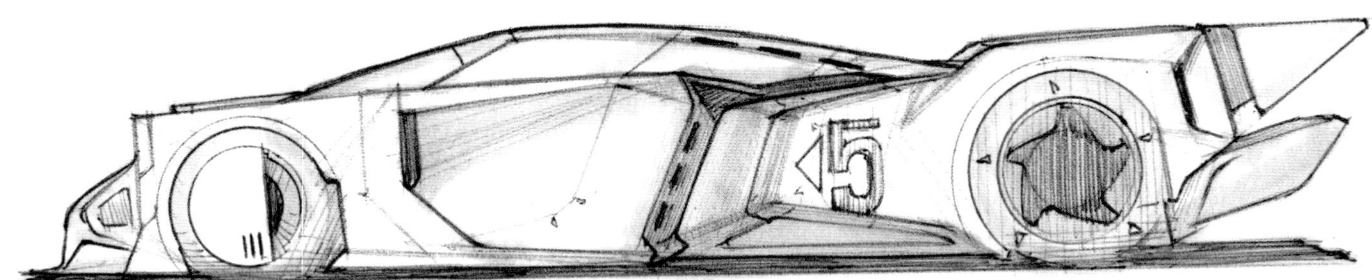

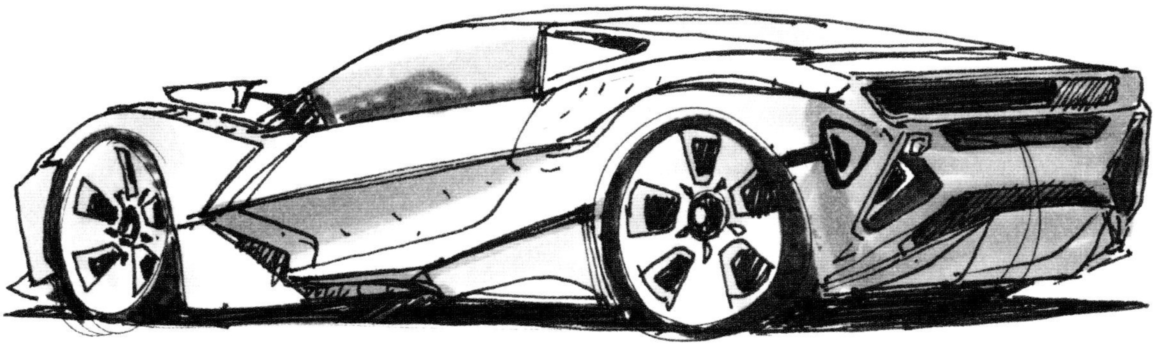

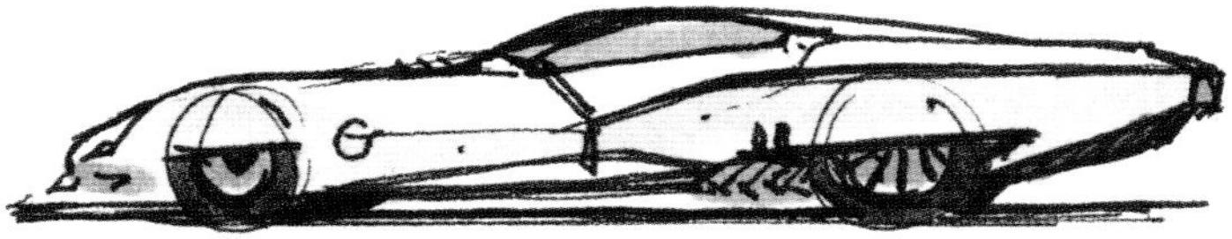

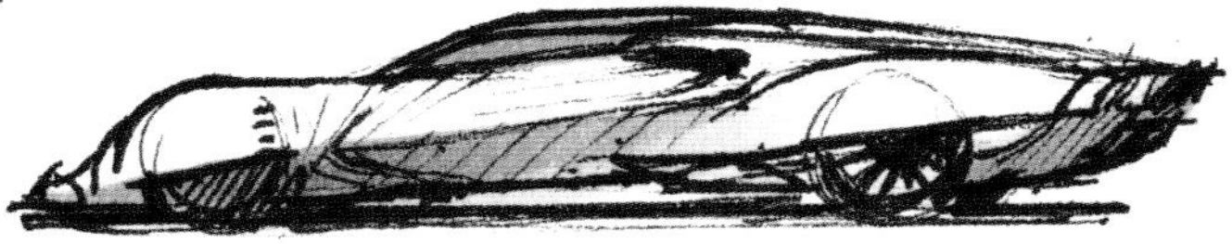

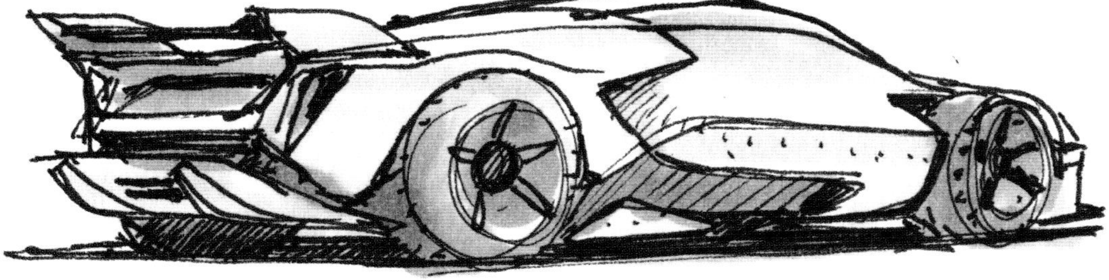

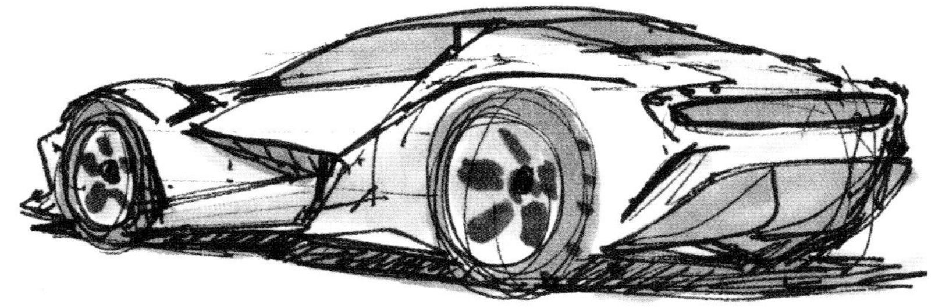

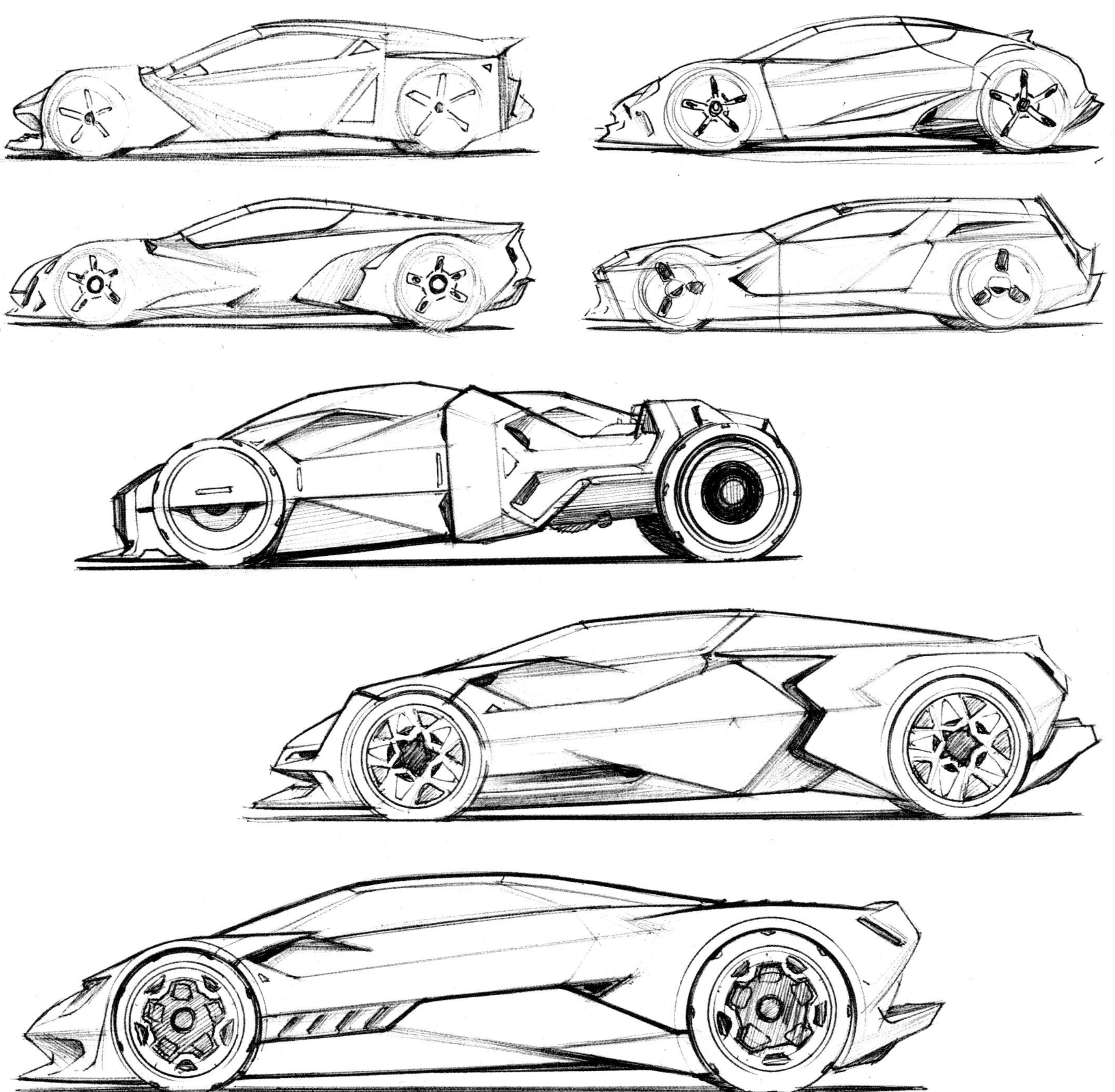

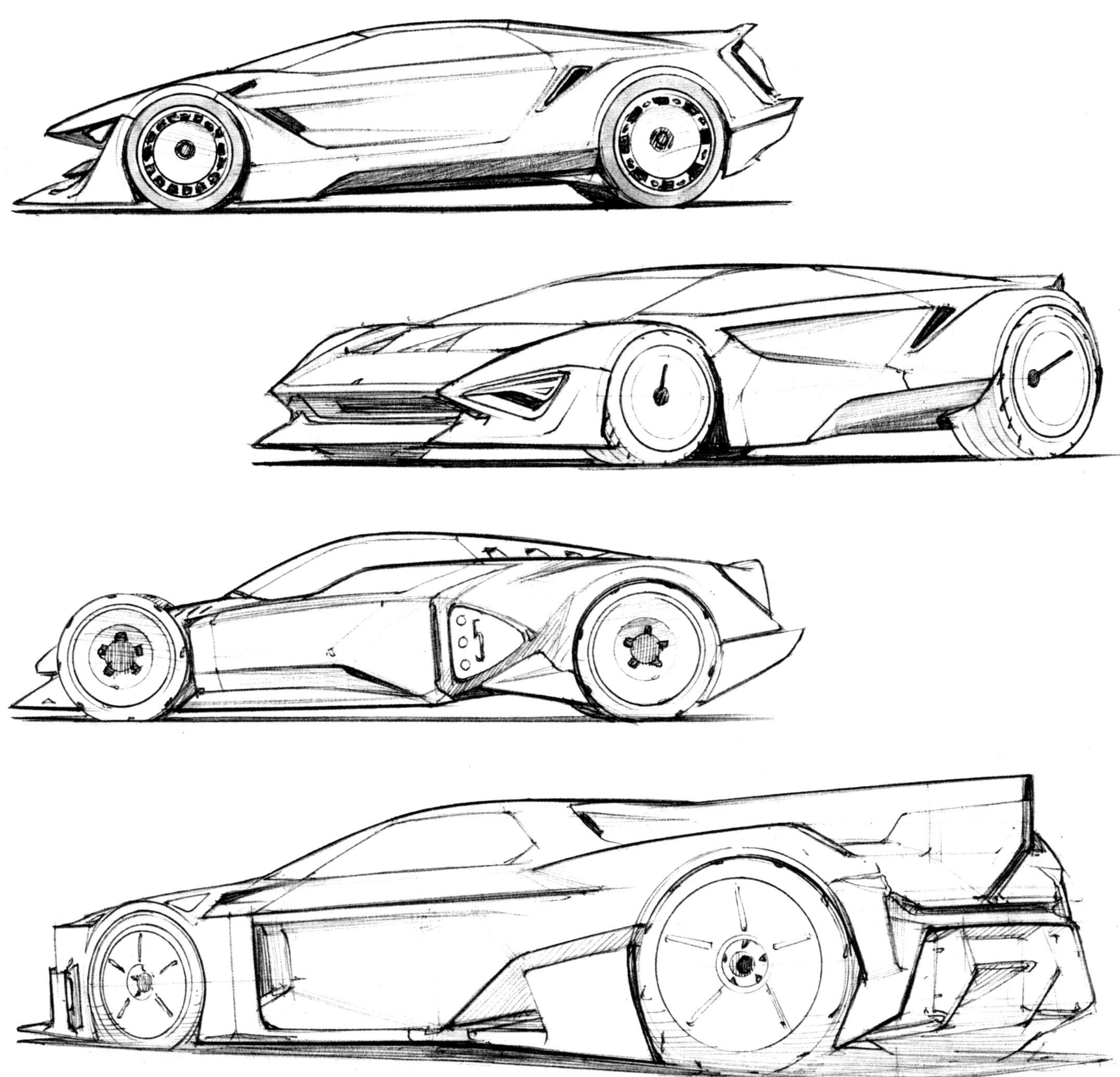

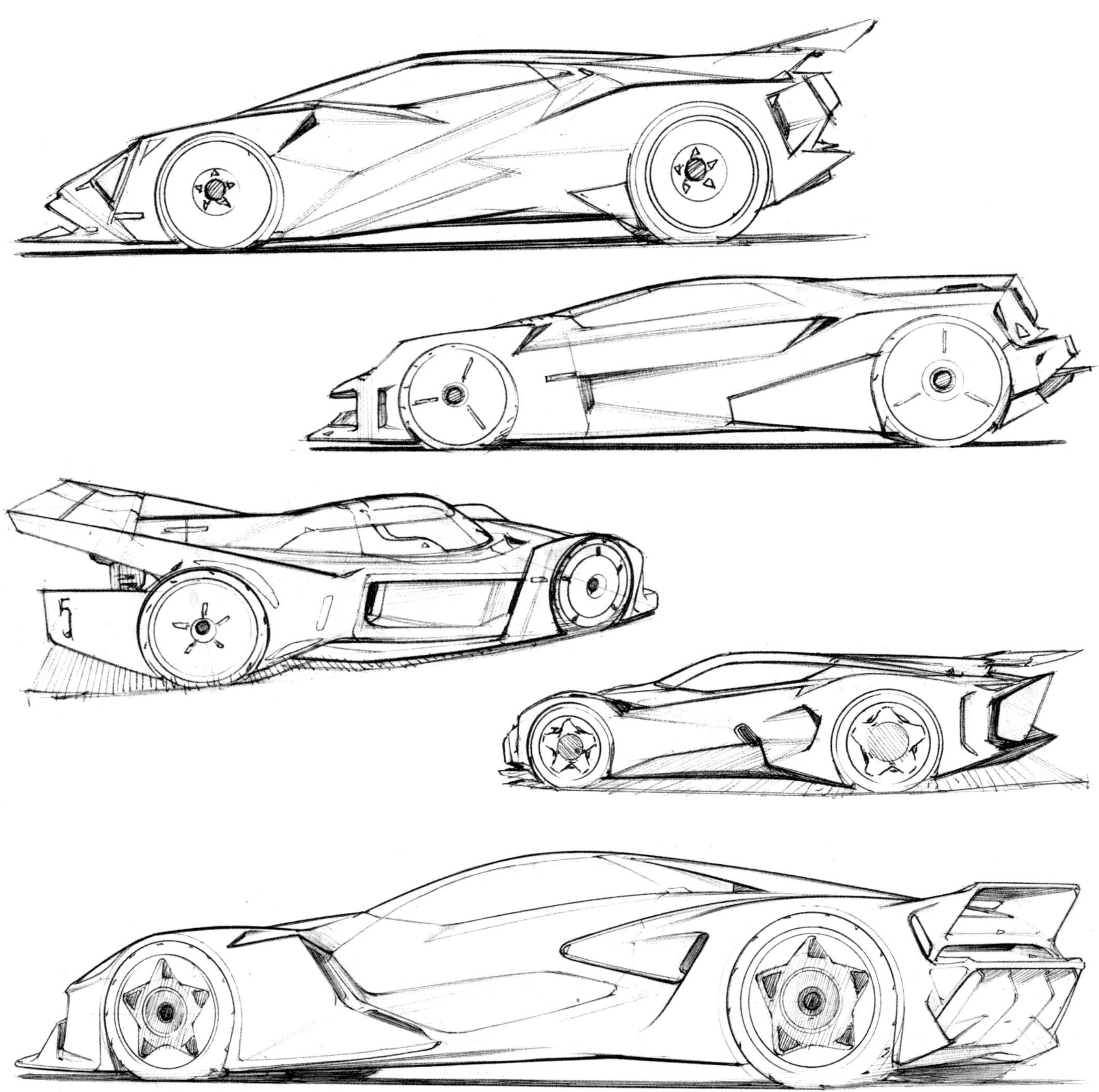

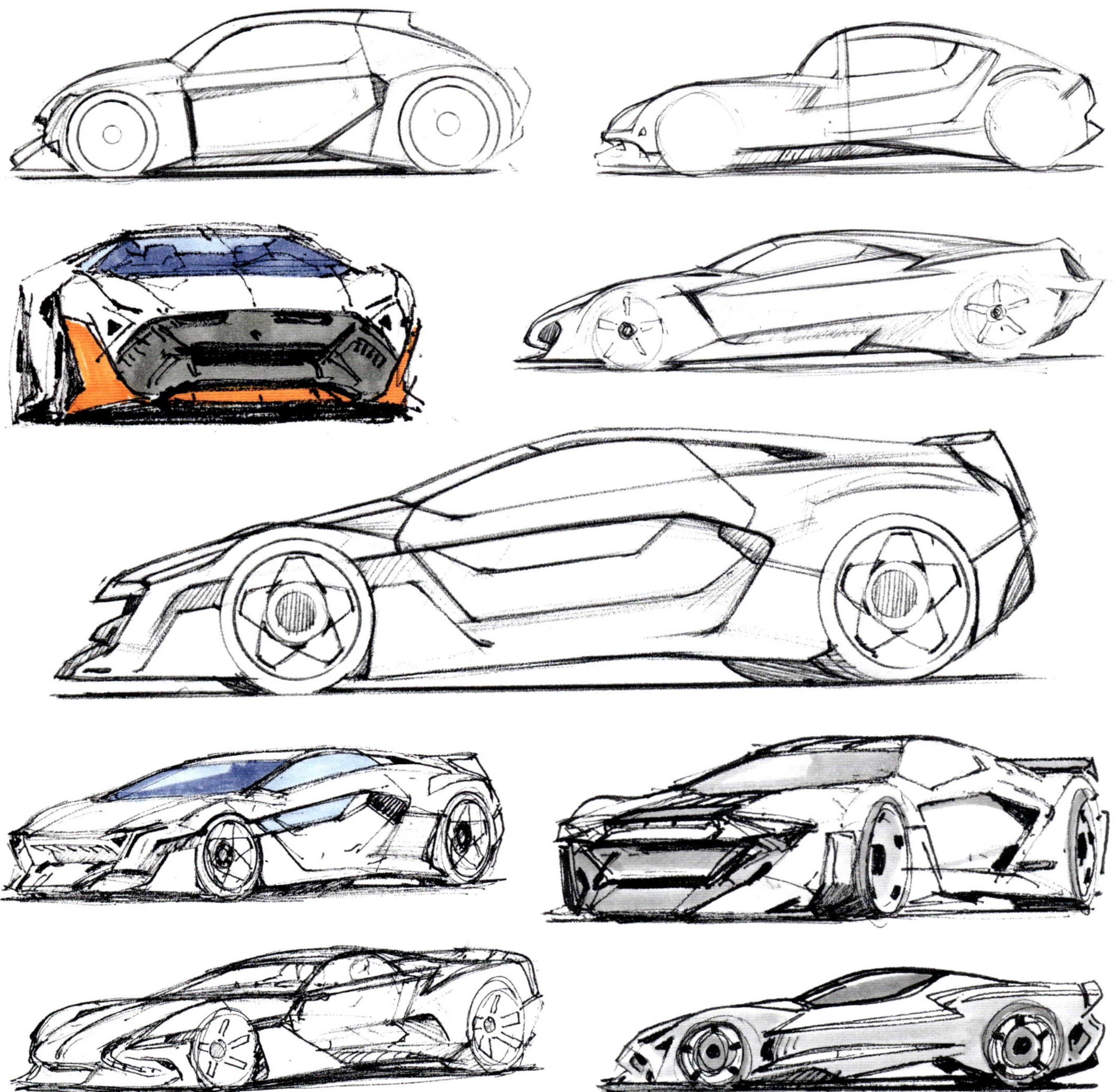

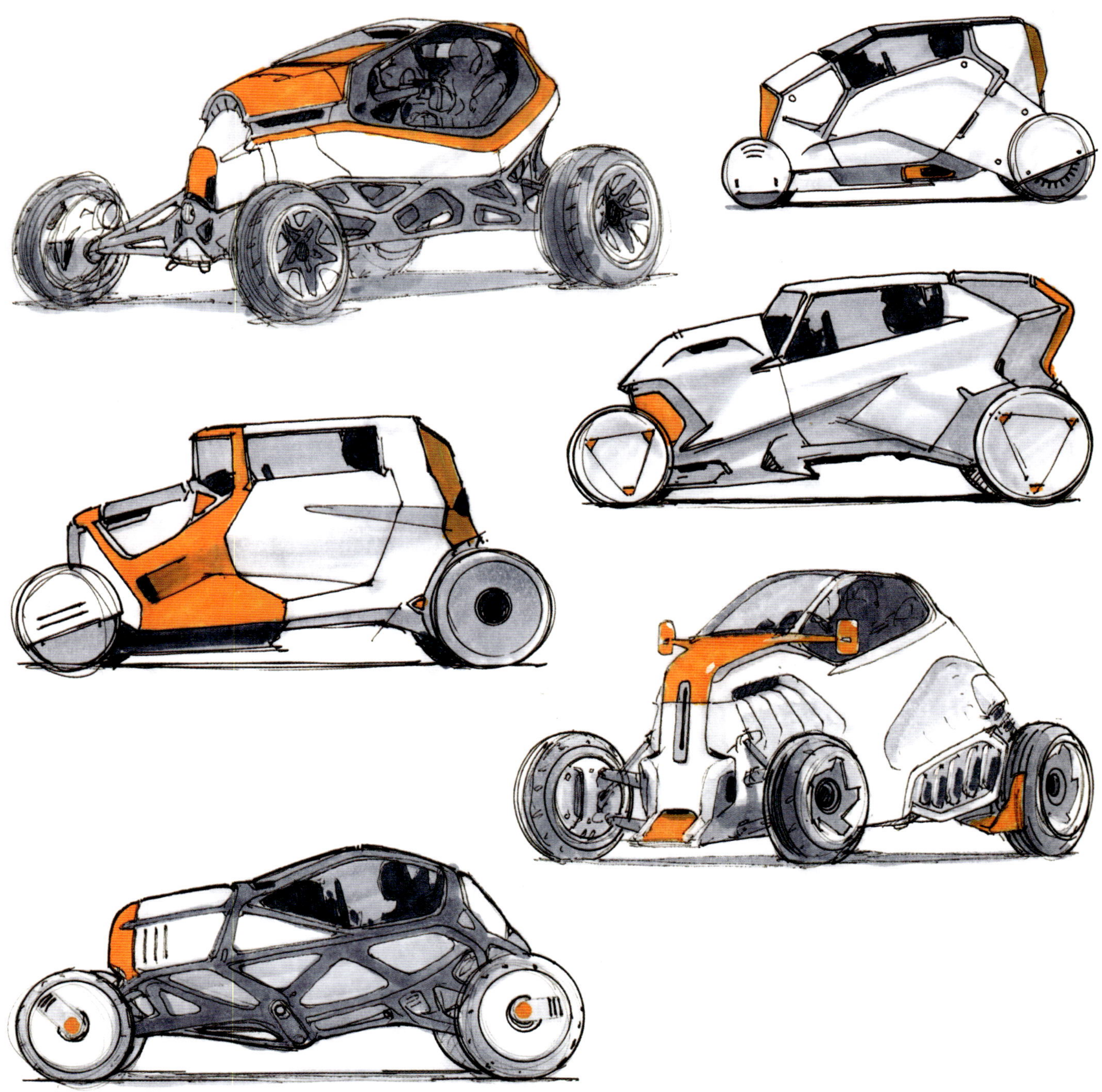

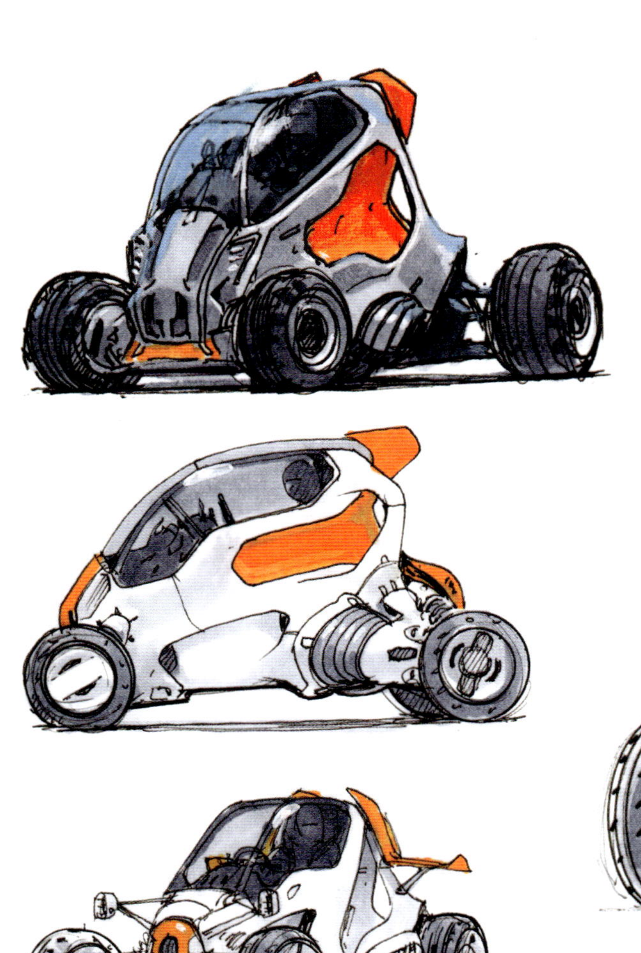
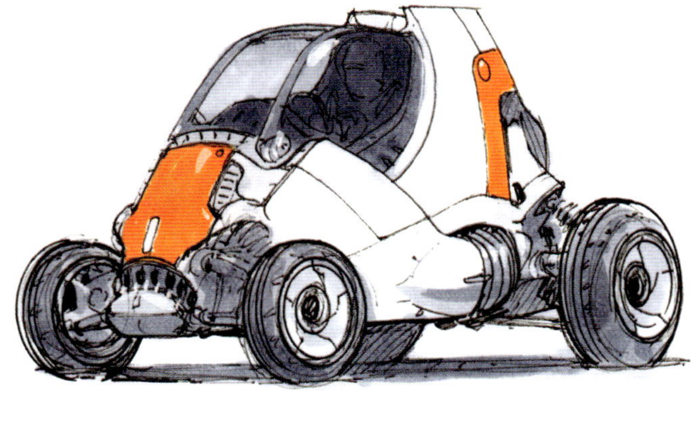
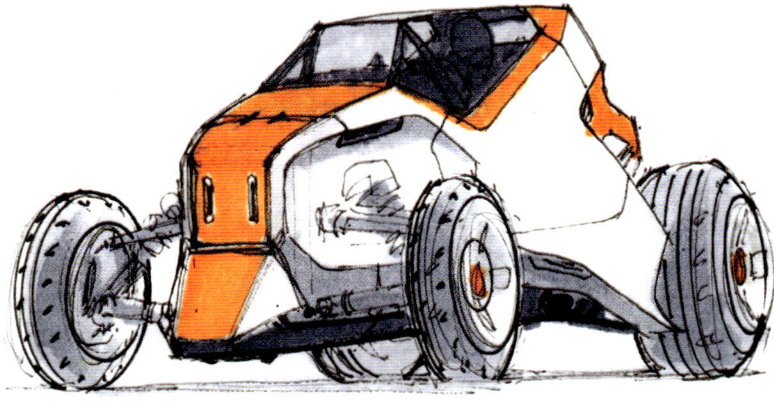
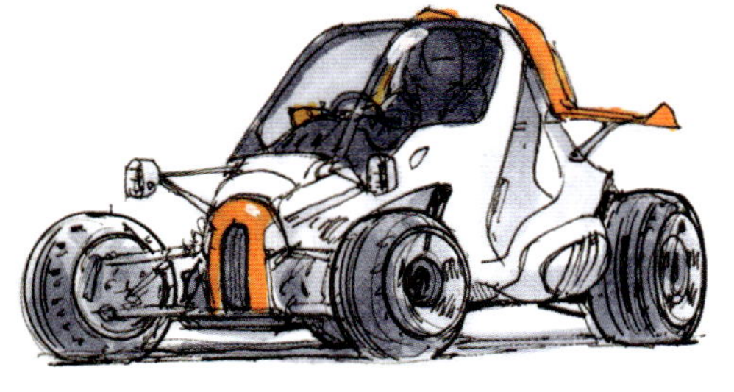
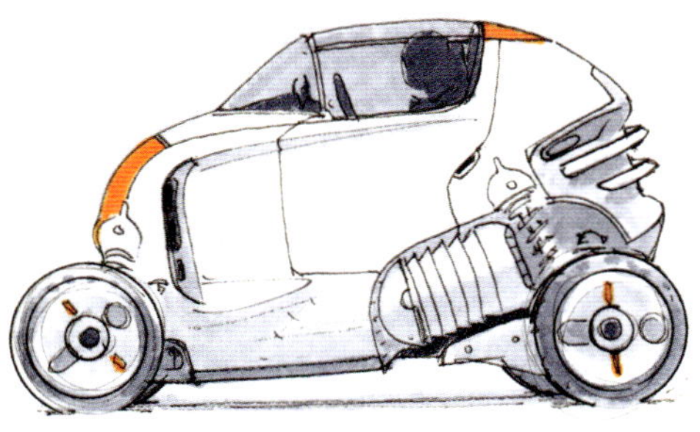
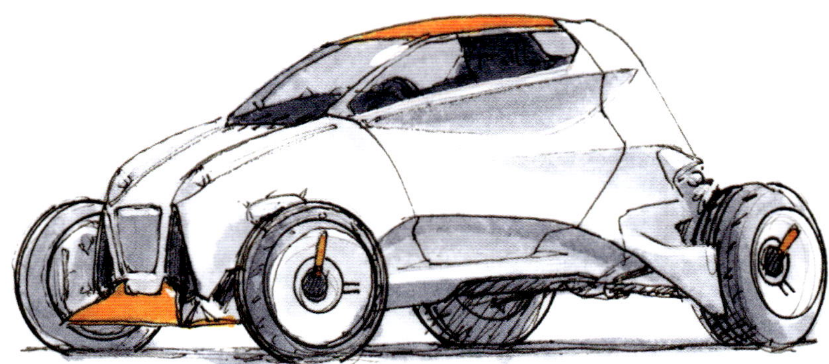

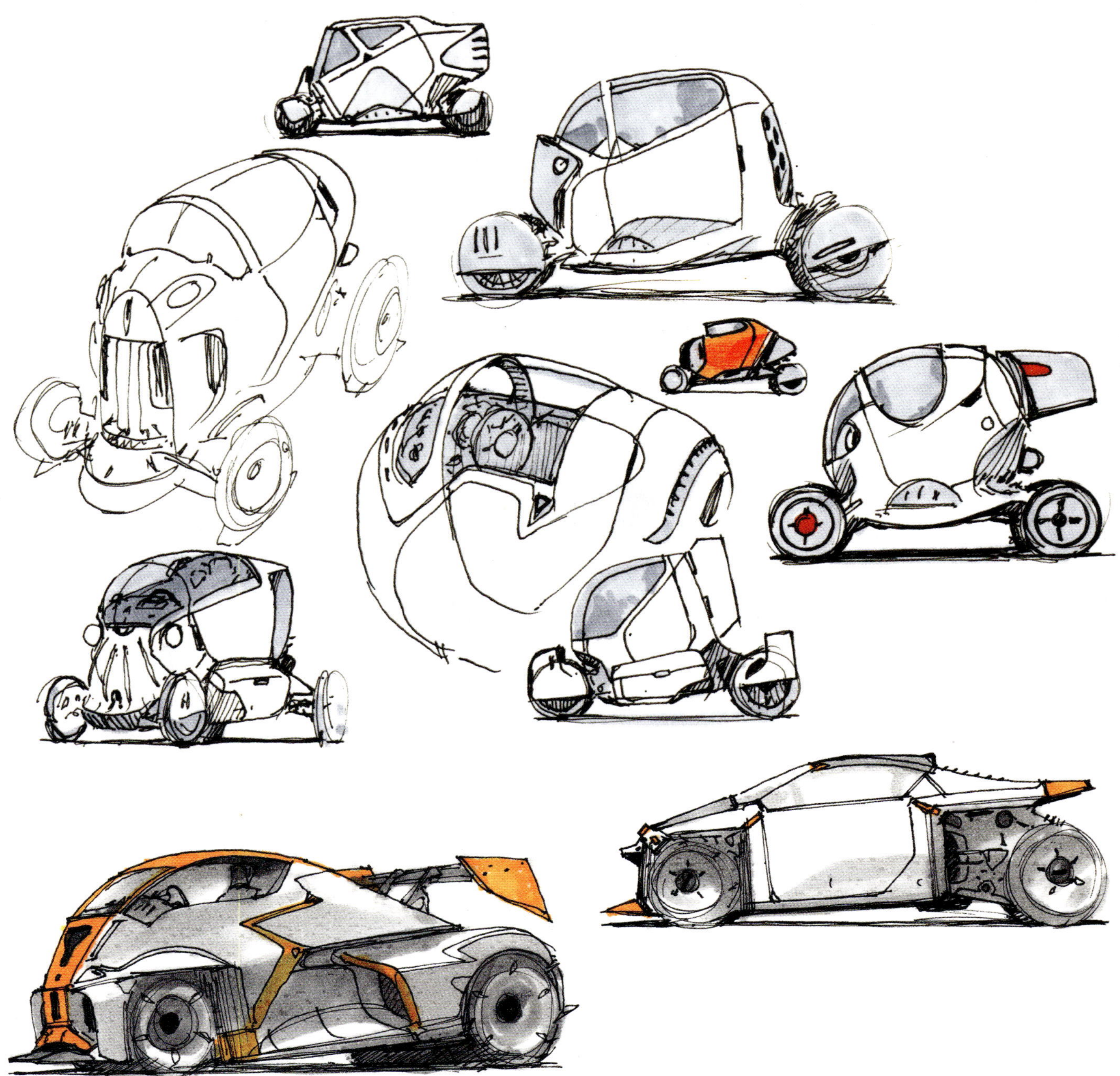

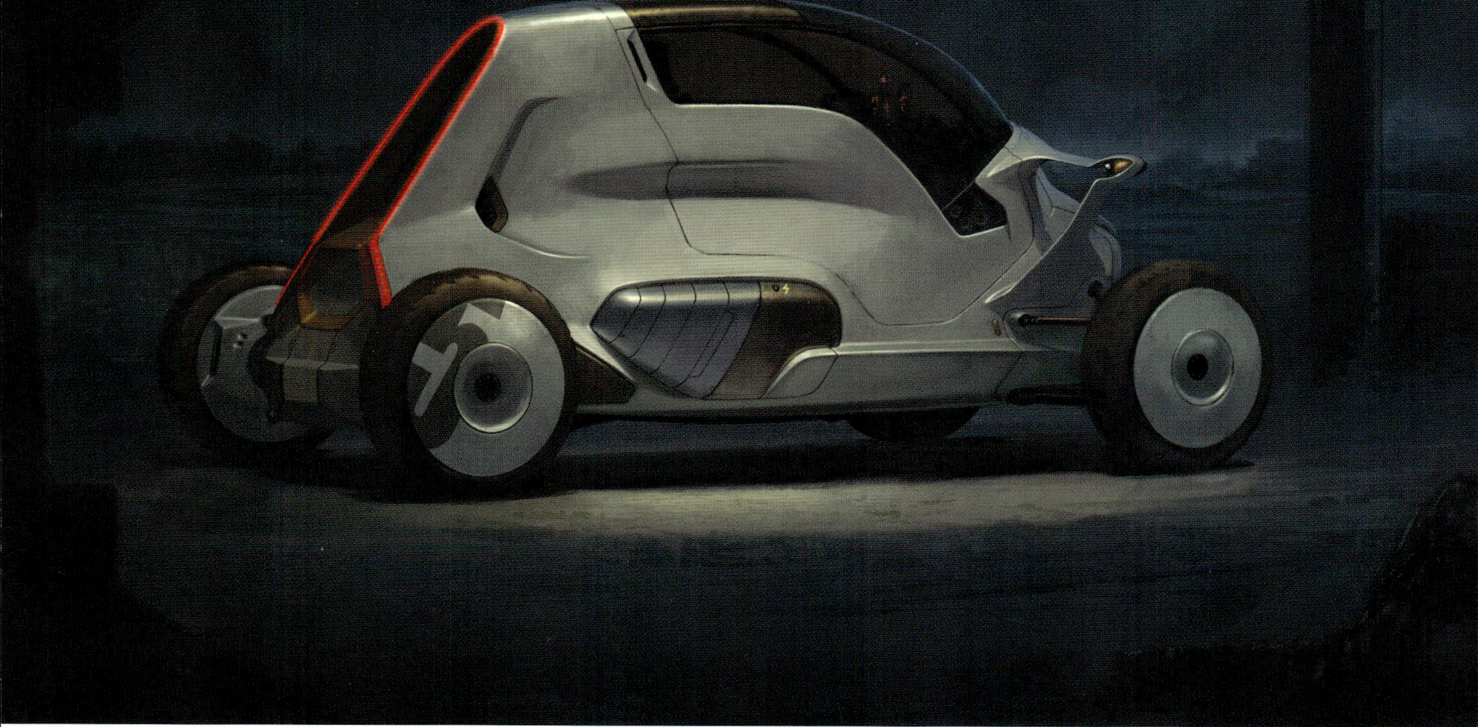

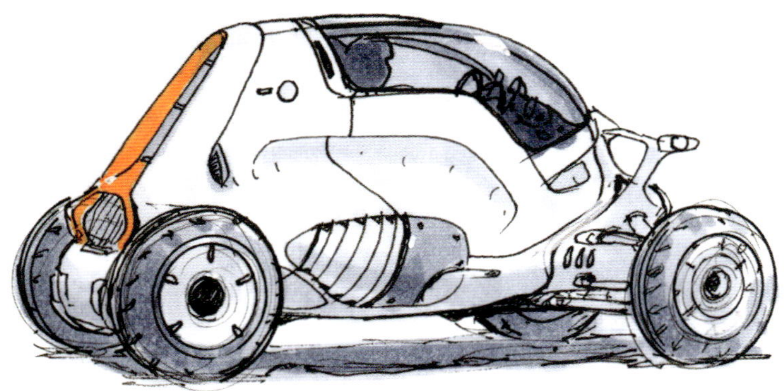

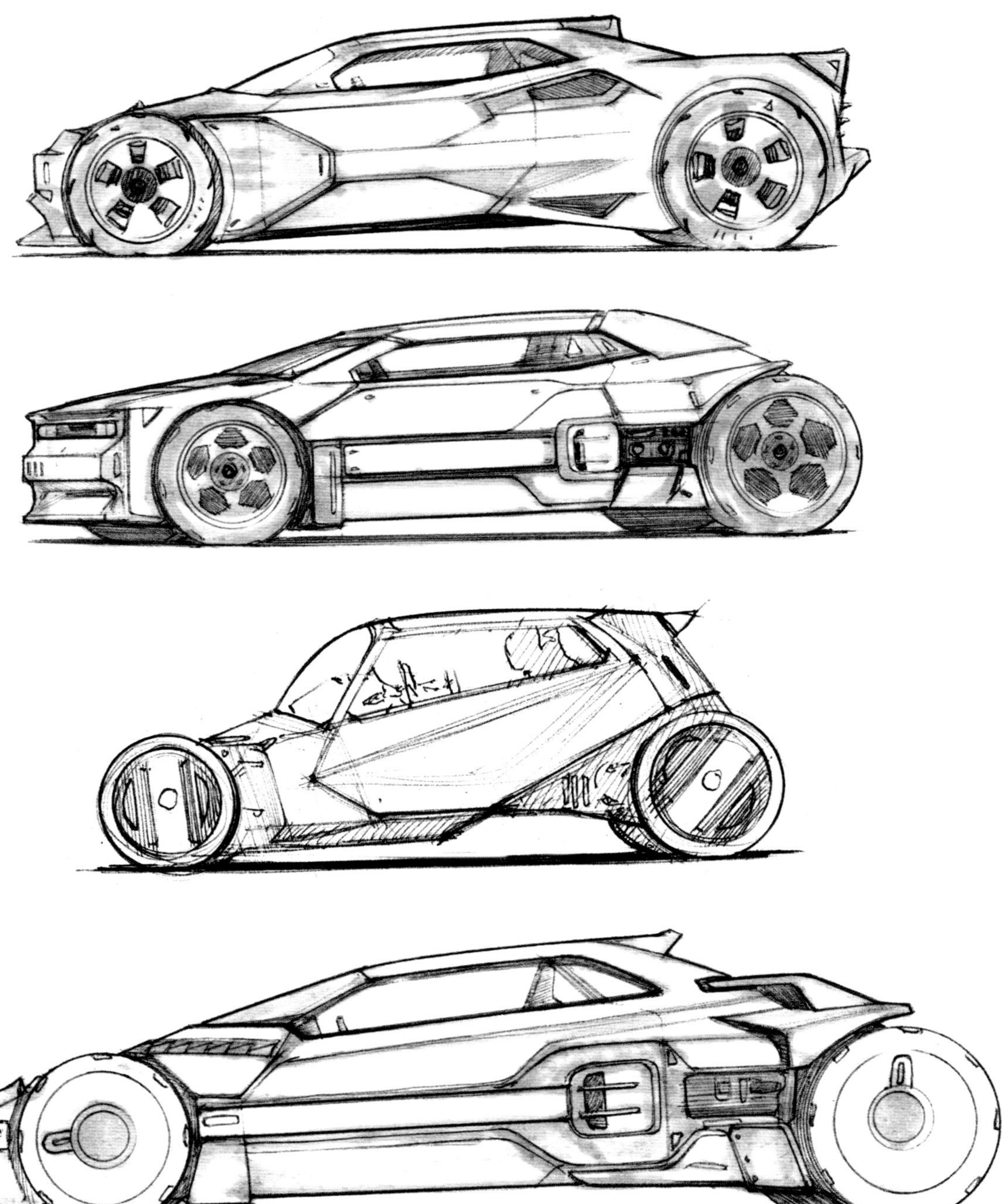

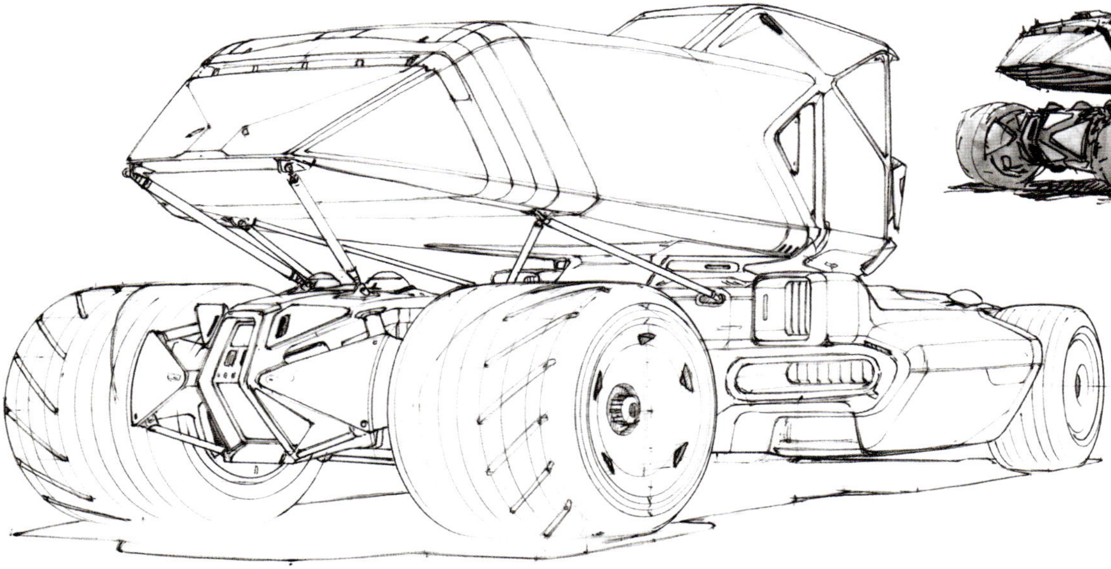

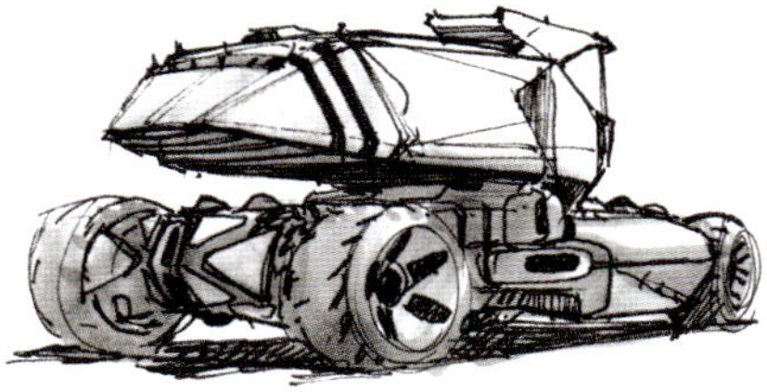

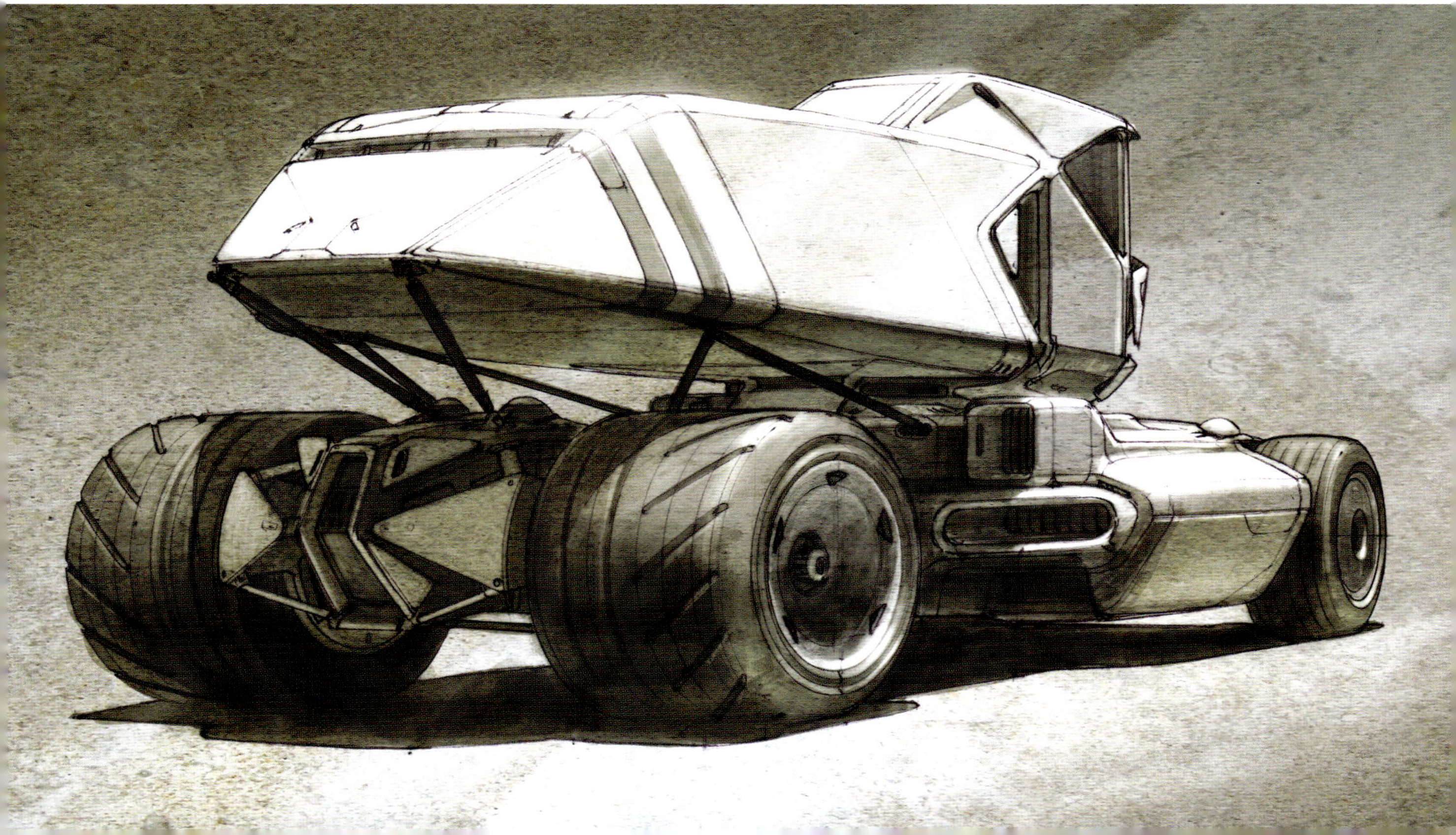

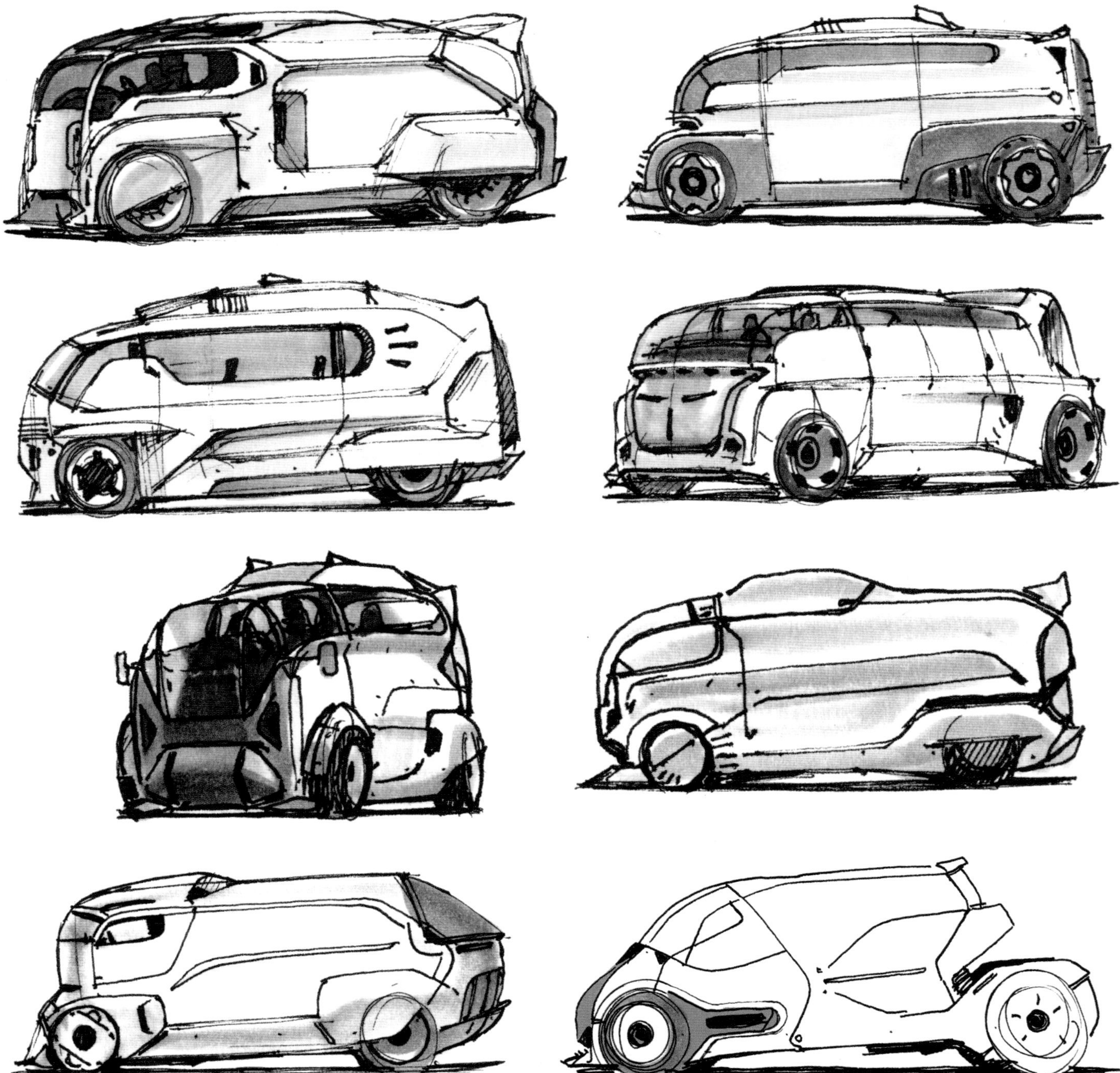

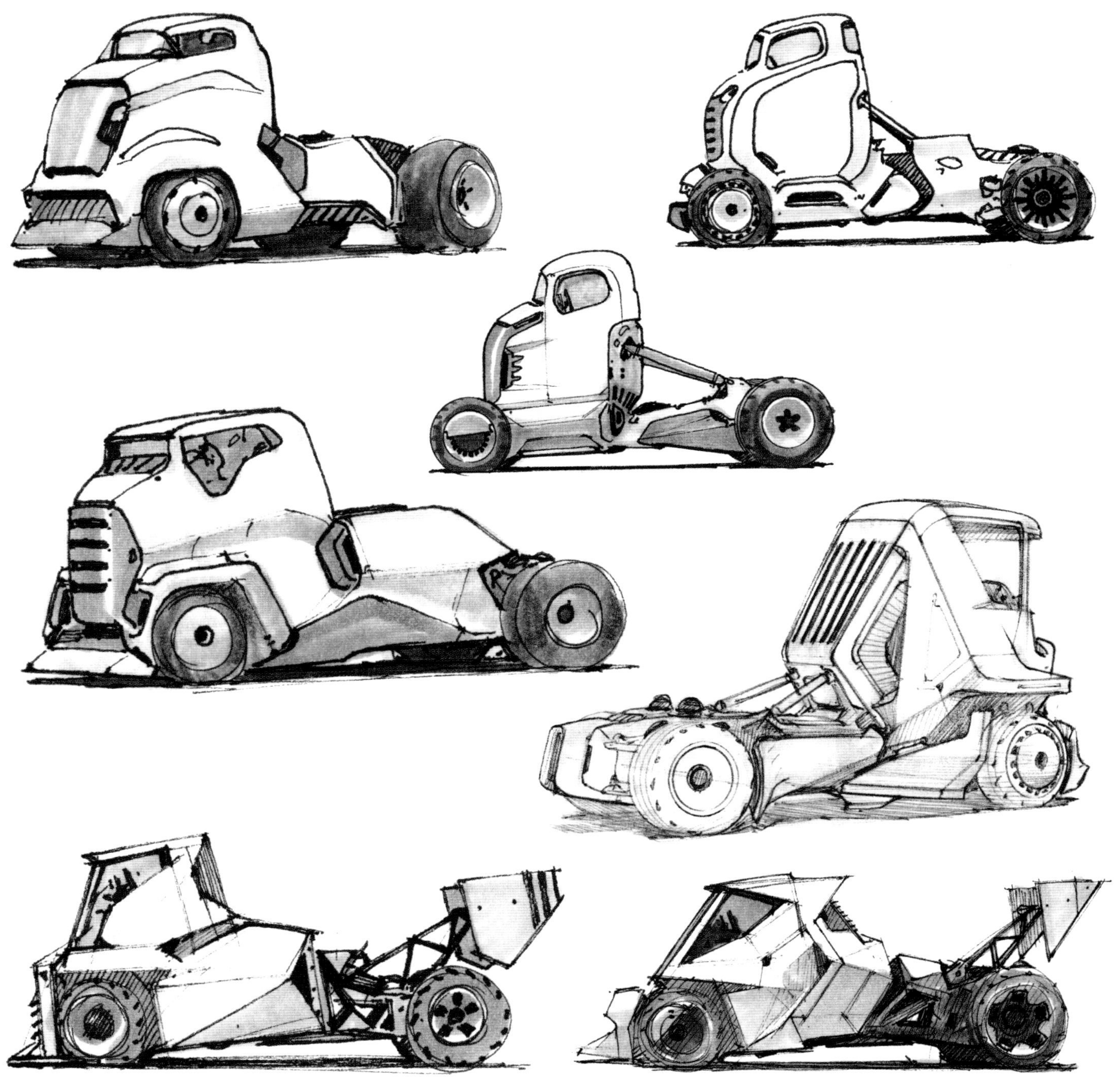

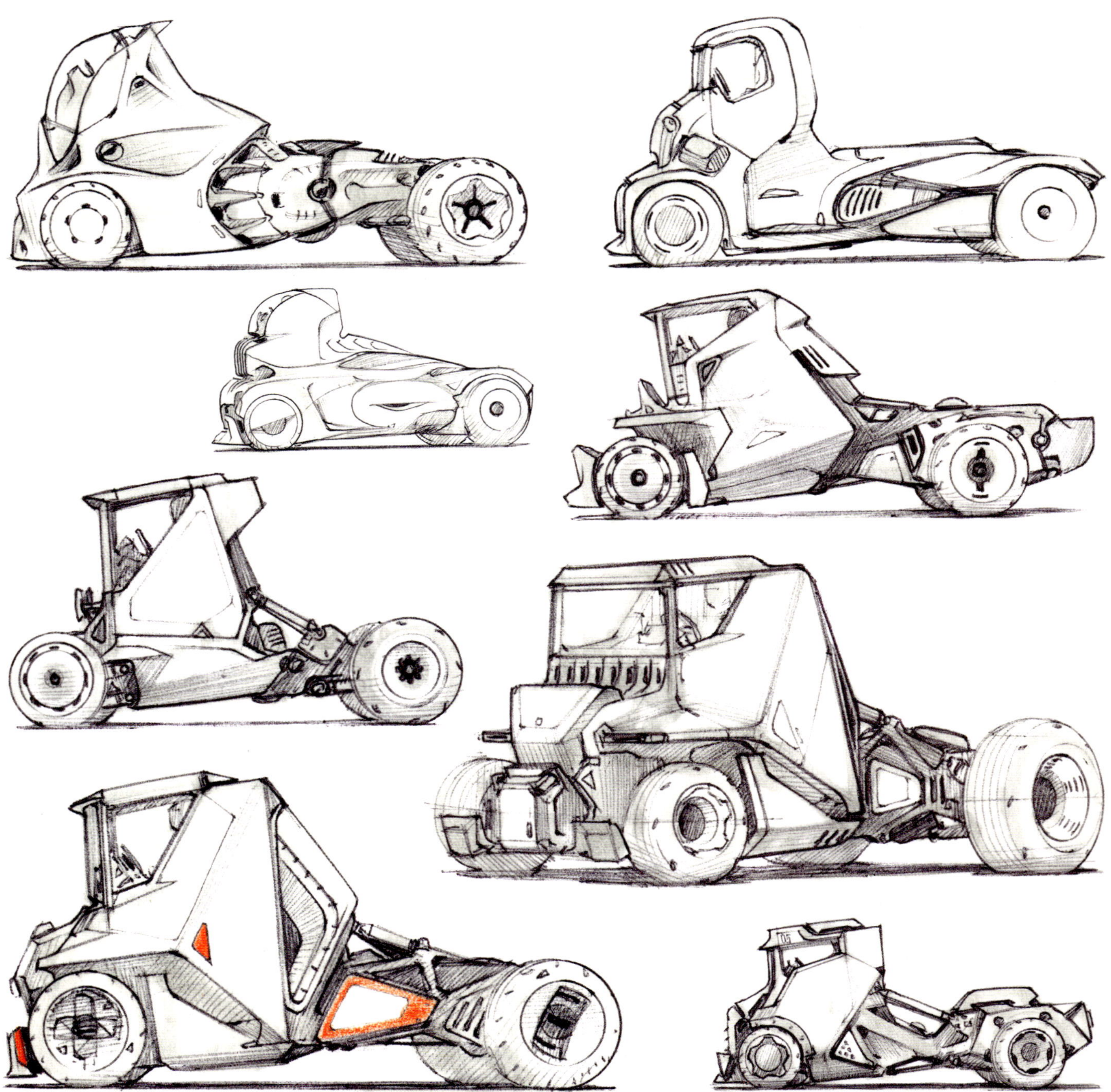

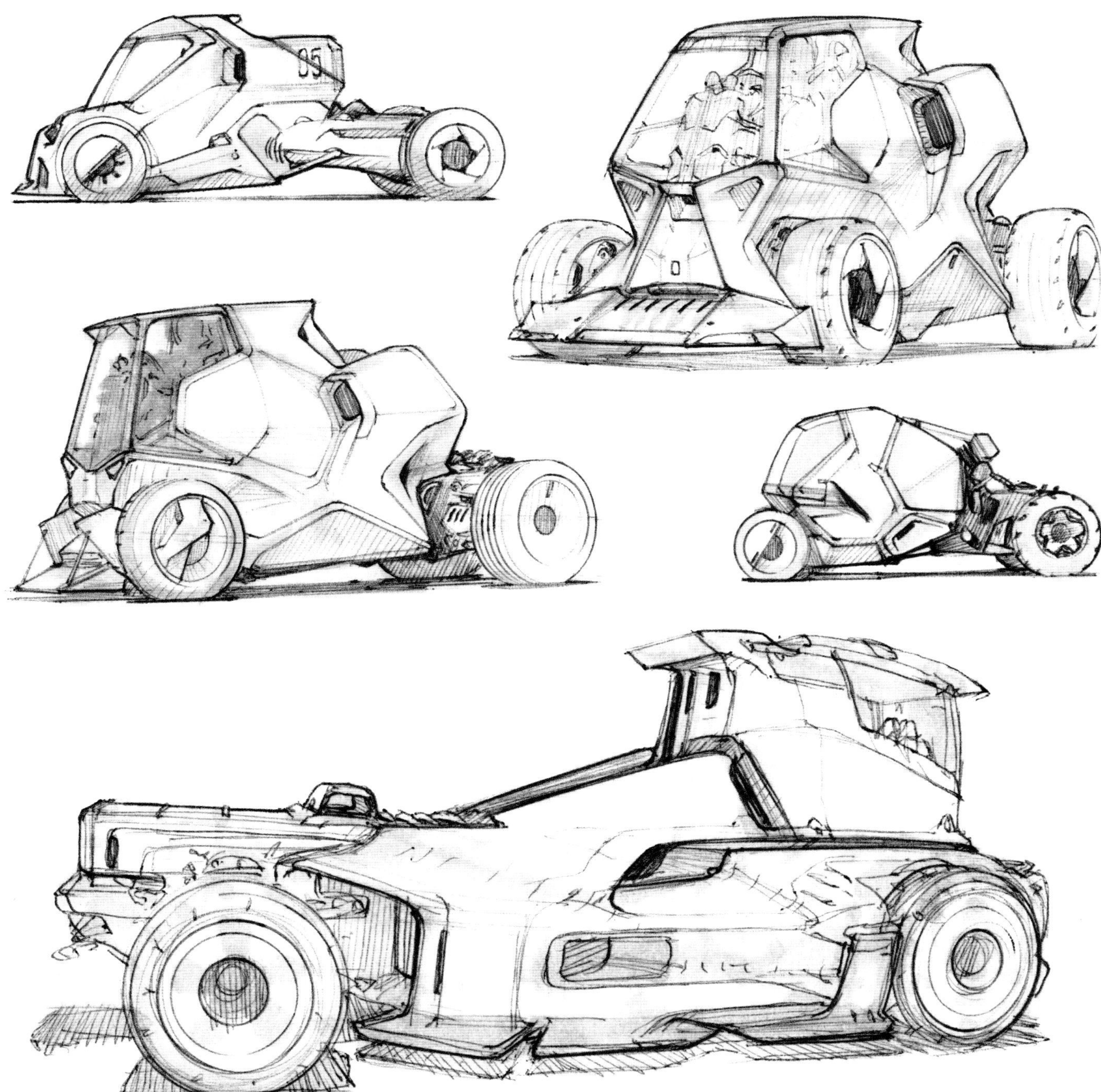

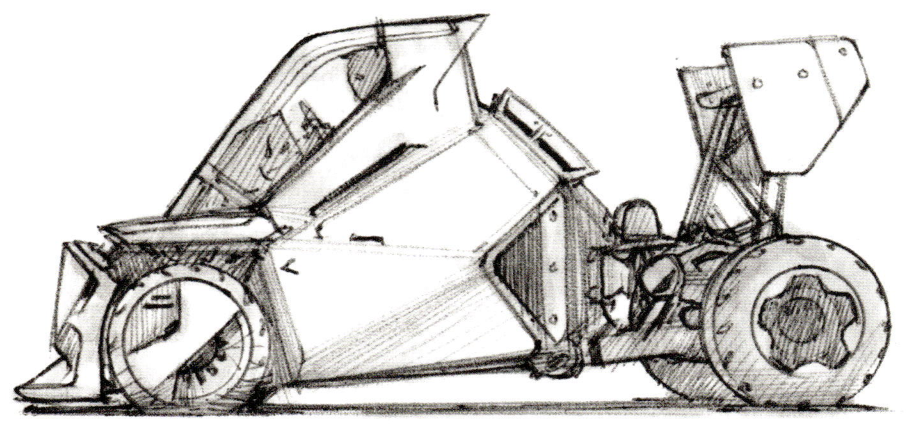

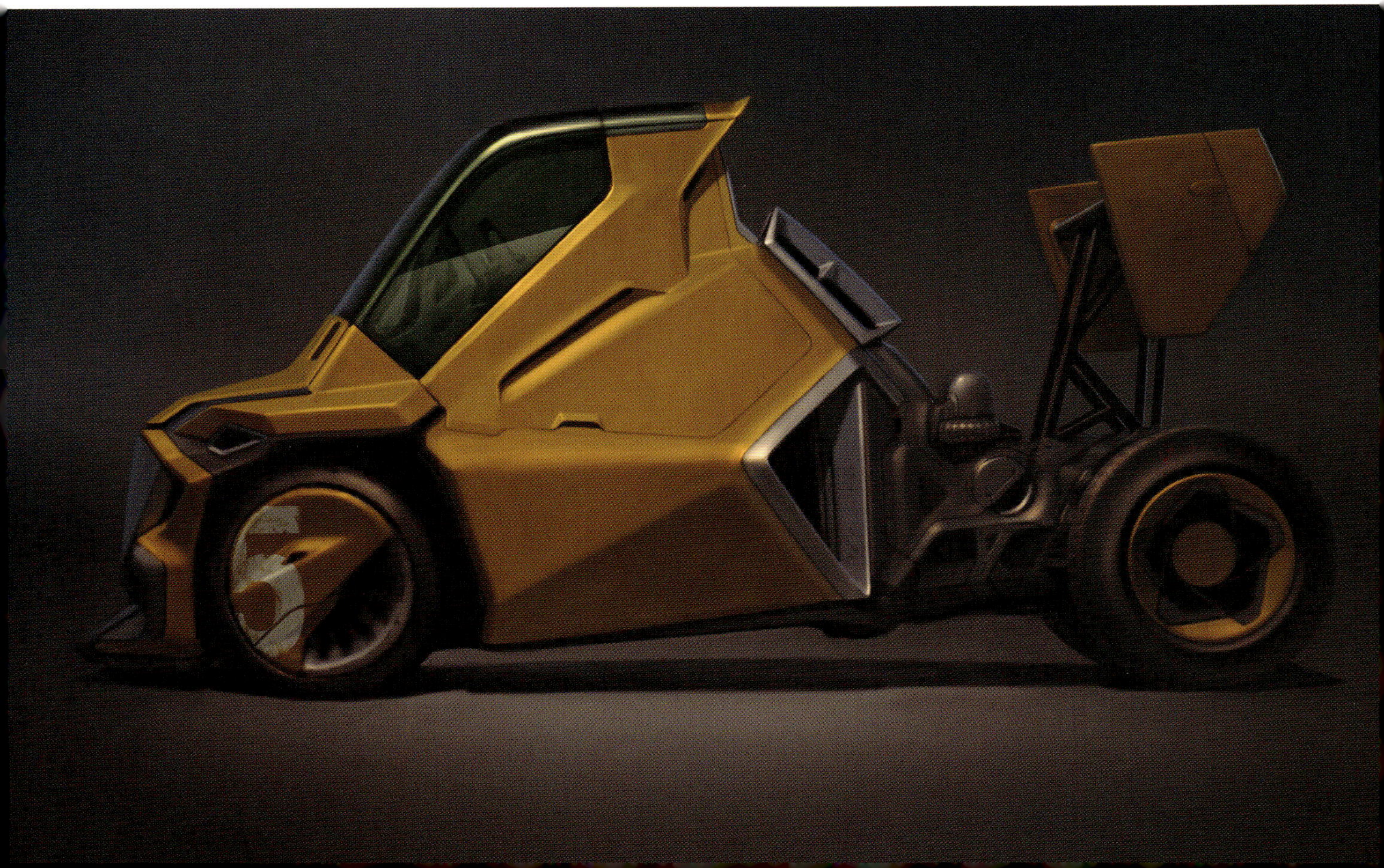

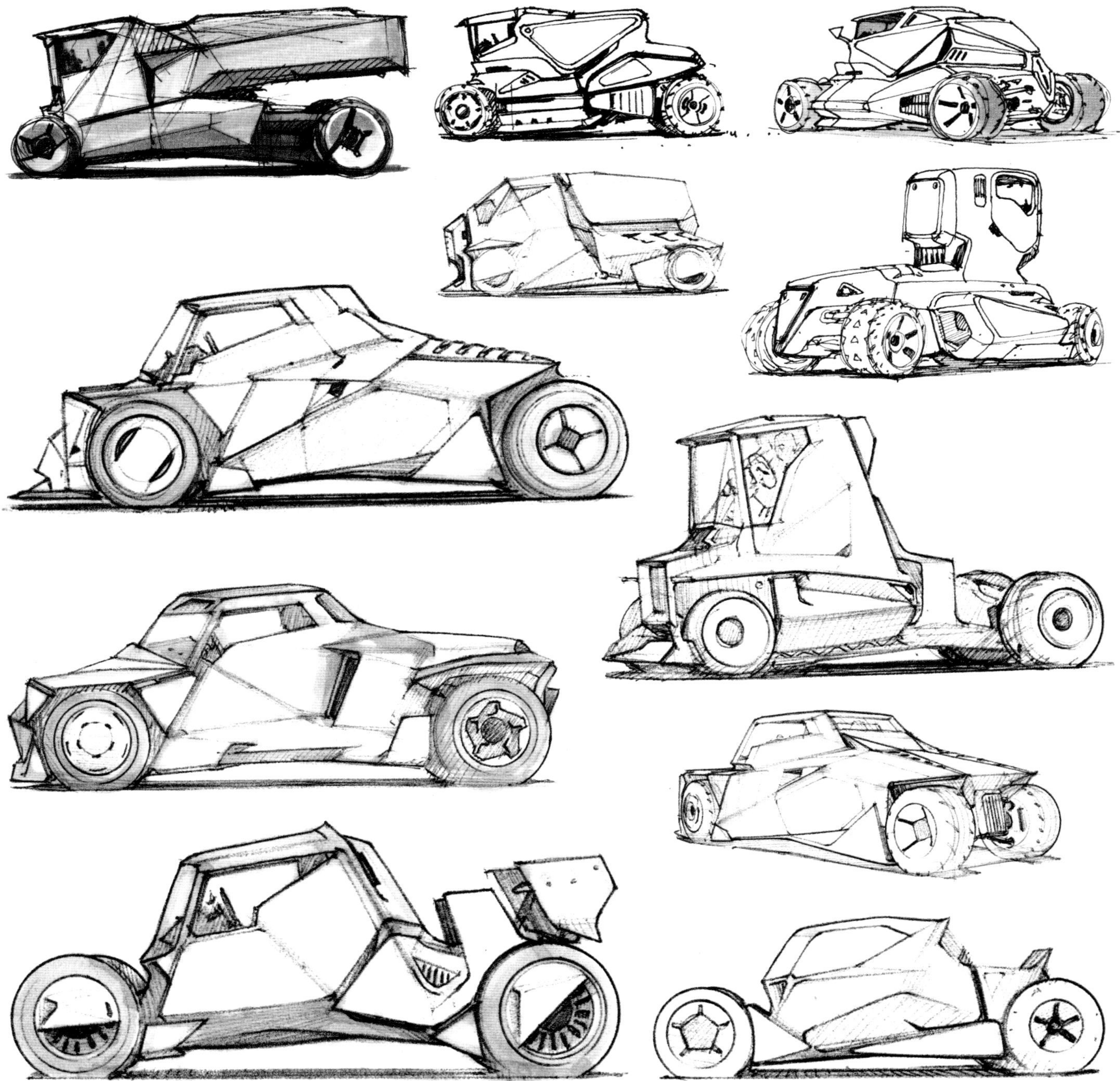

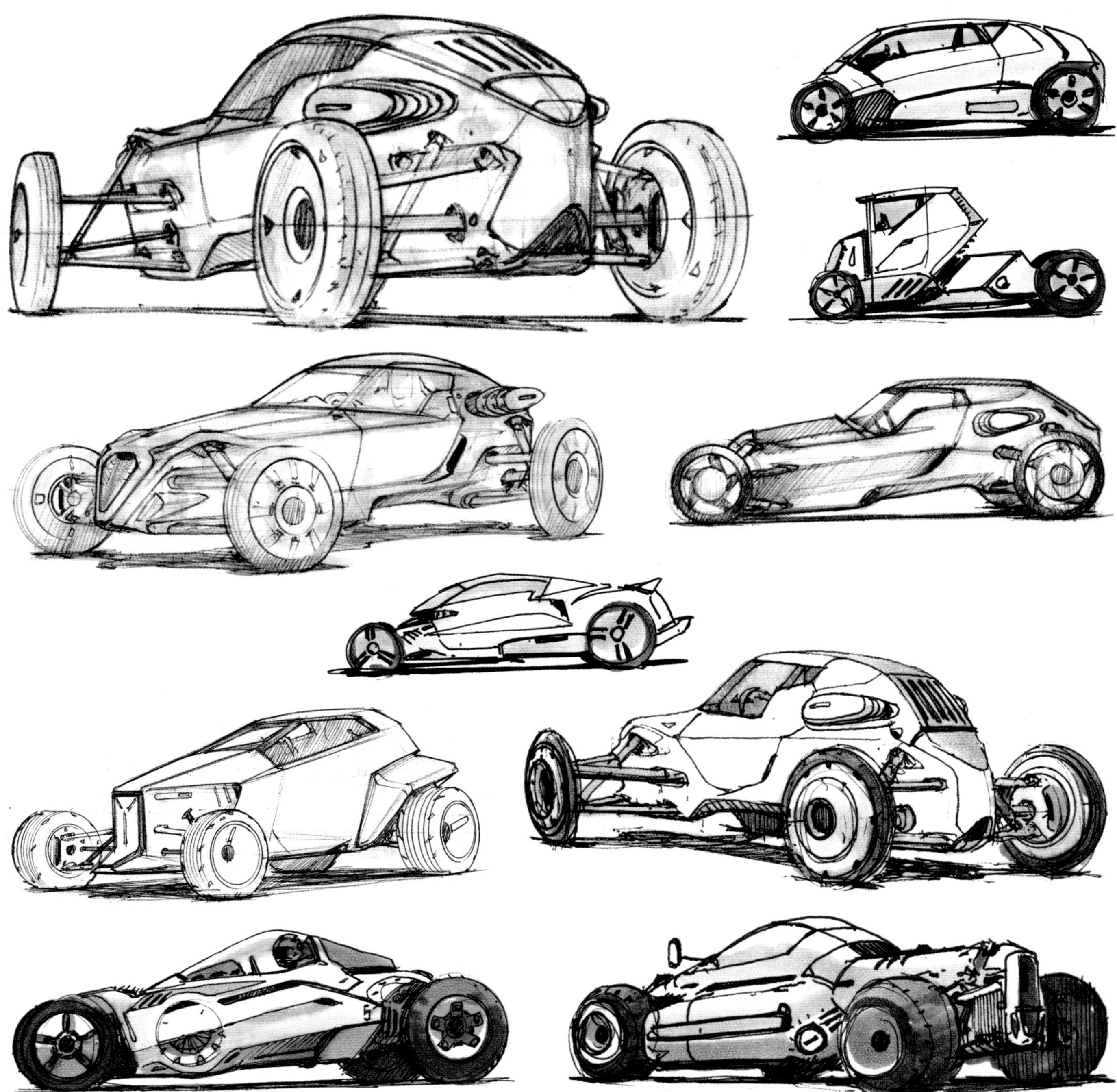

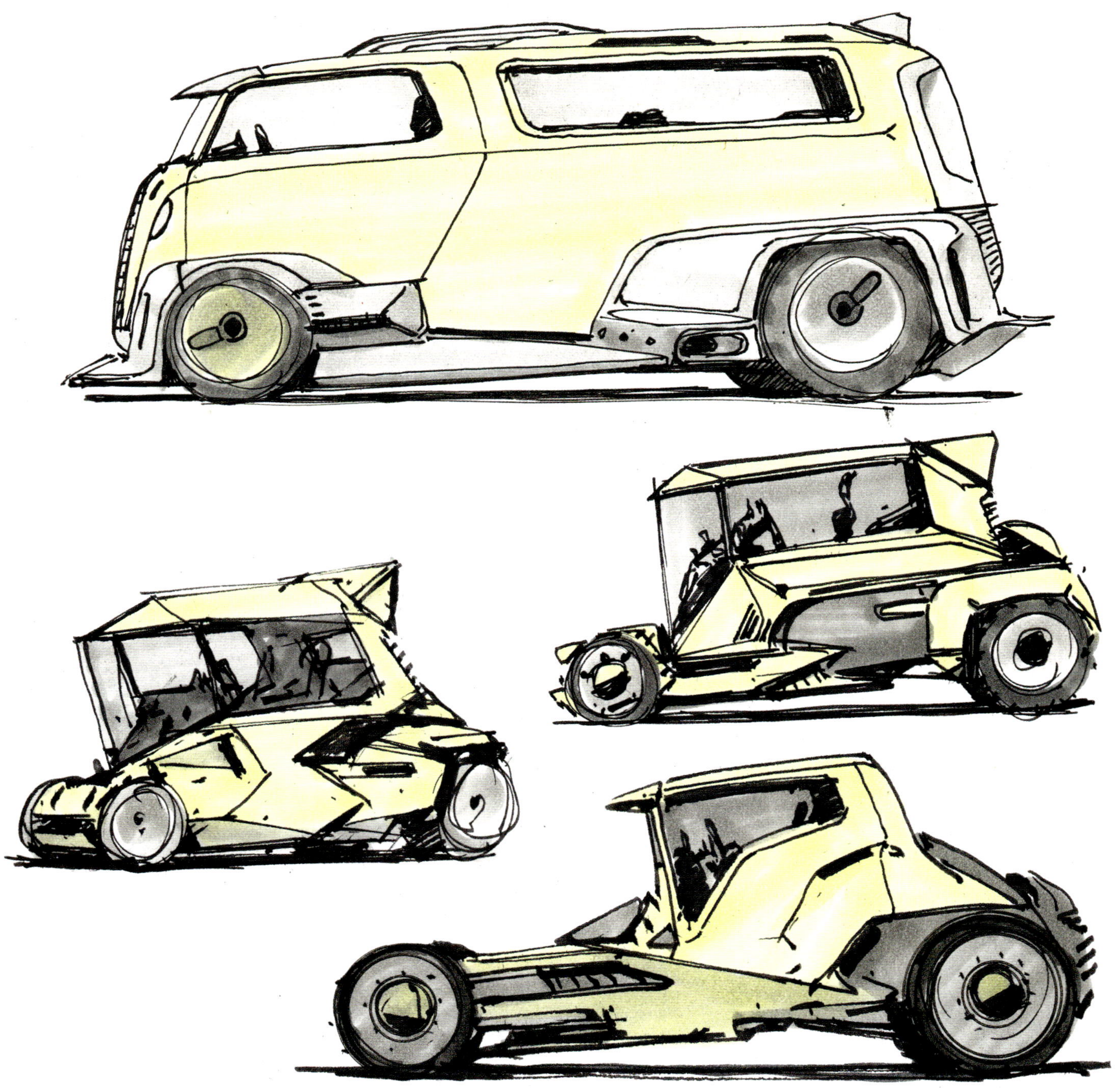

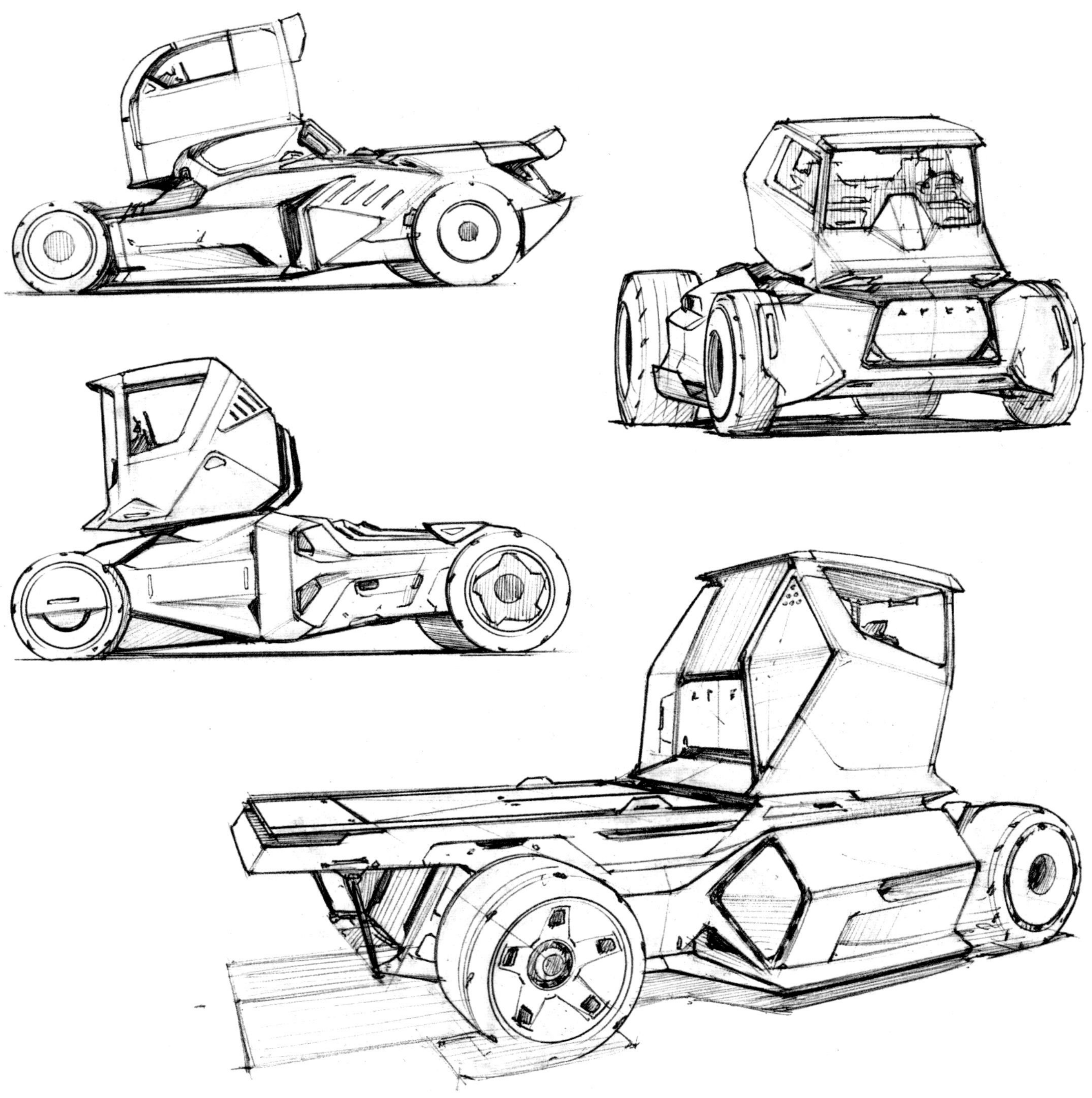

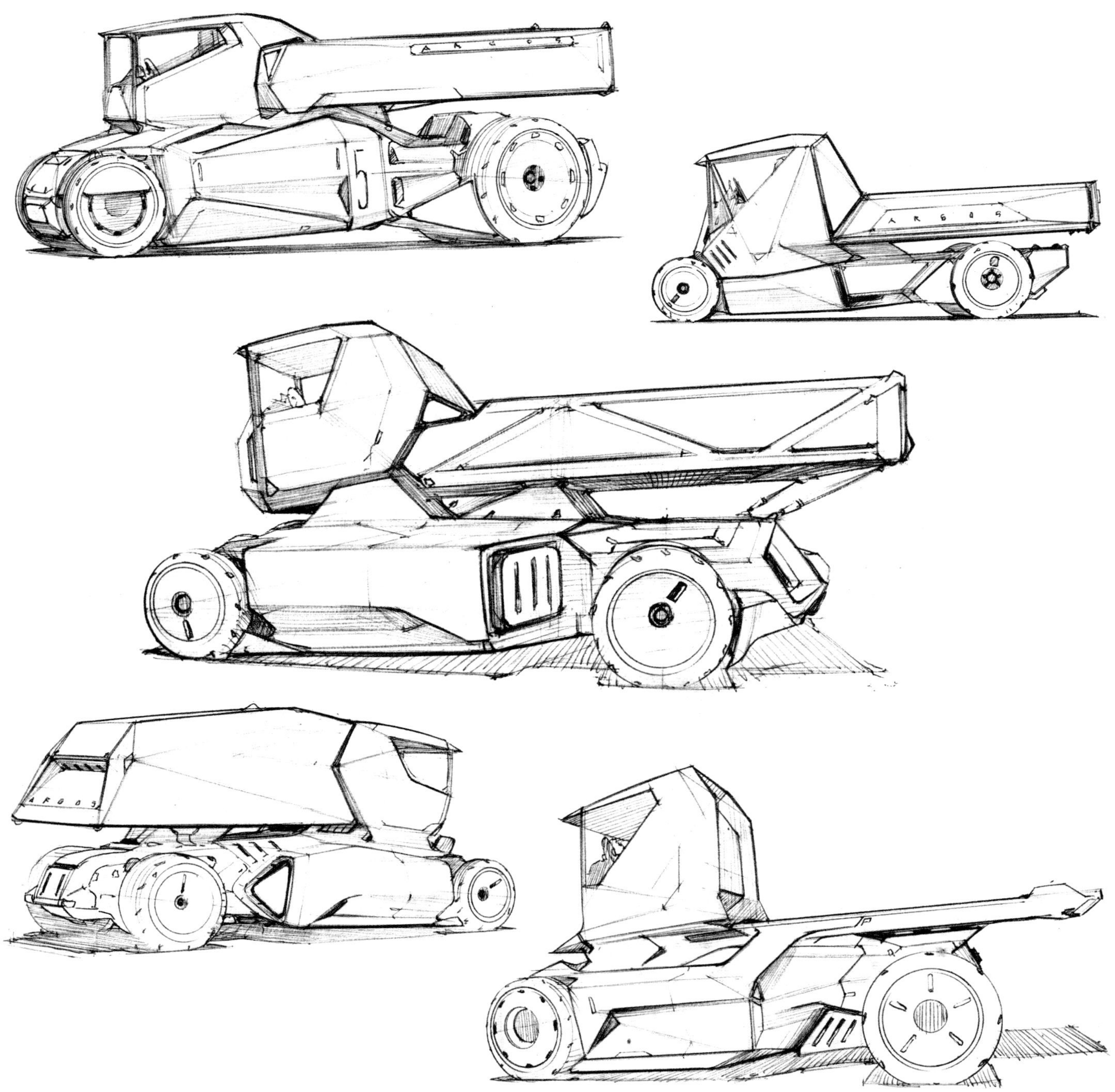

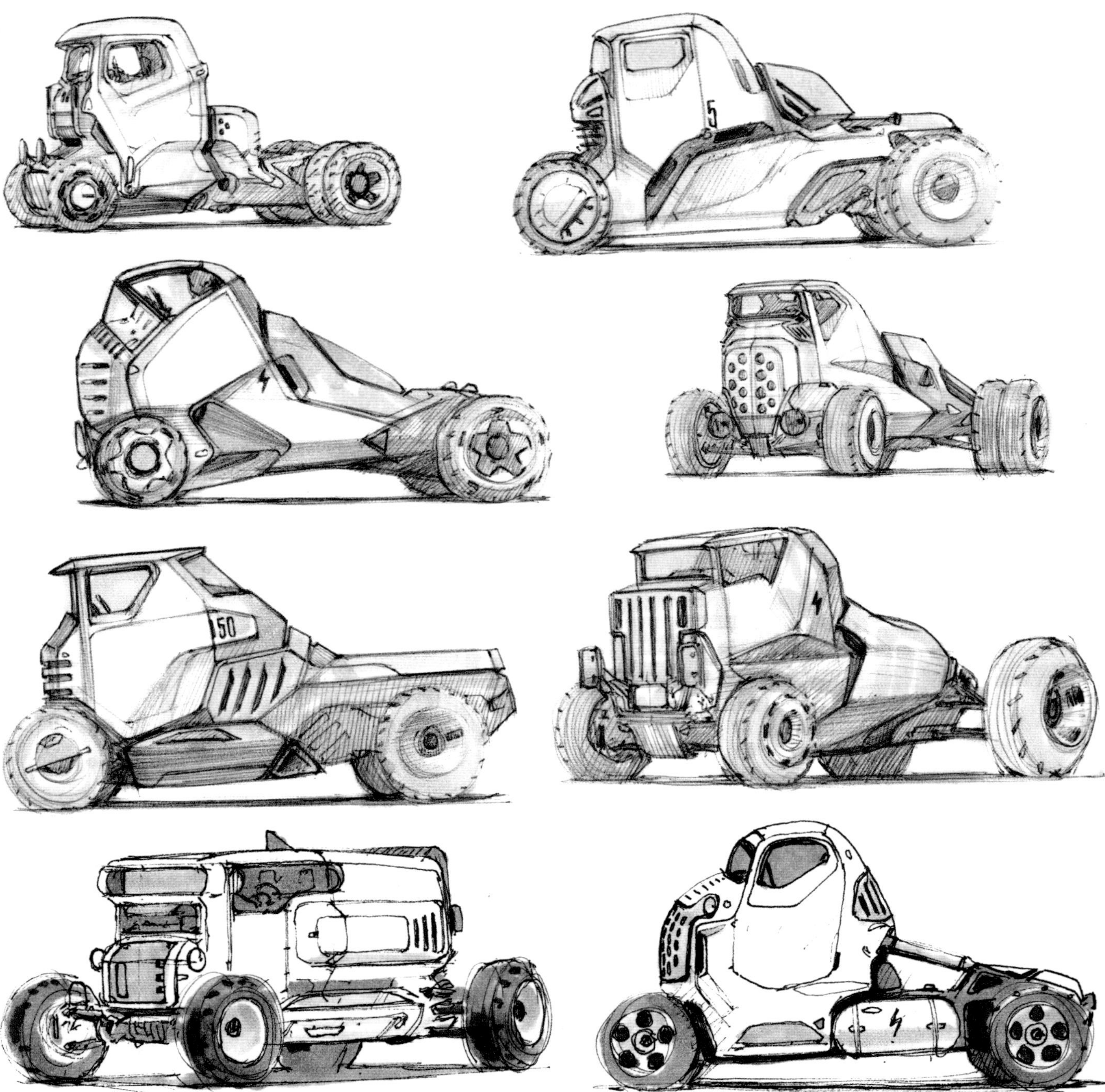

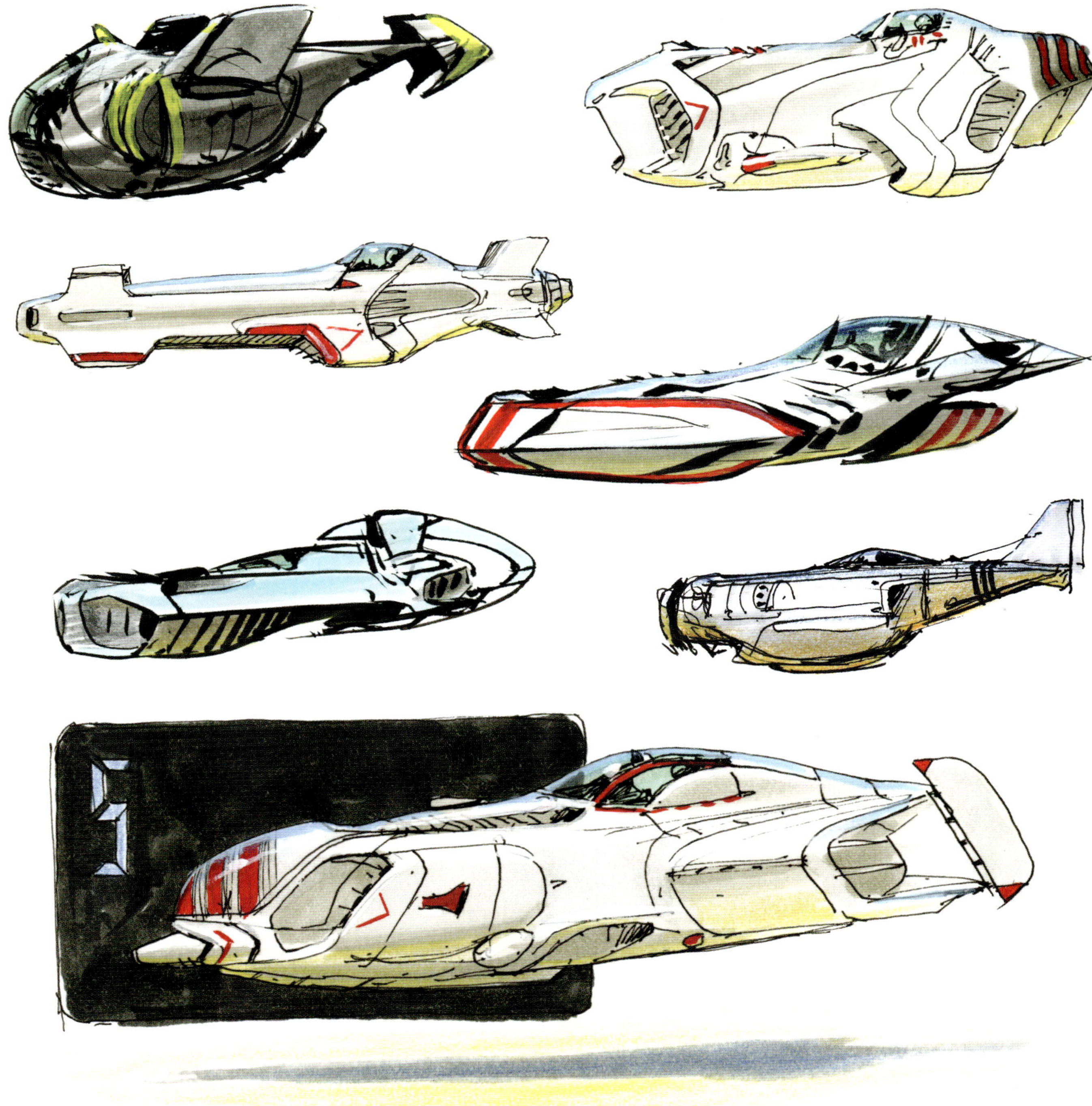

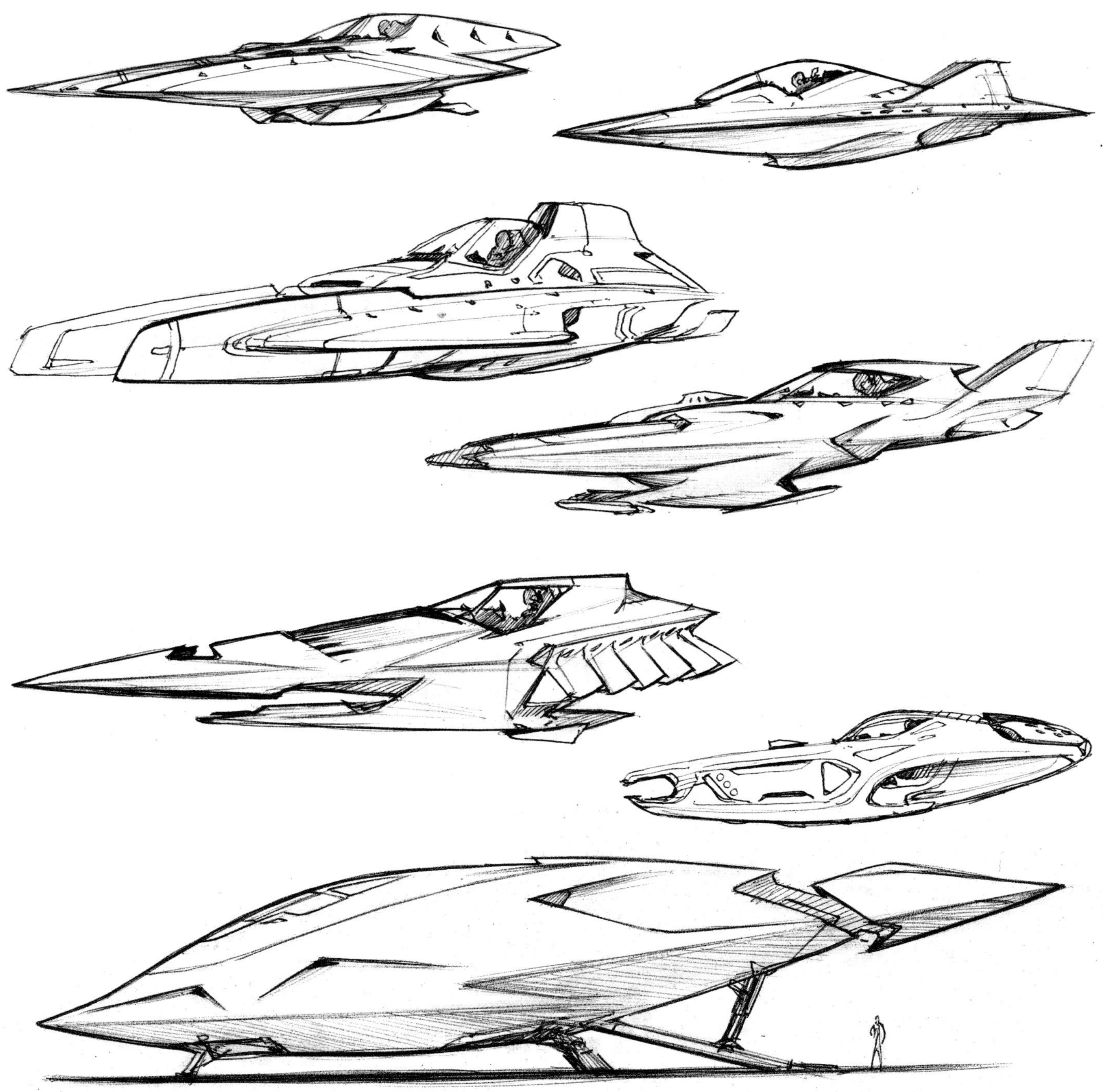

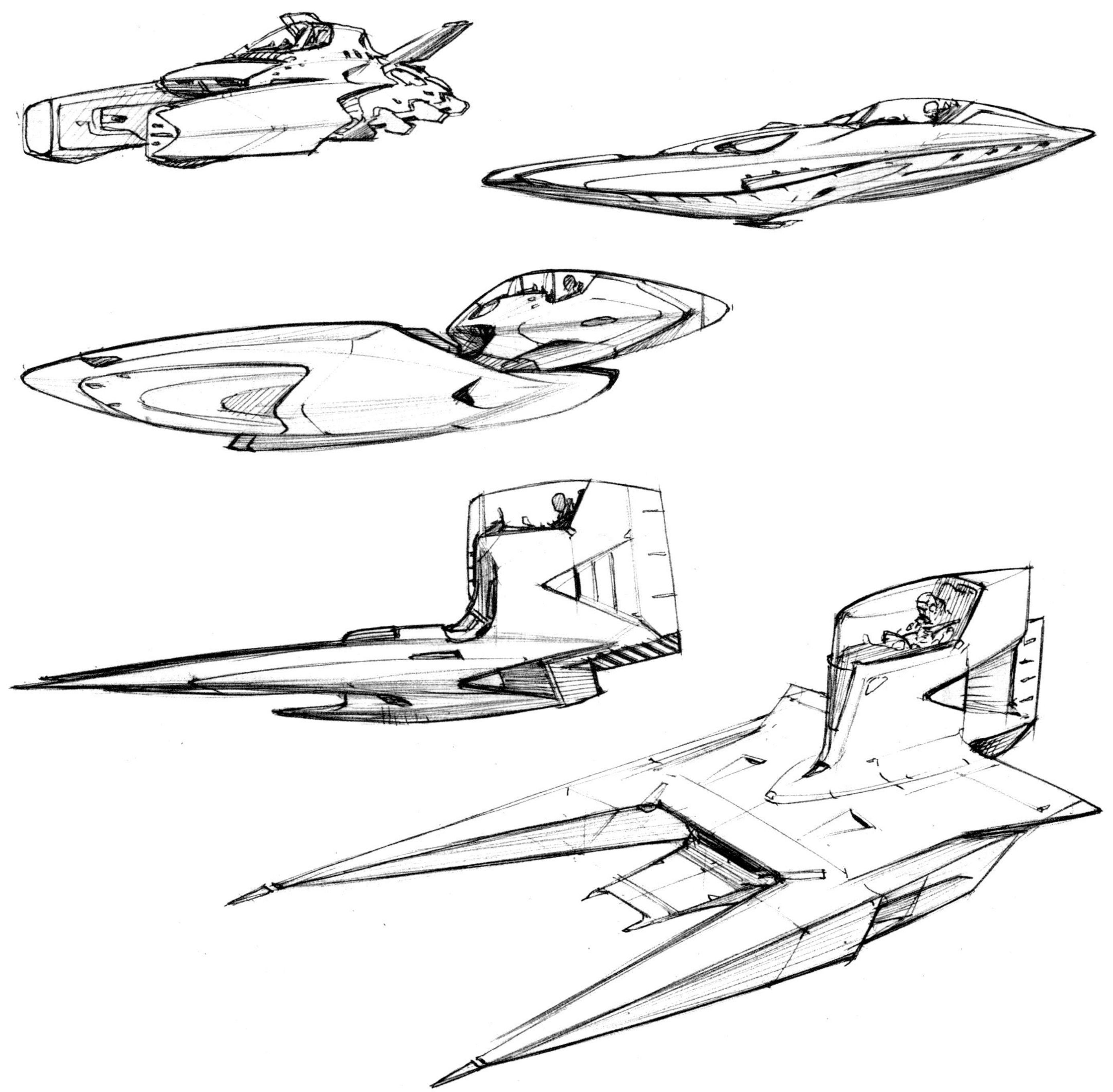

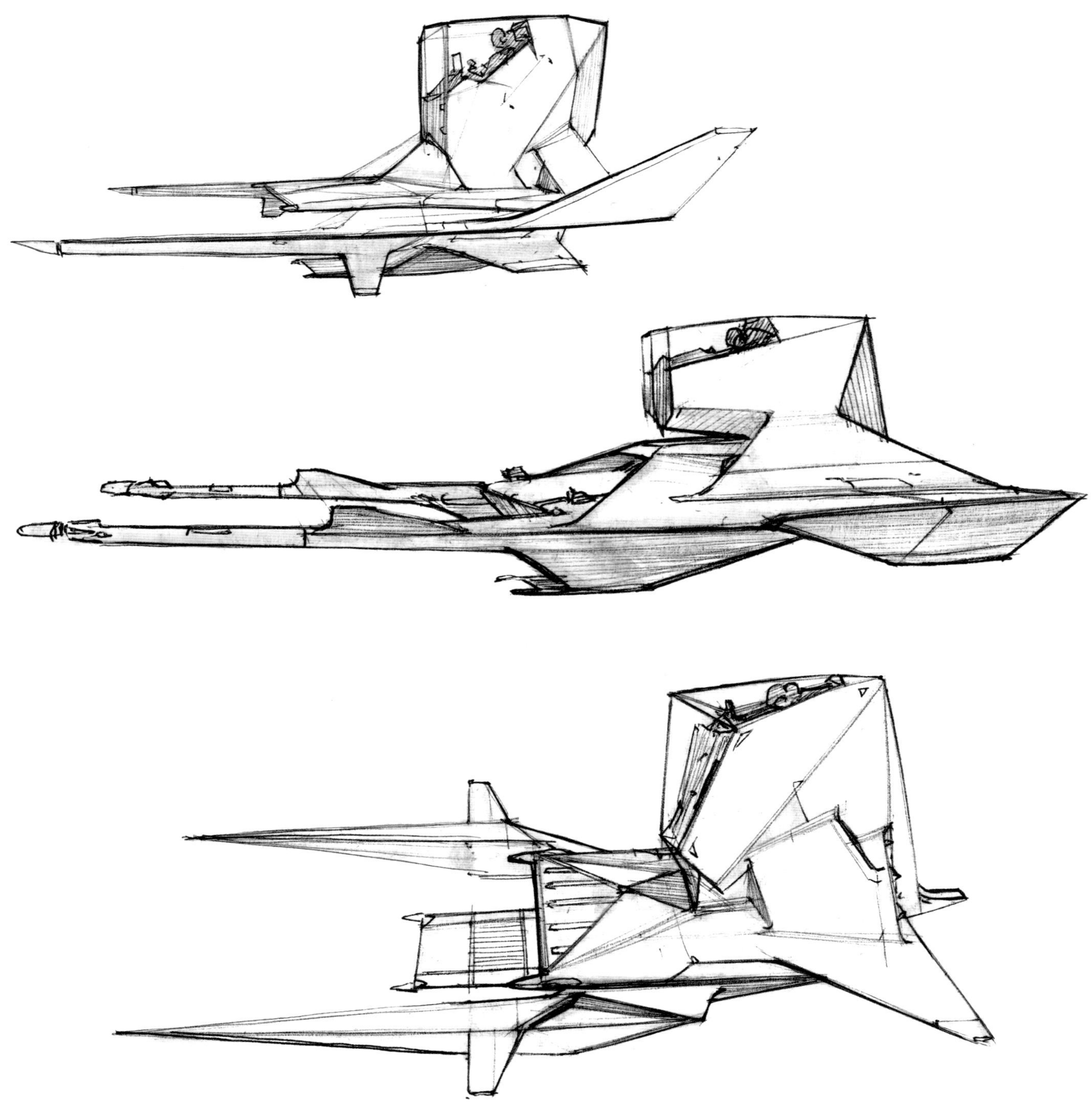

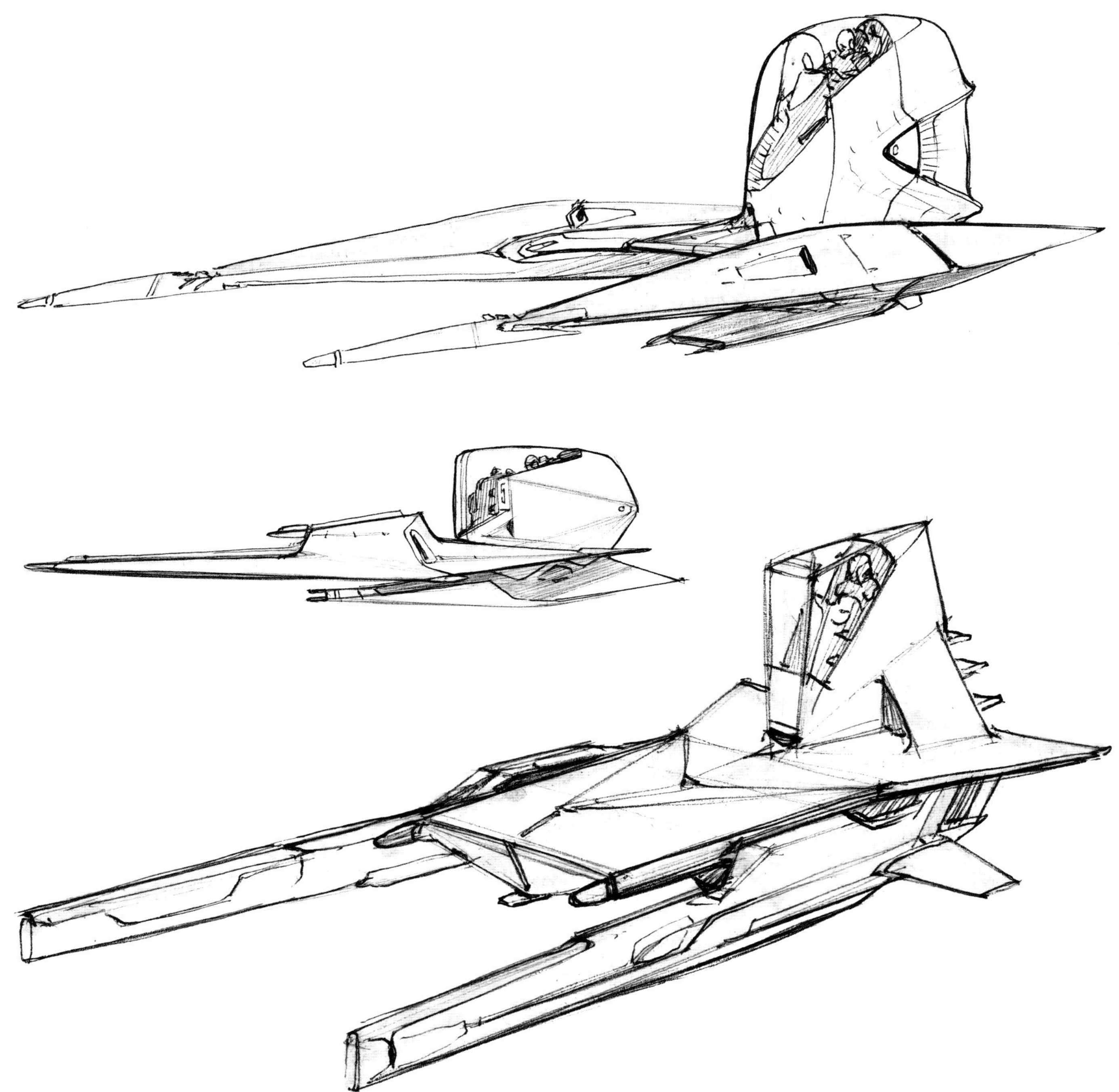

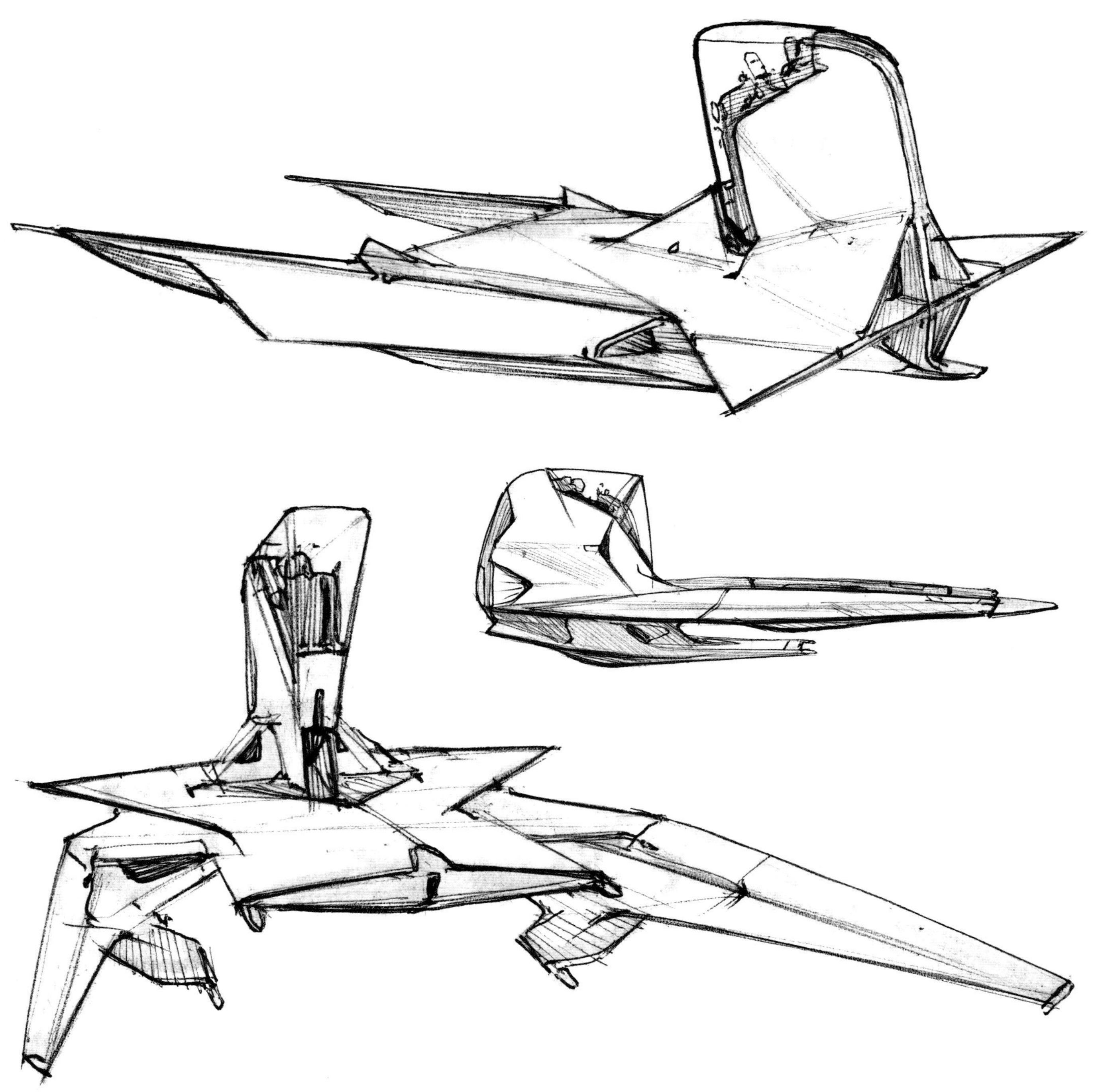

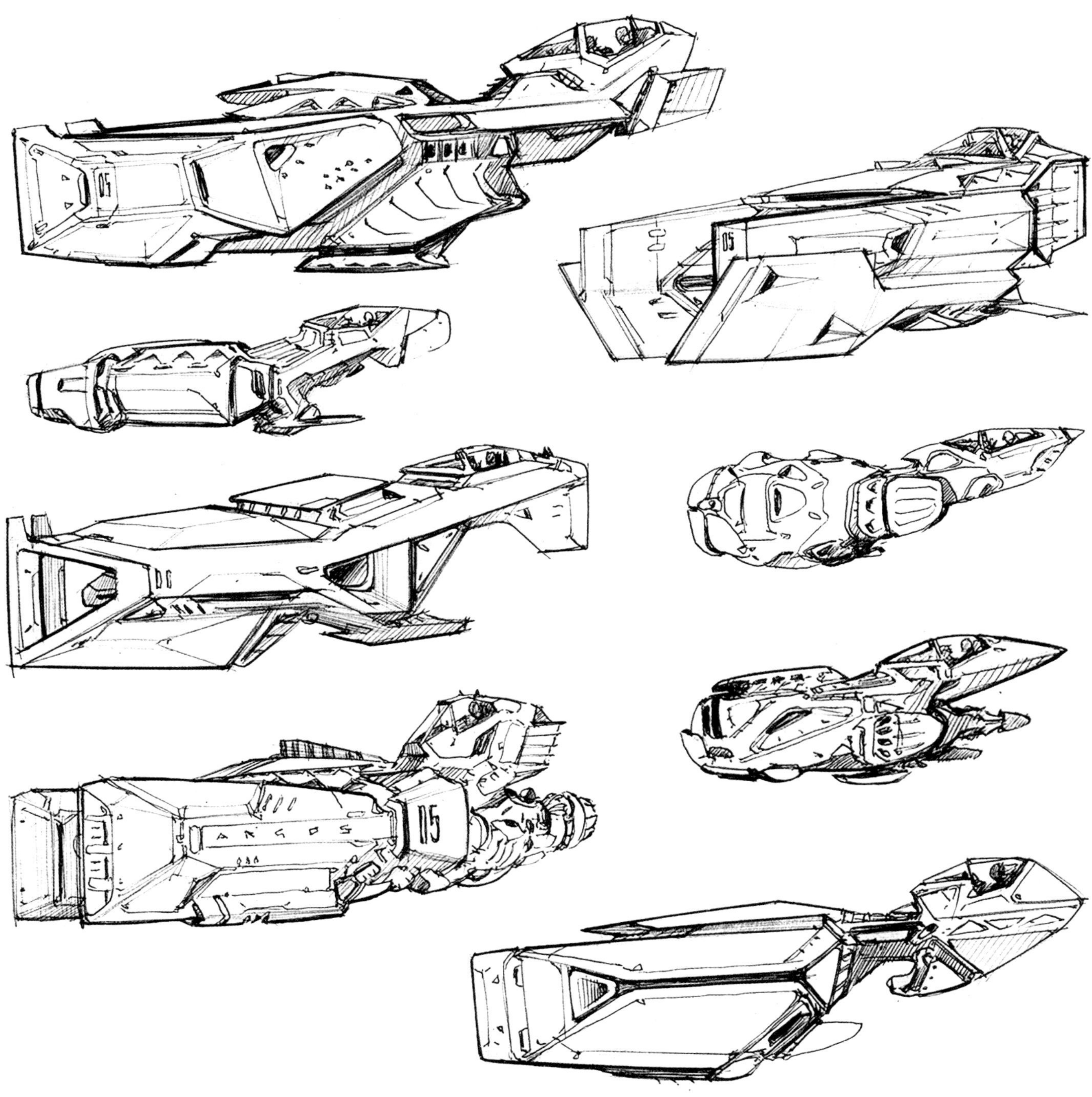

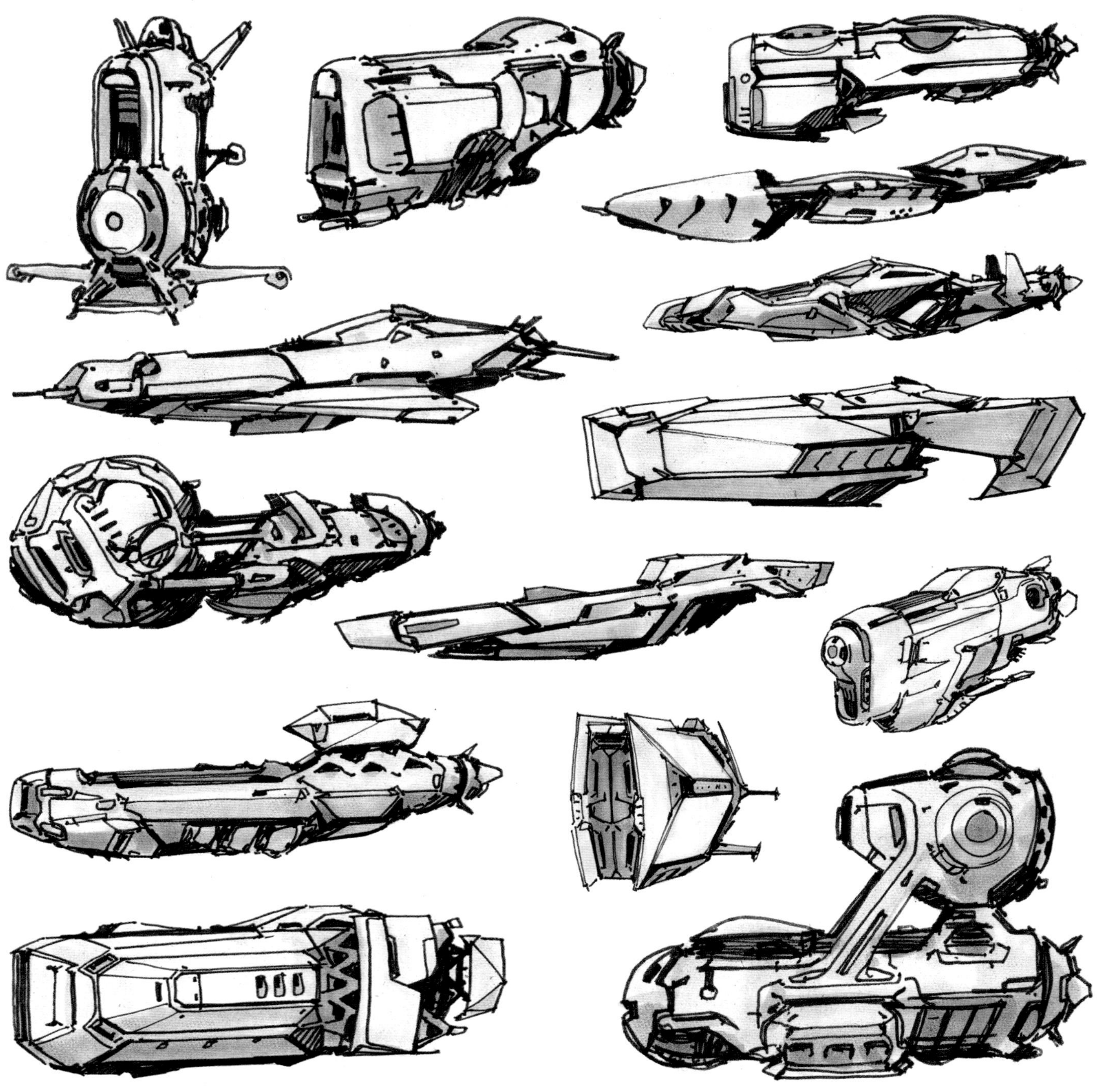

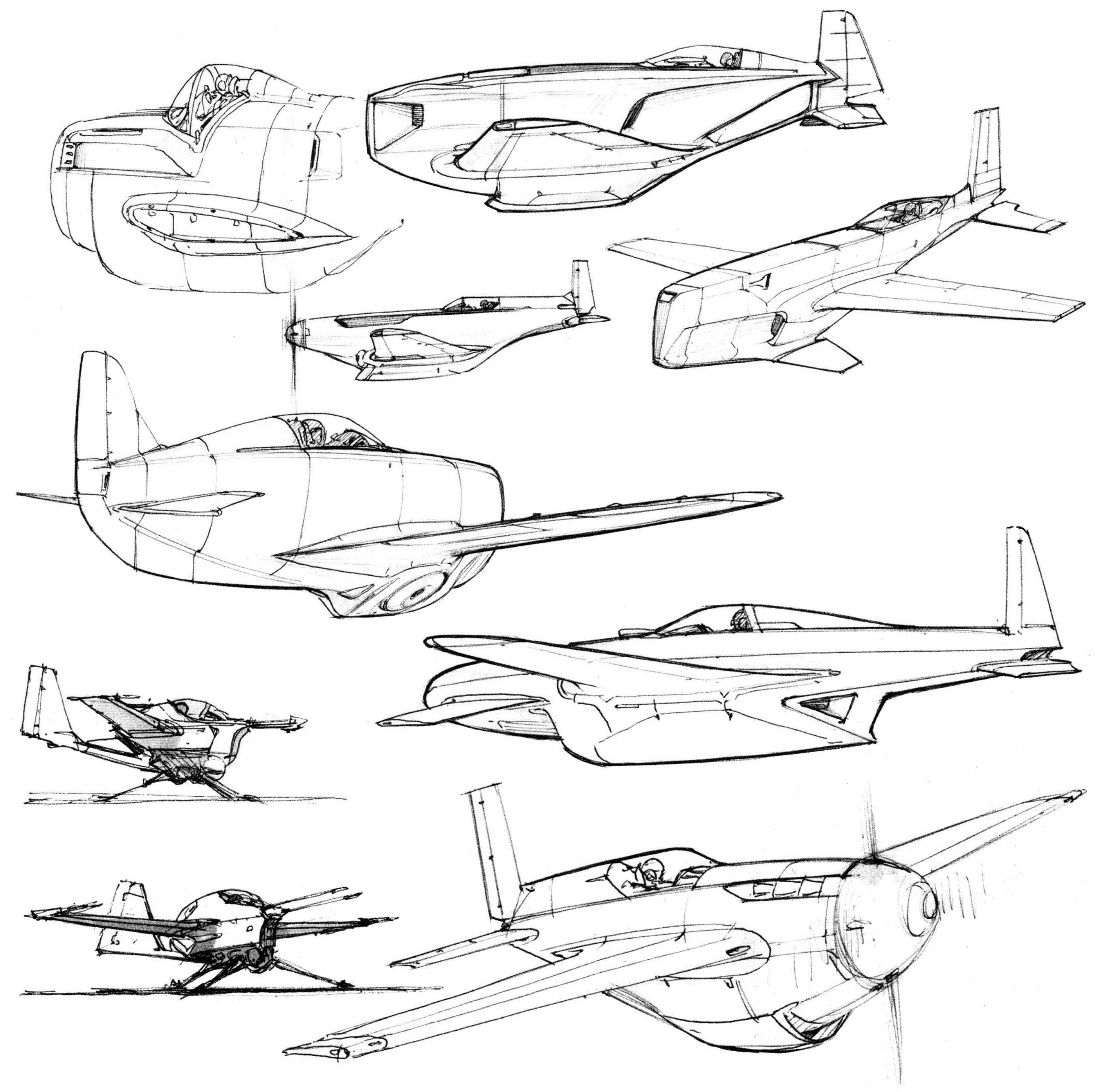

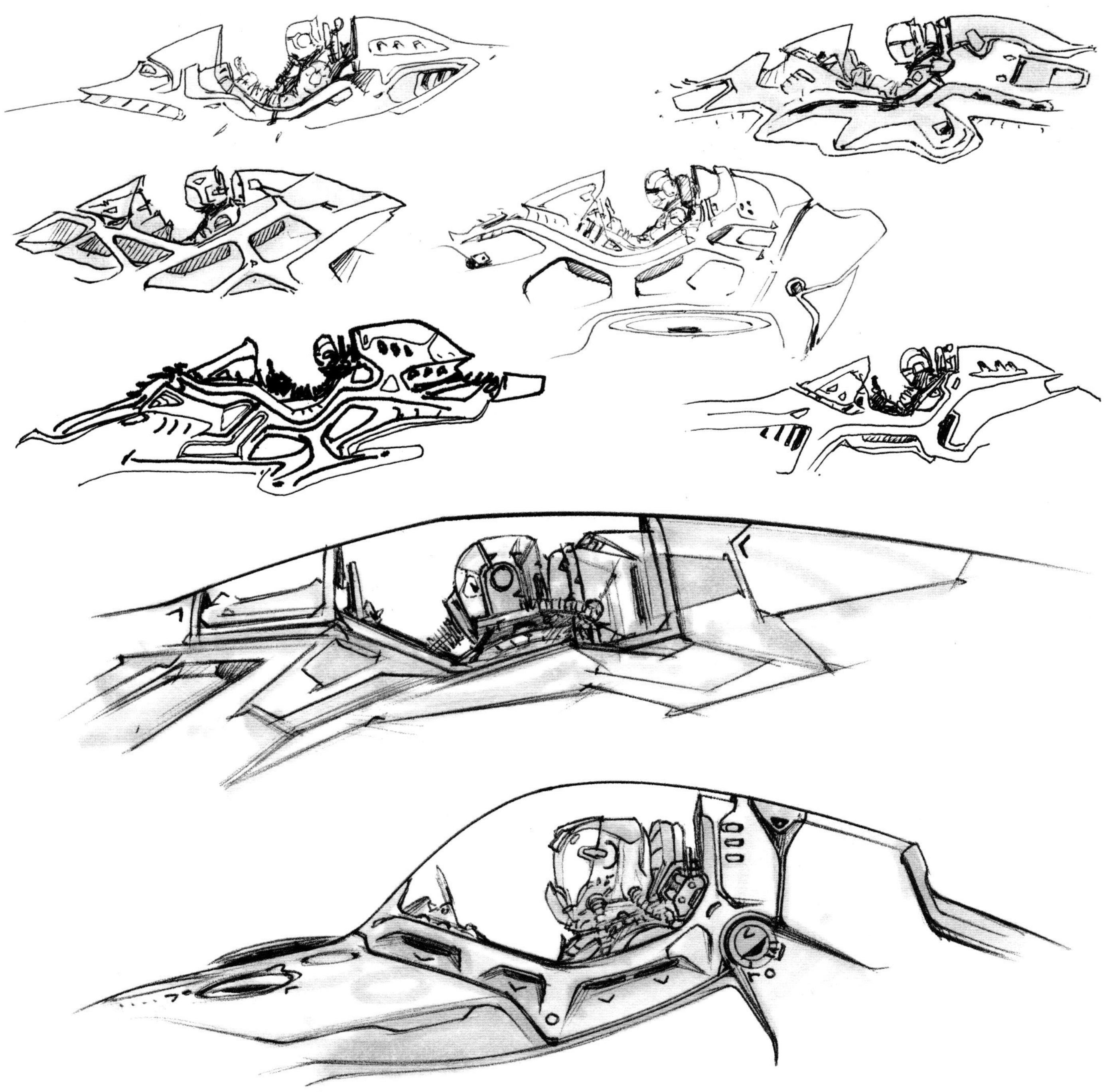

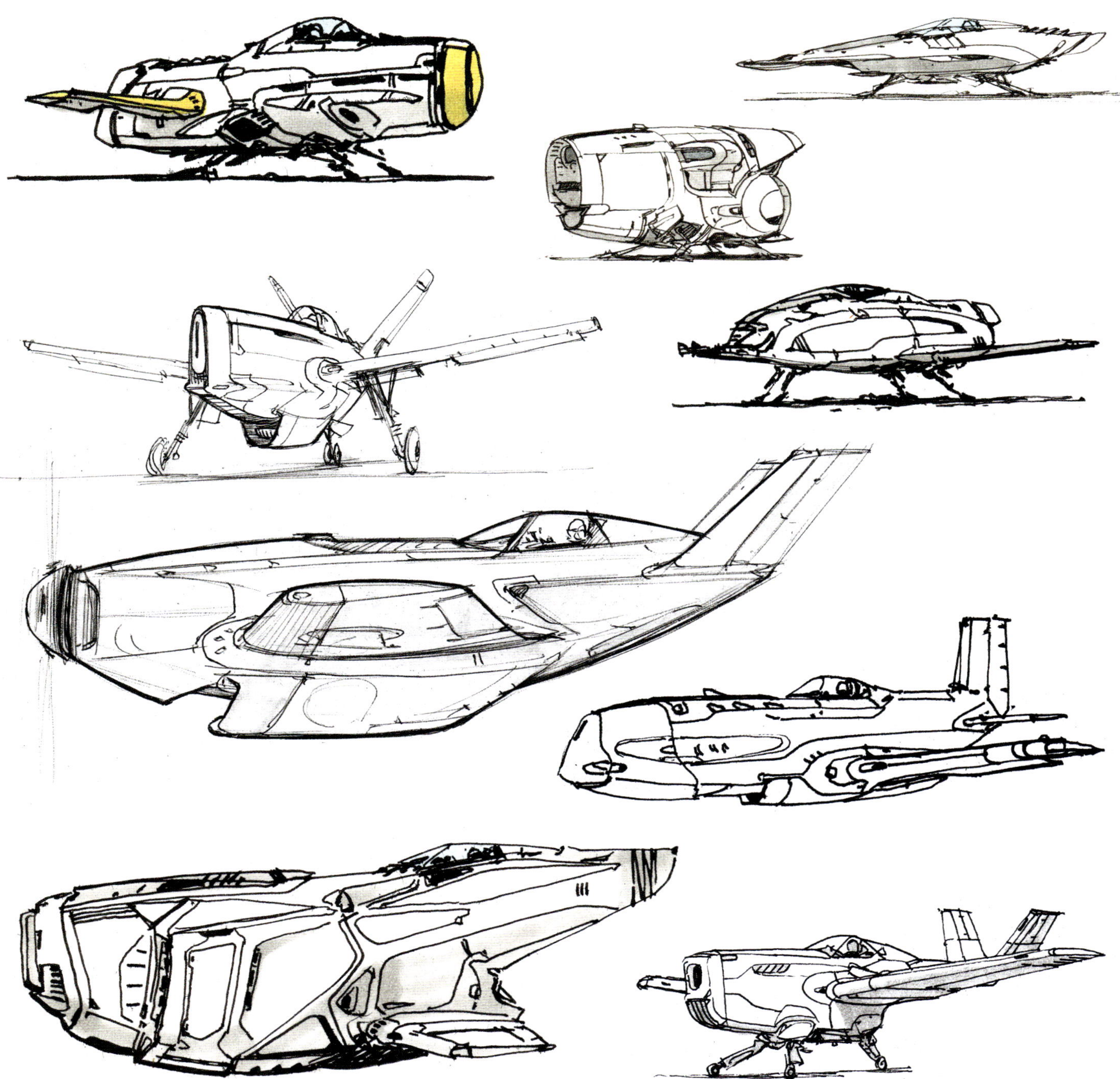

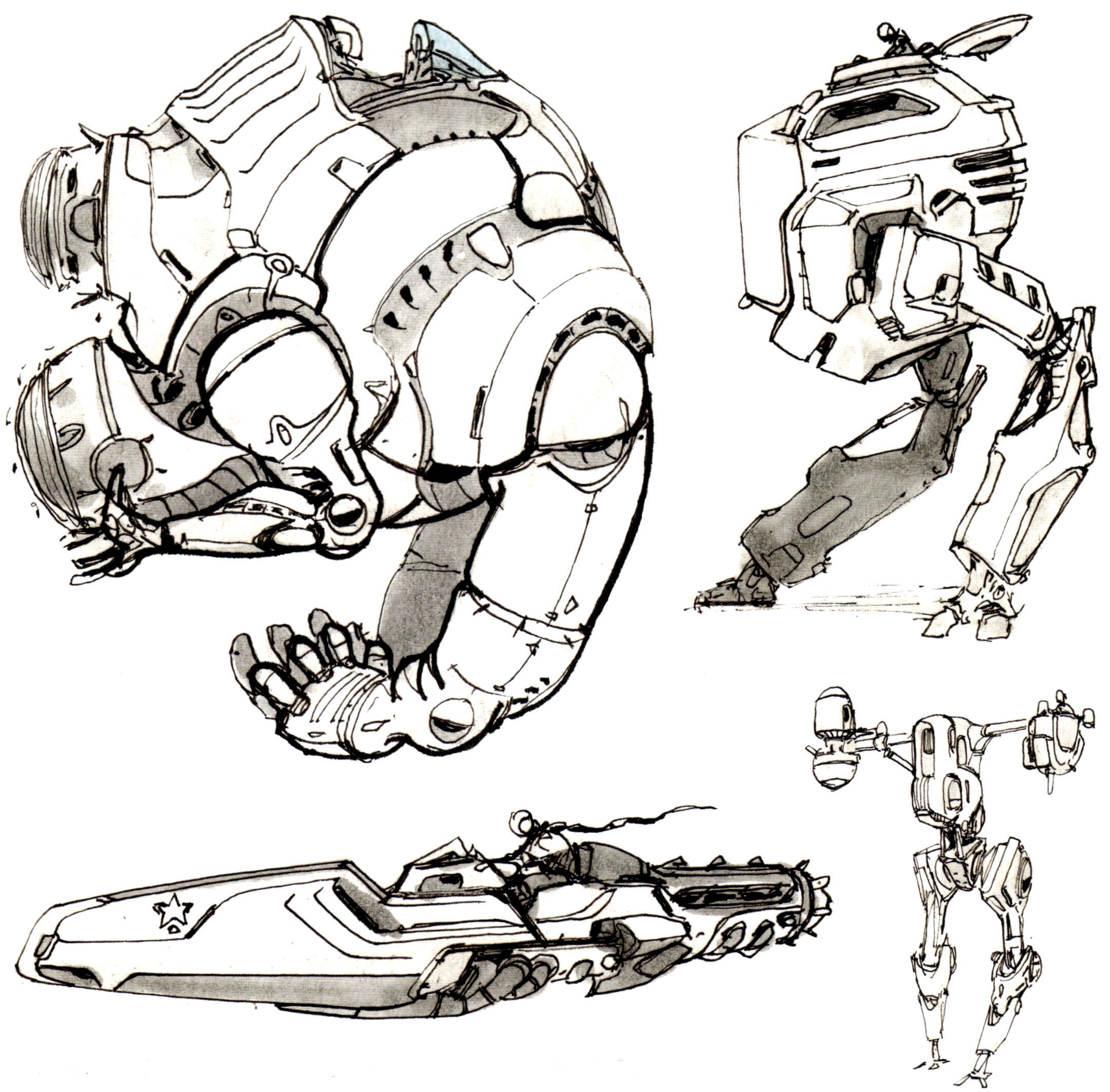

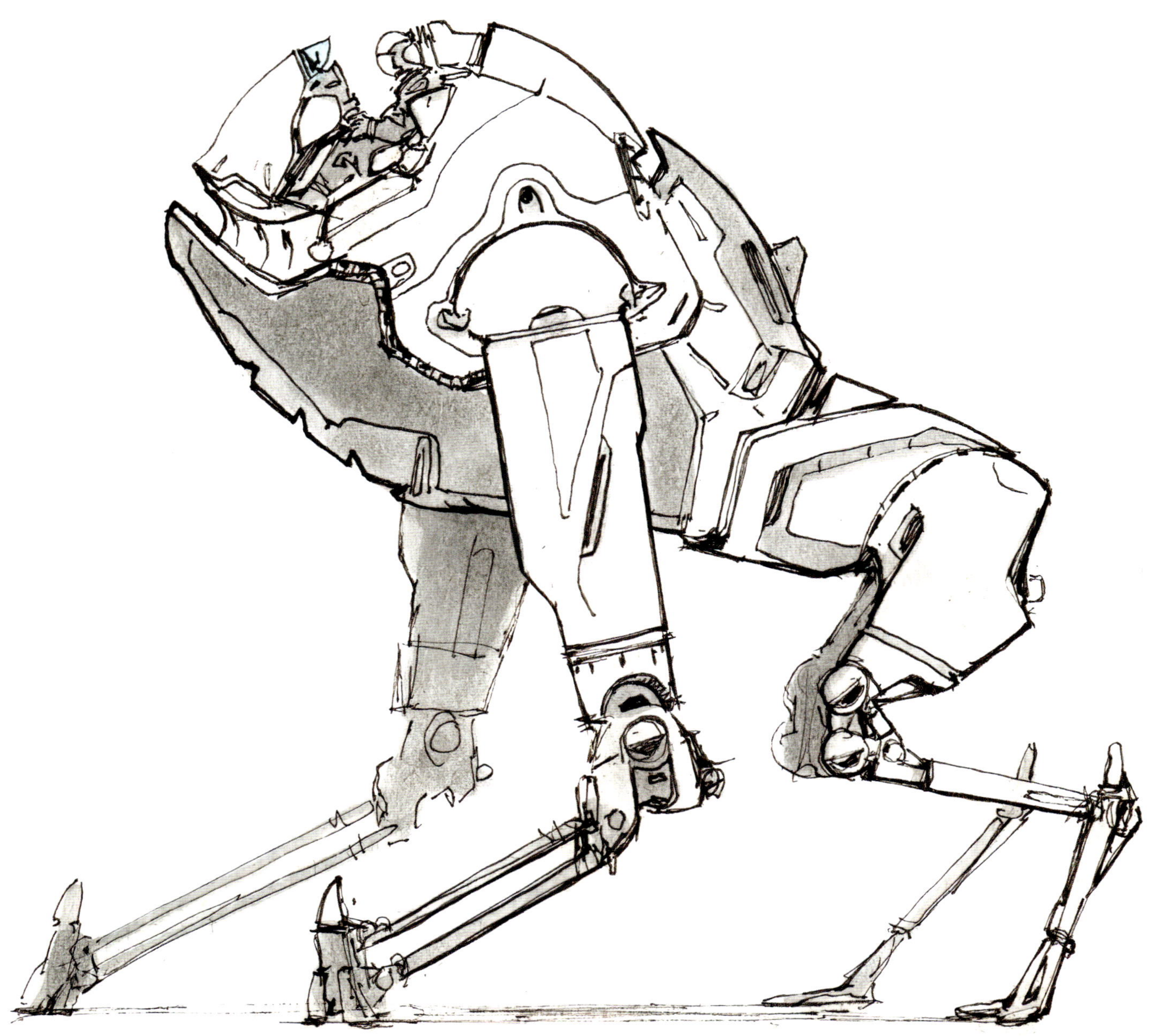

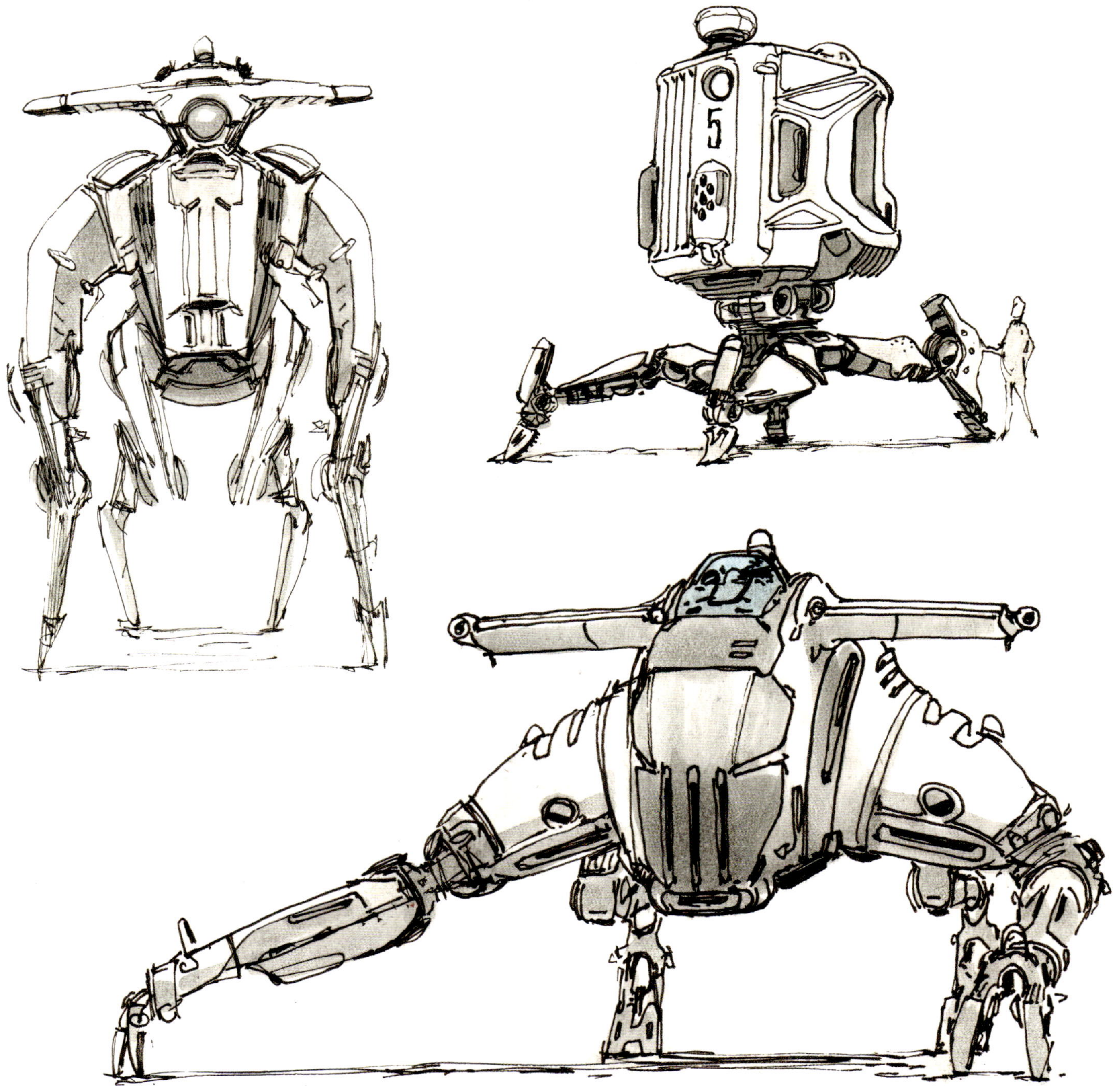

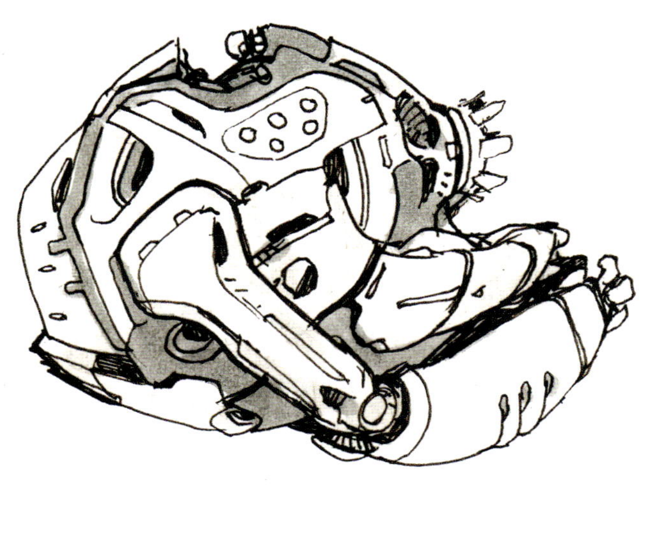

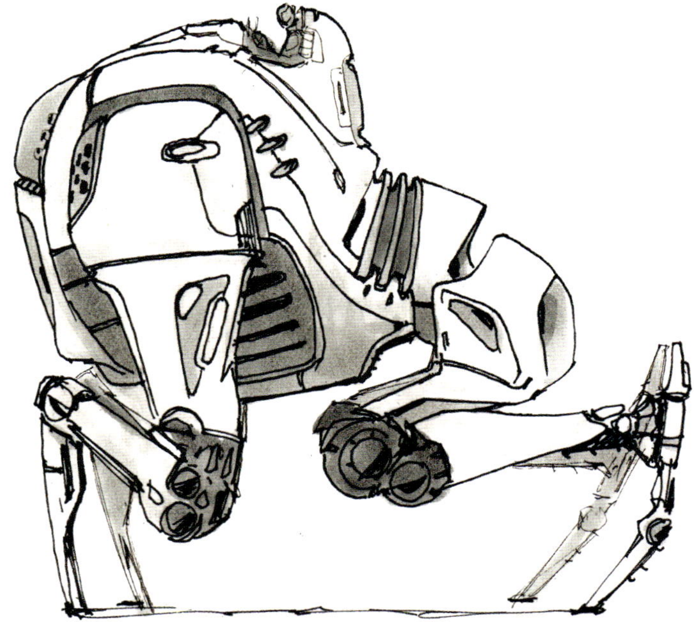

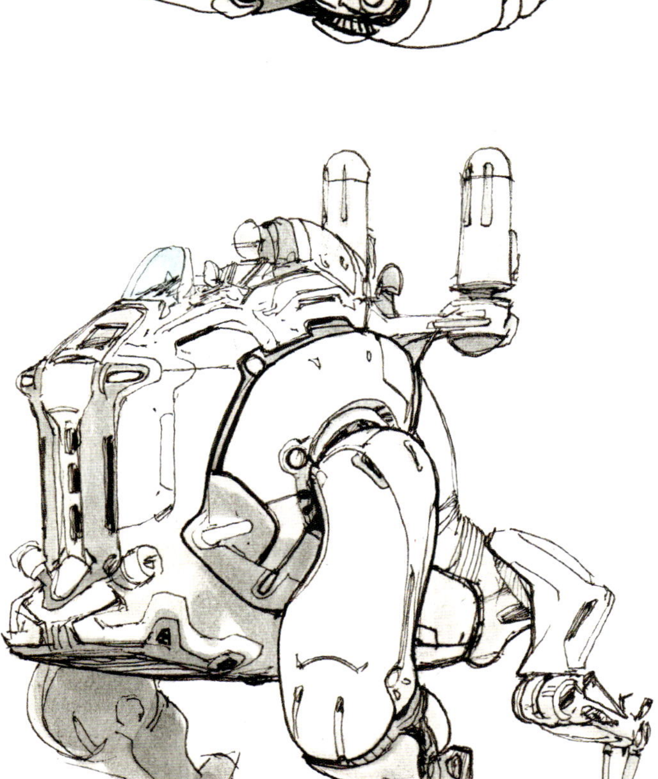

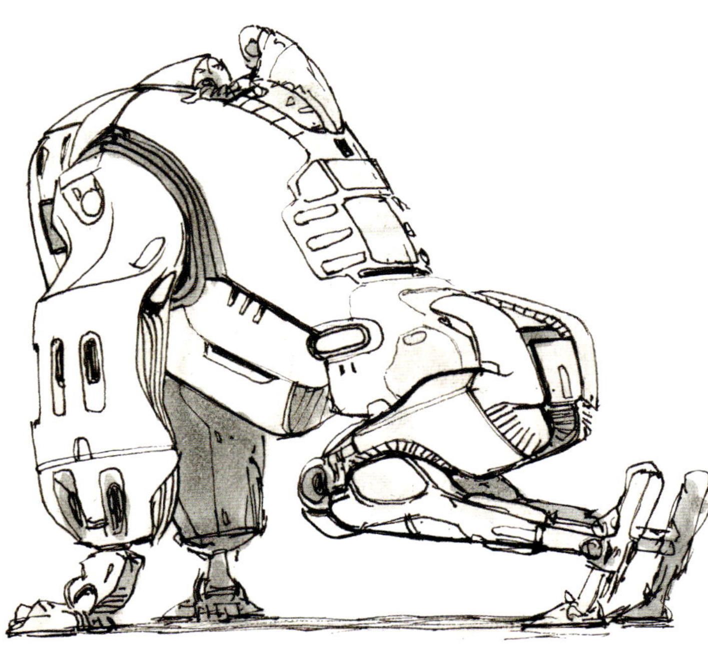

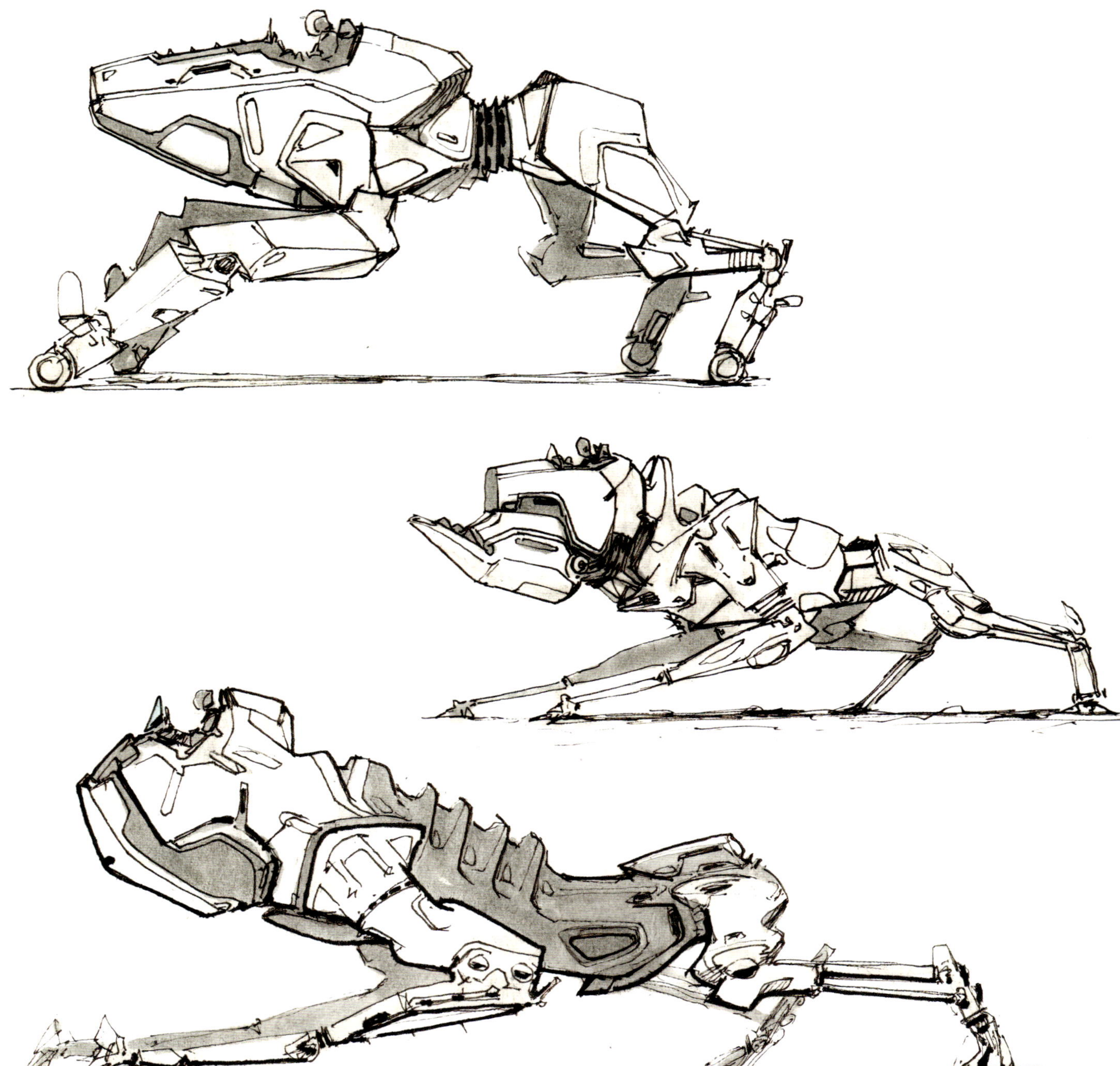

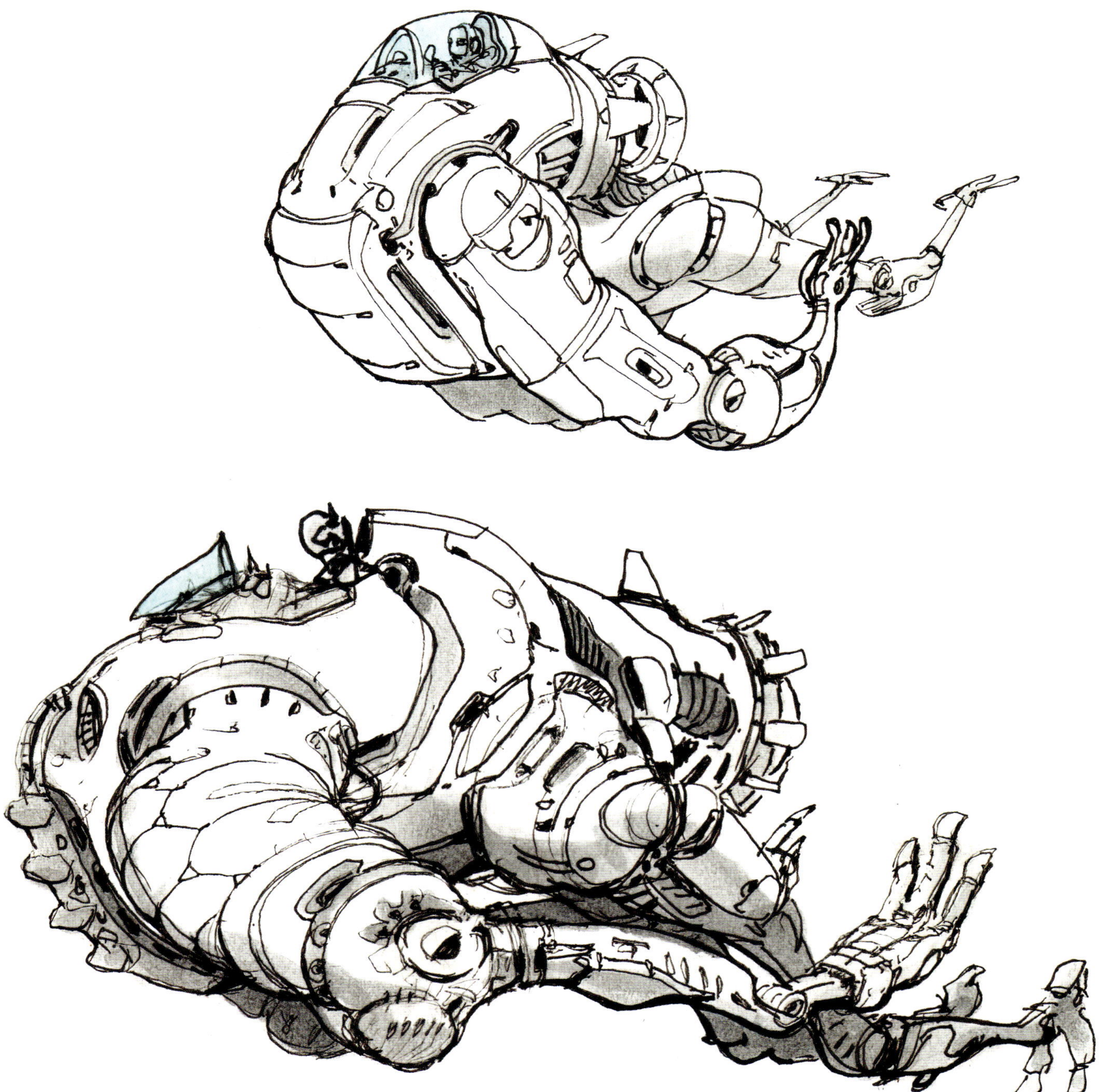

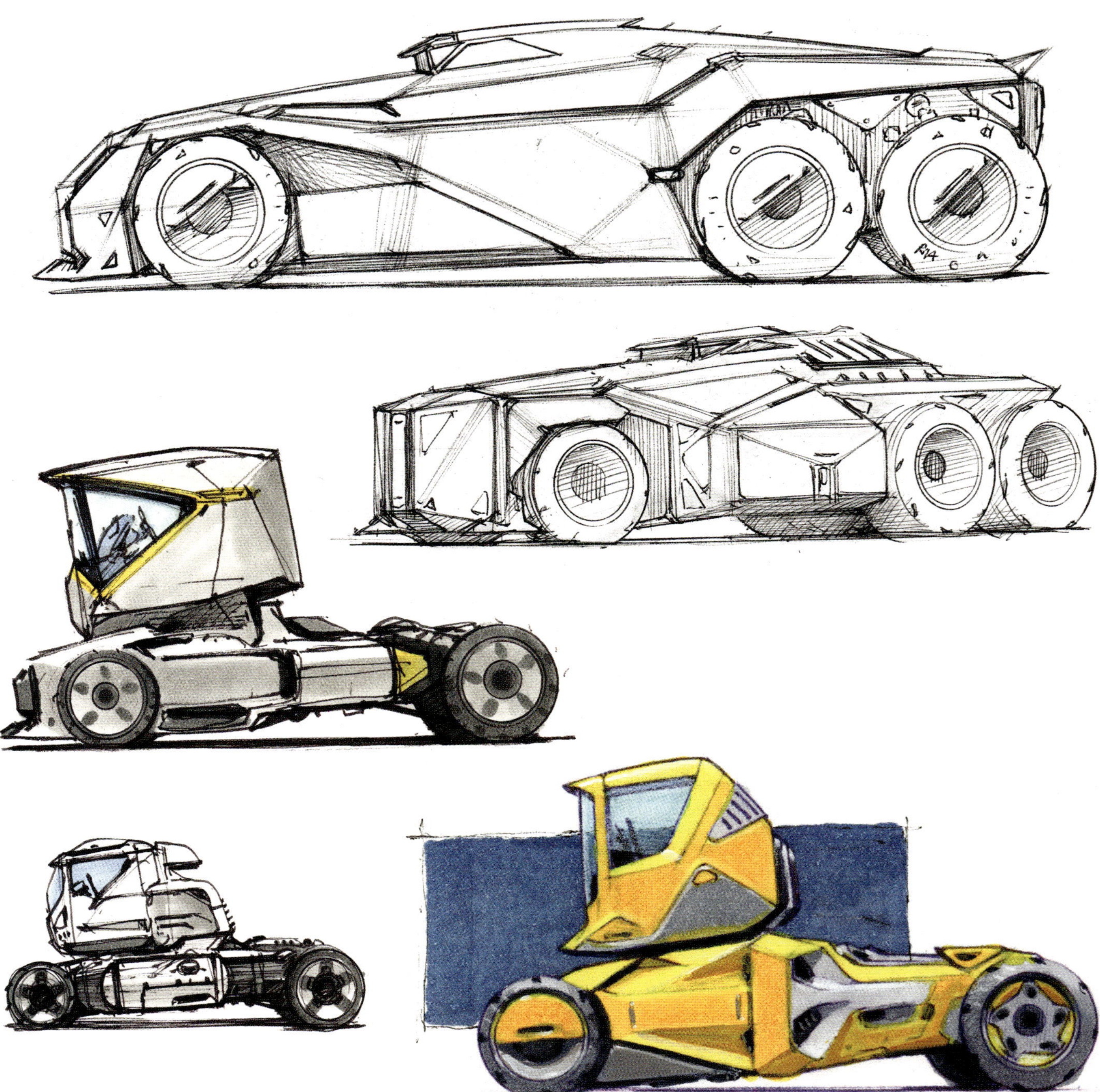

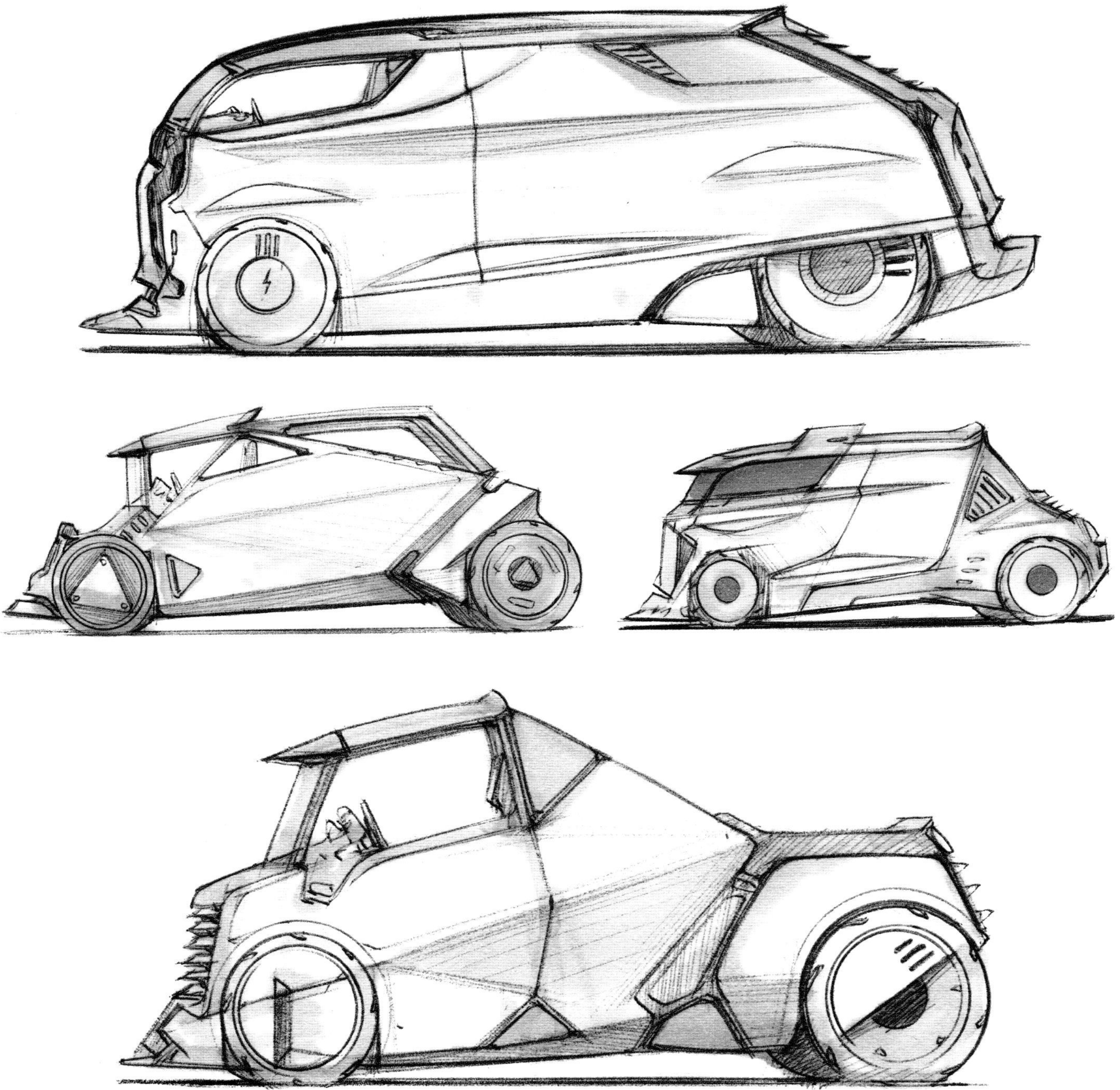

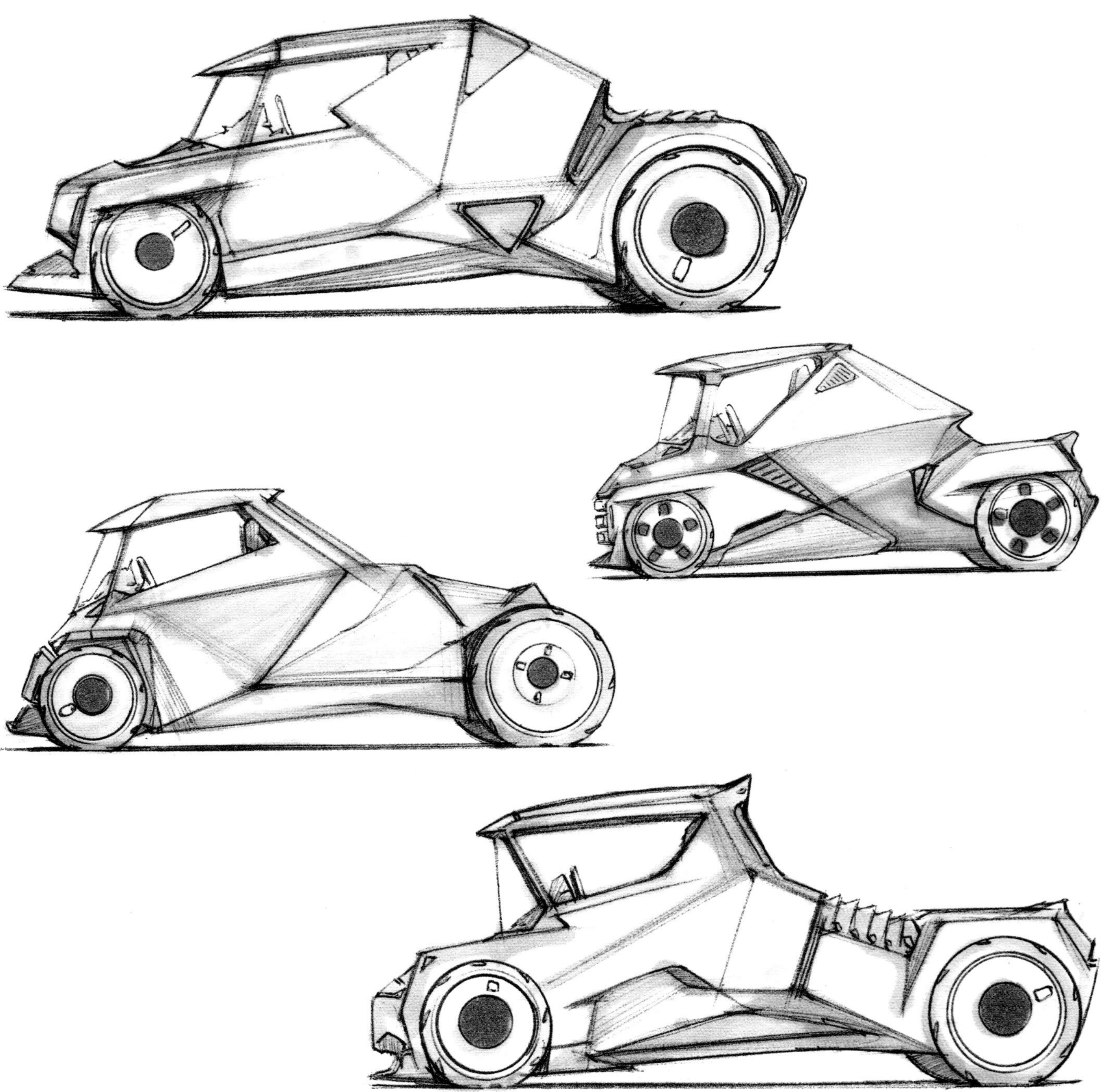

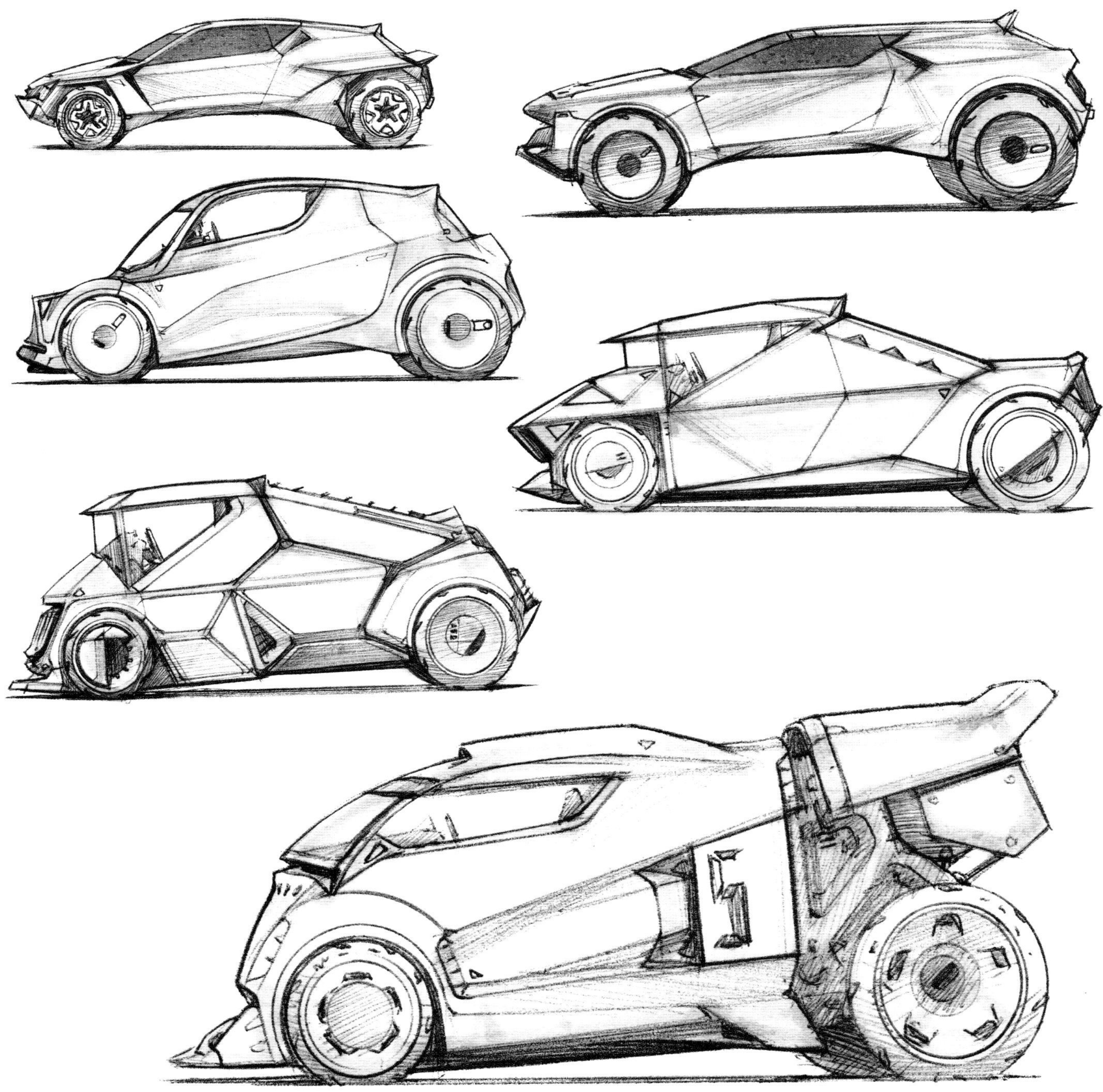

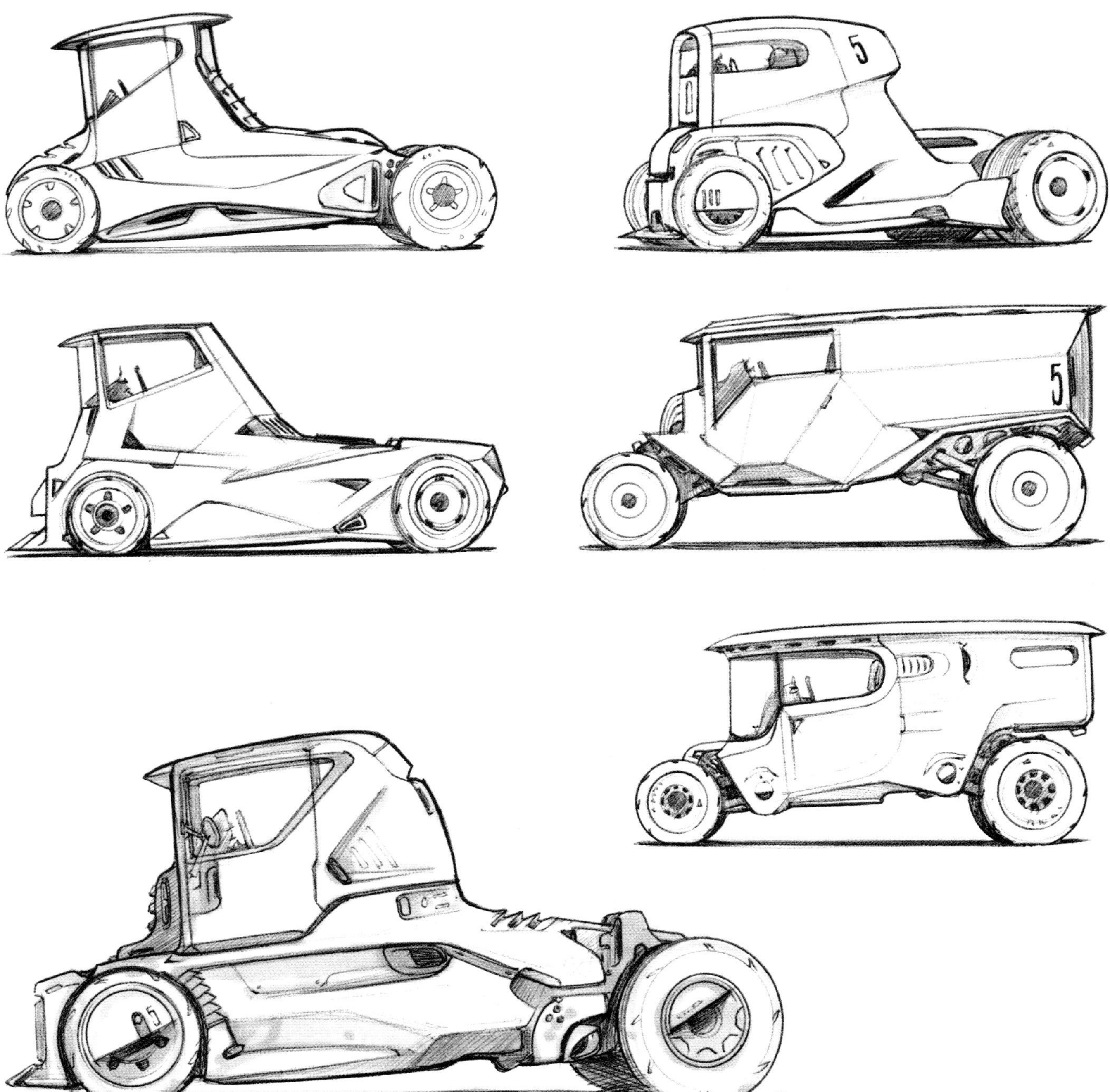

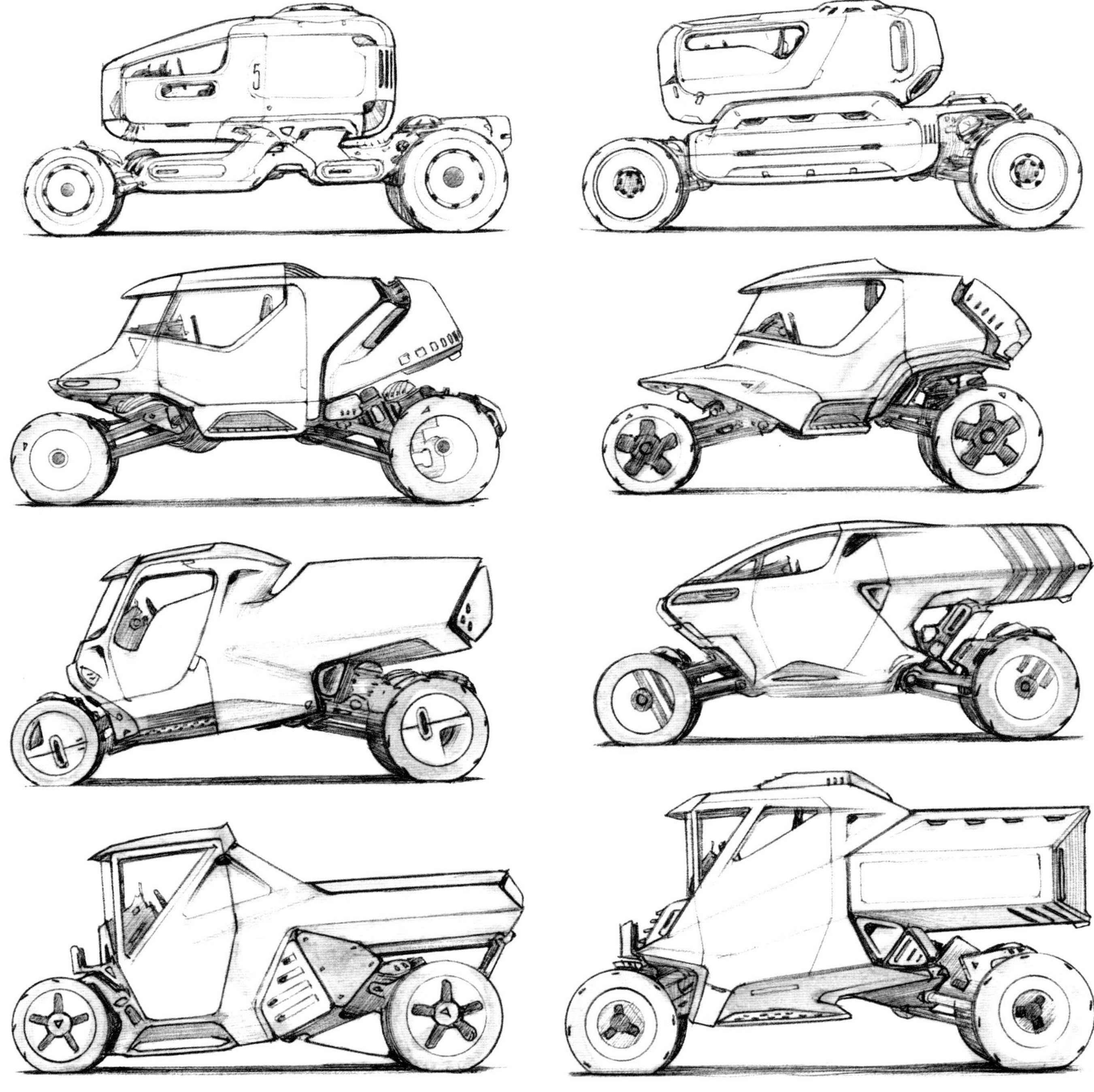

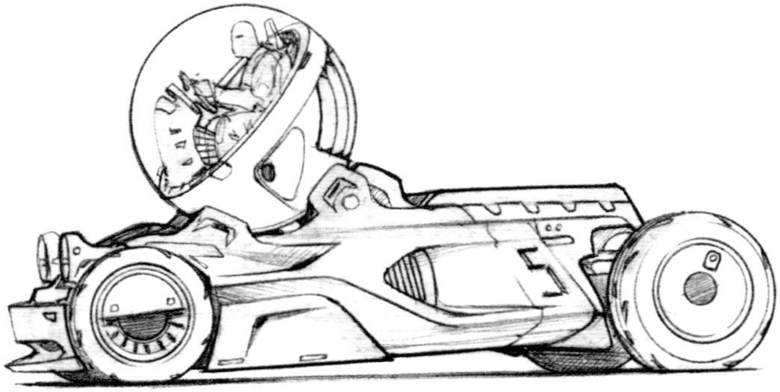

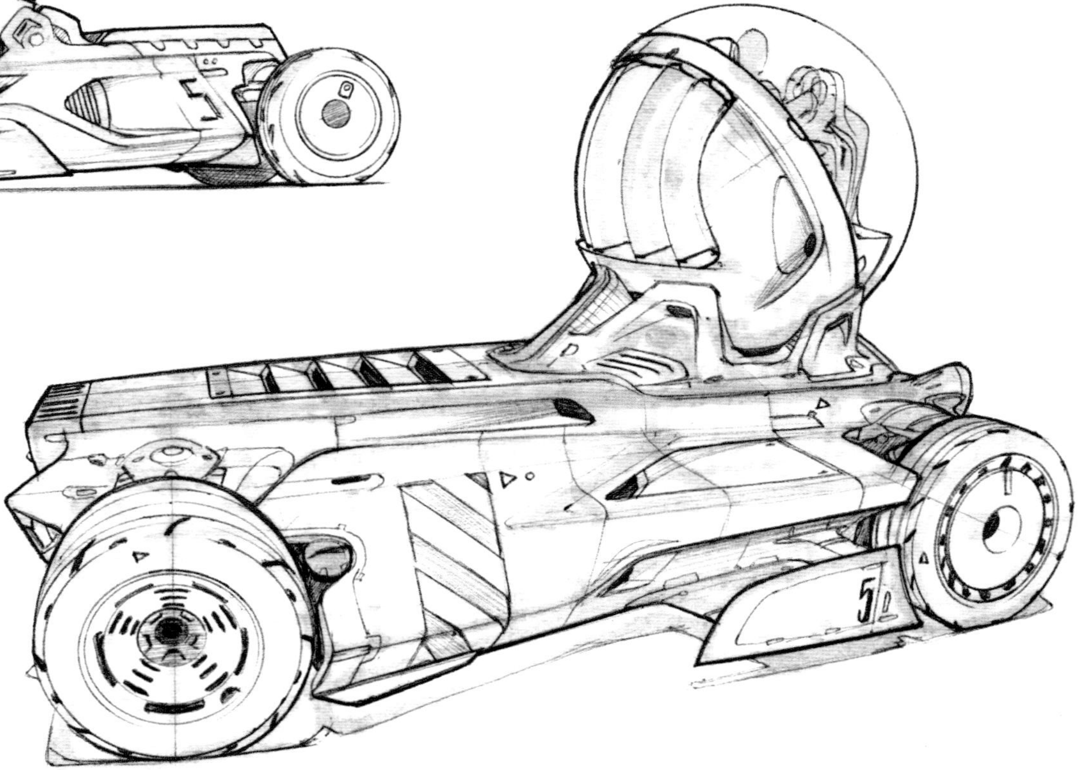

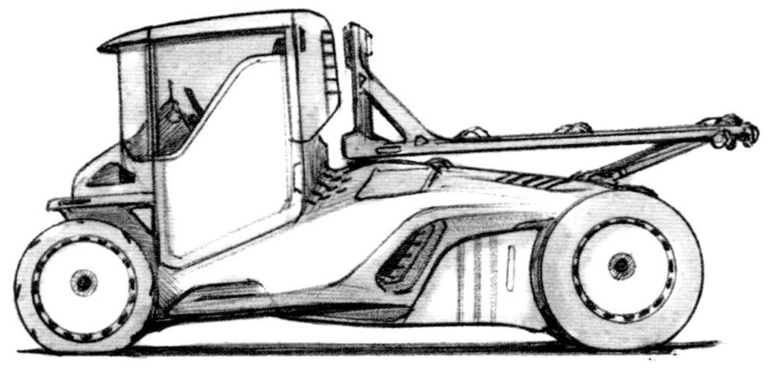

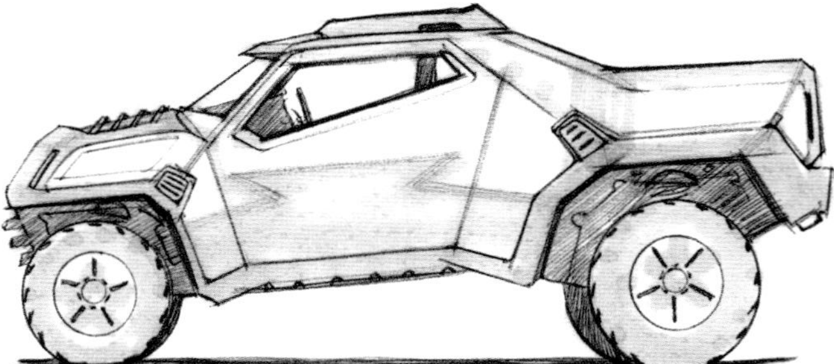

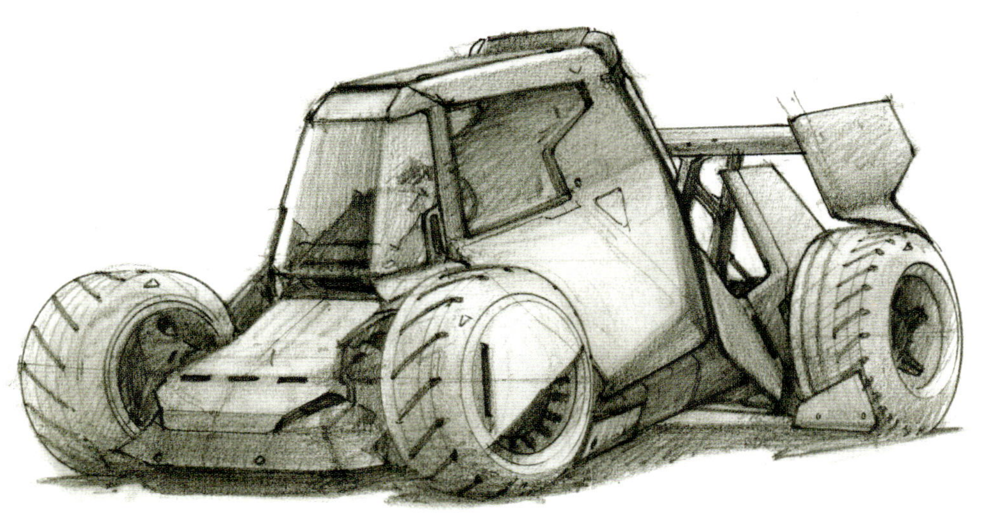
APEX
5

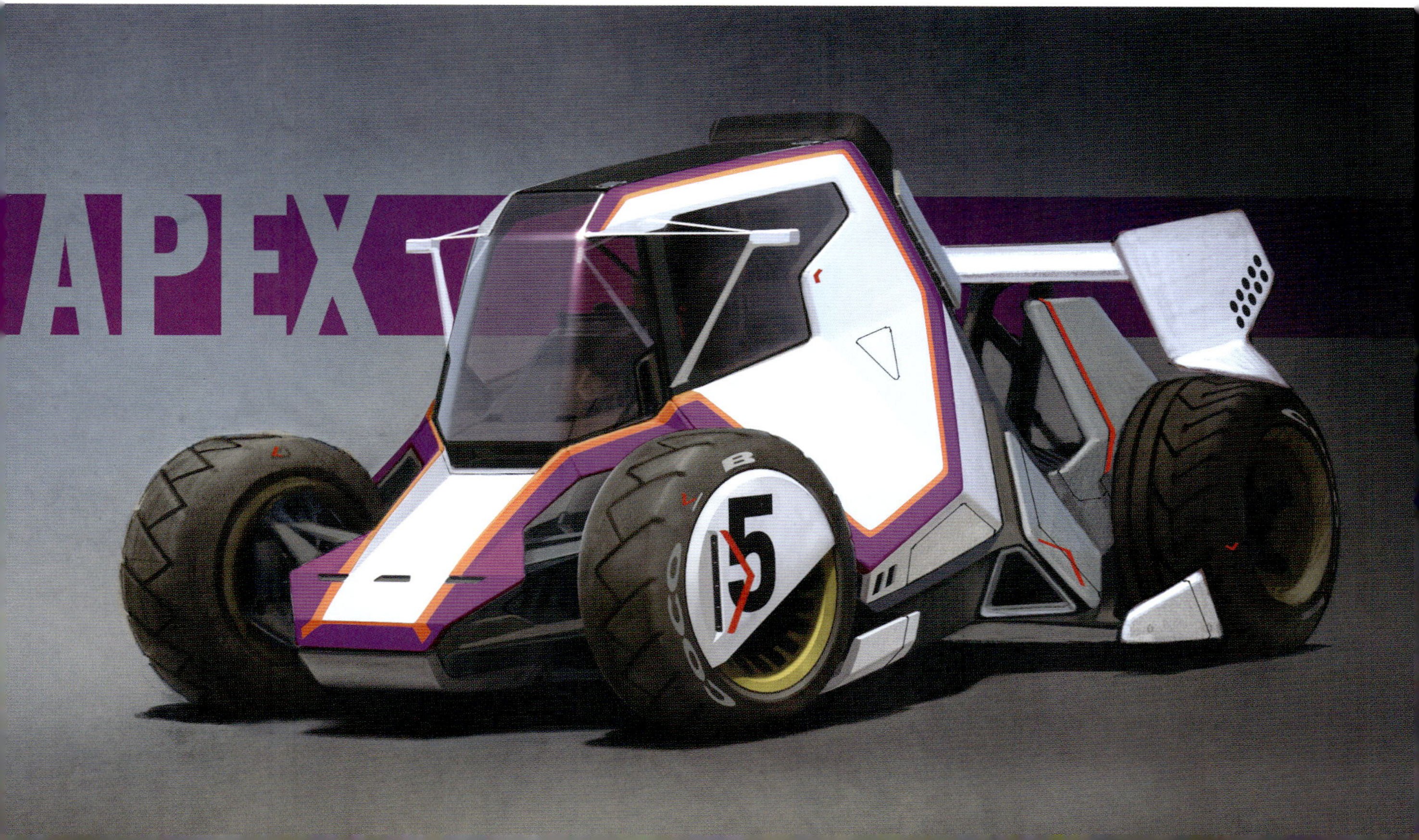

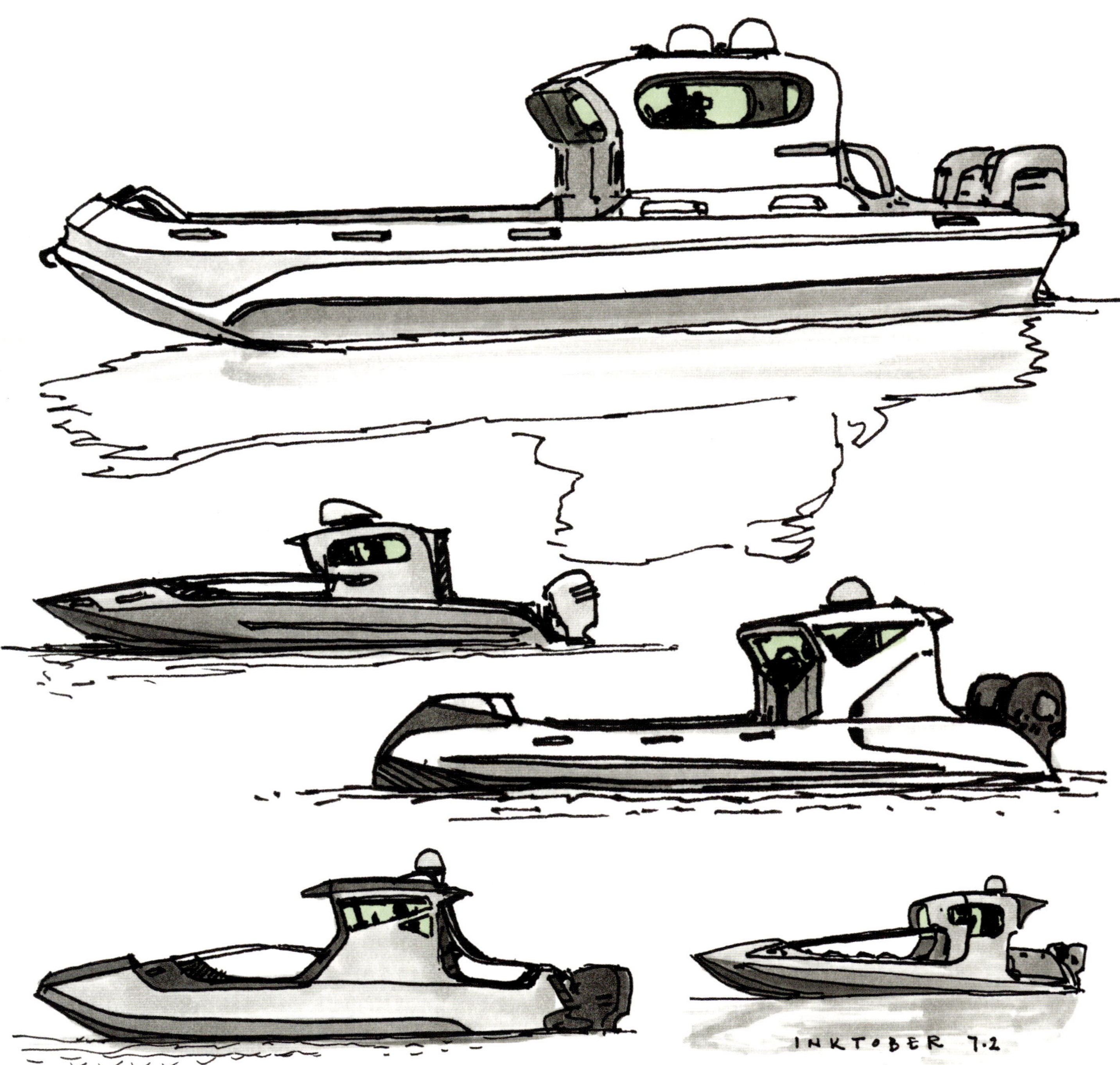

INKTOBER 7.2

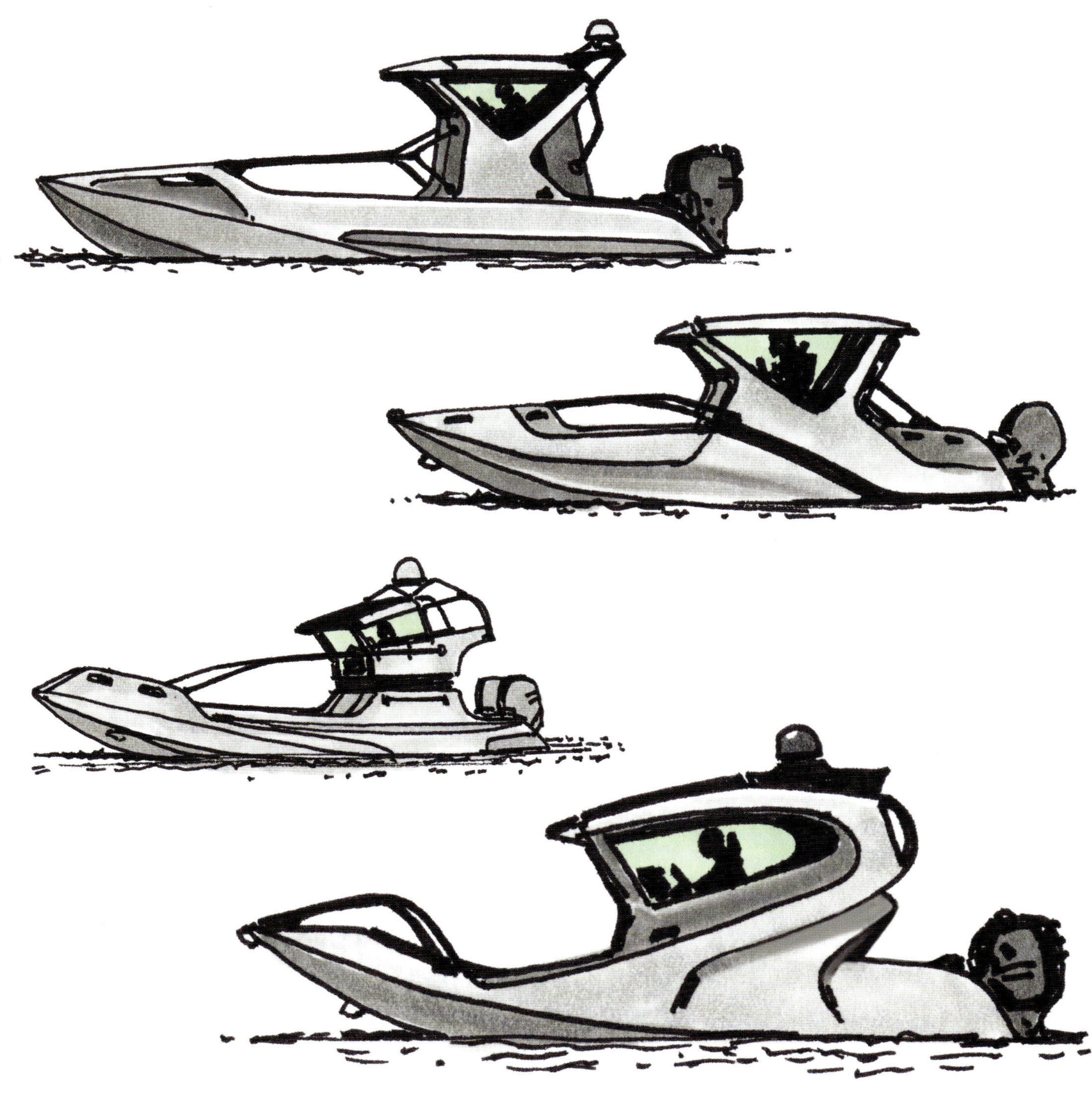

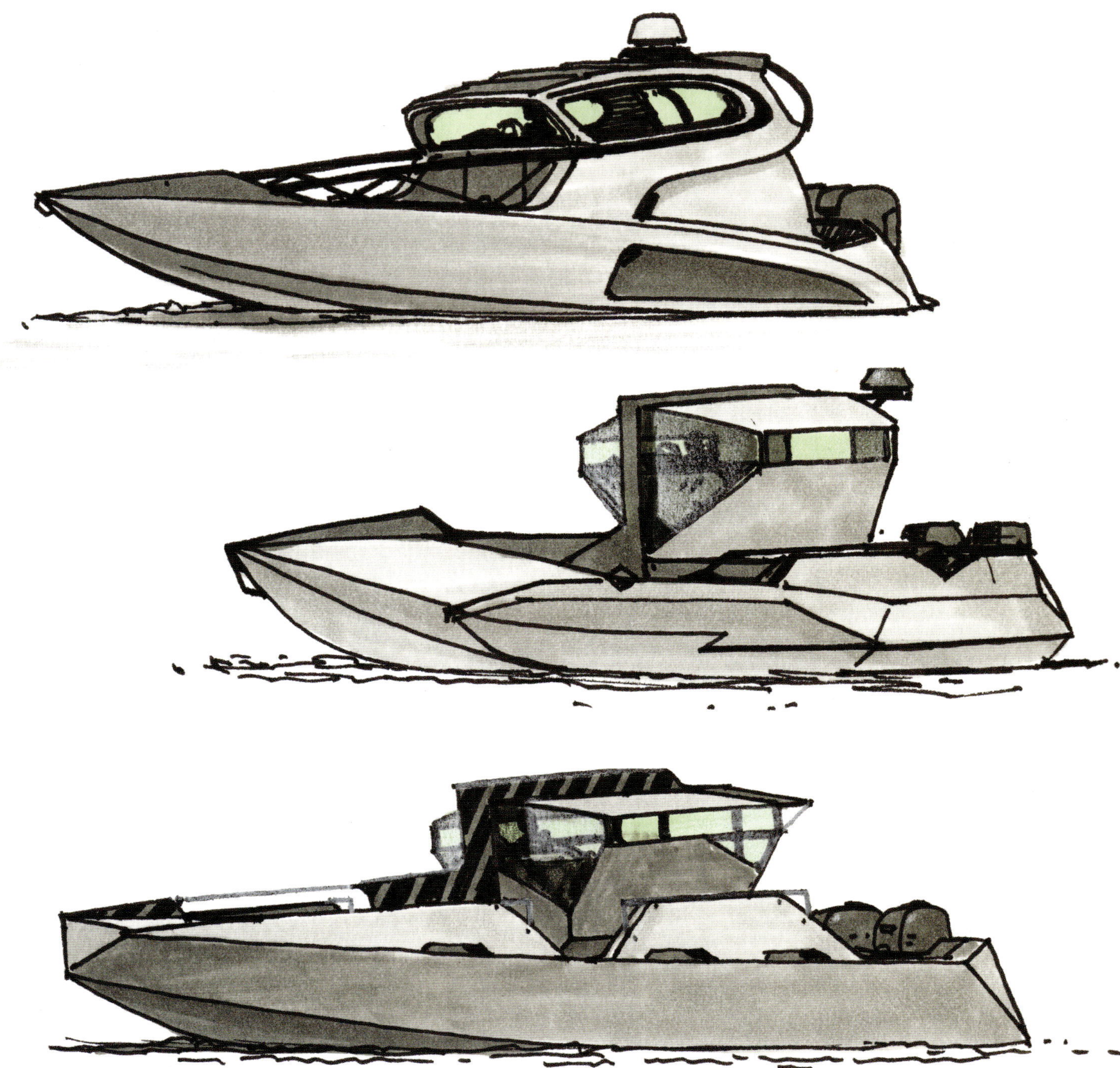

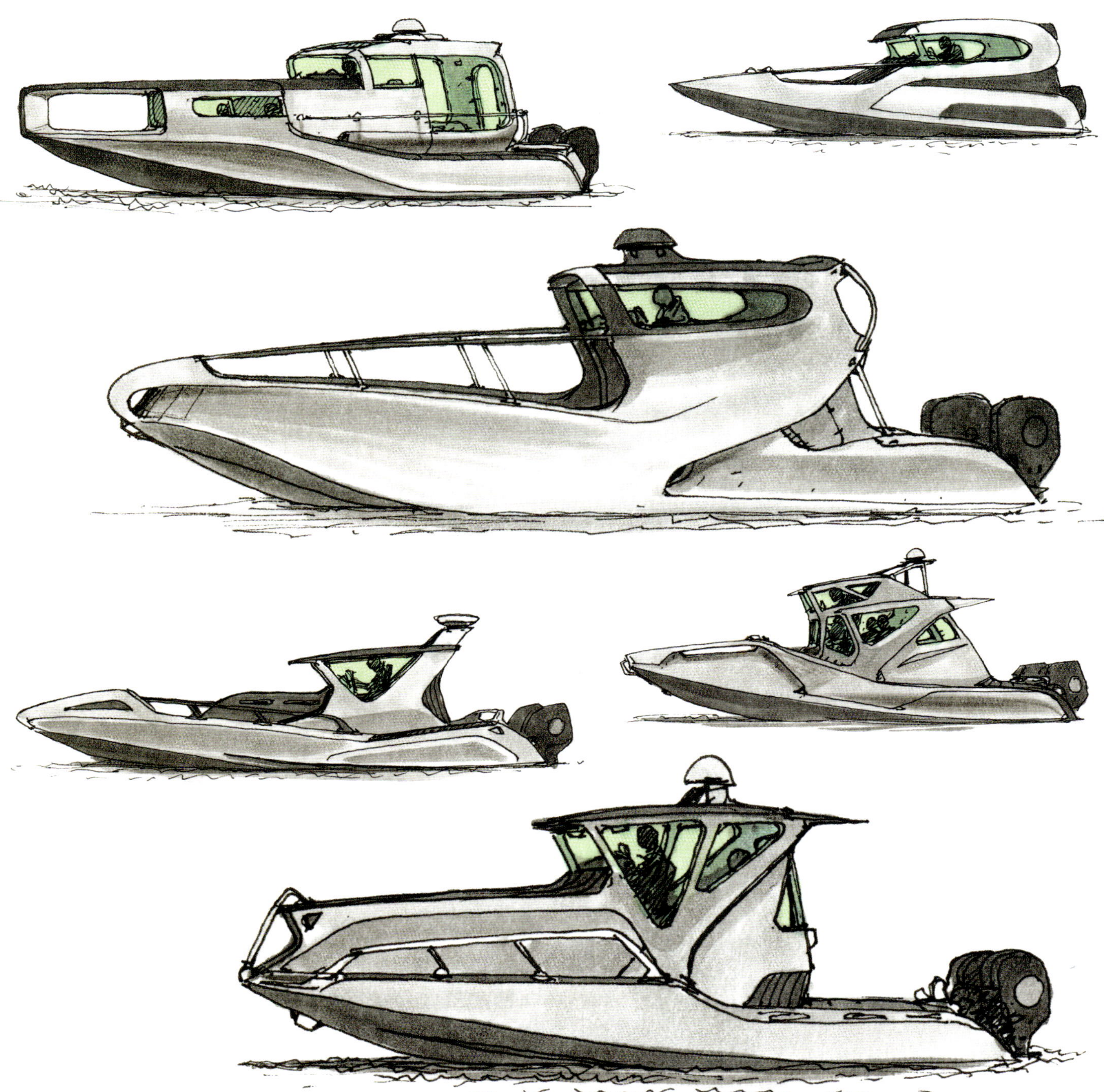

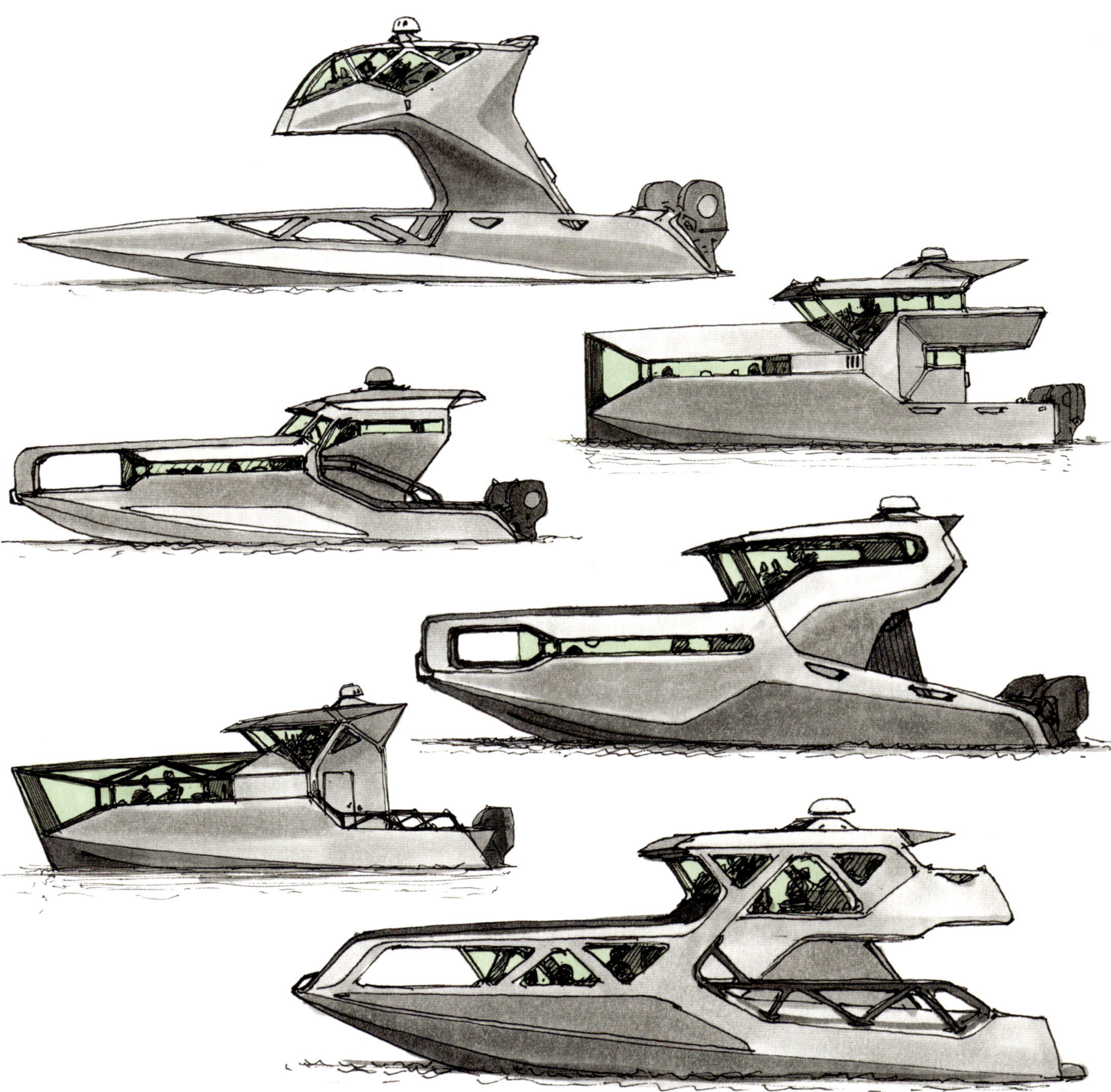

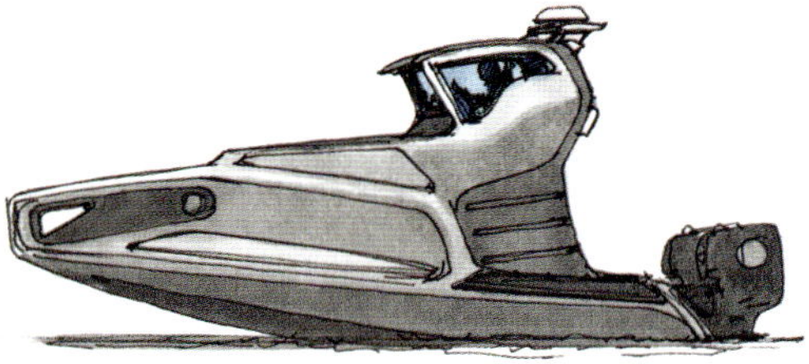

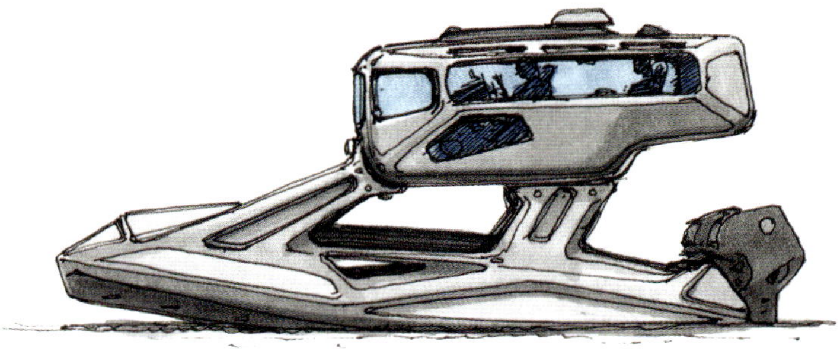

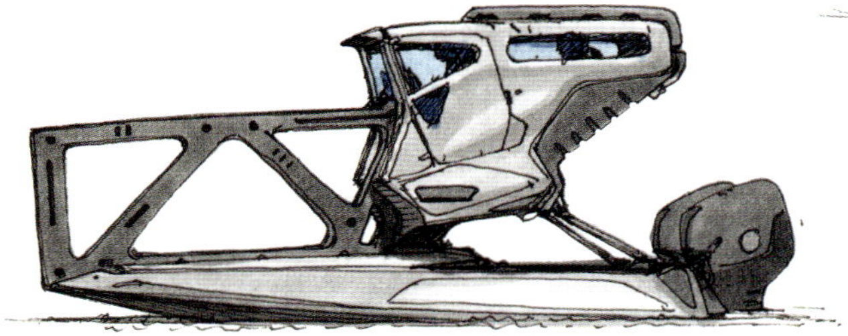

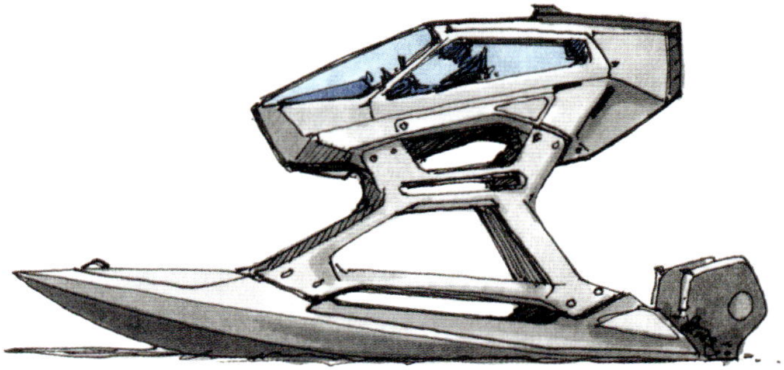

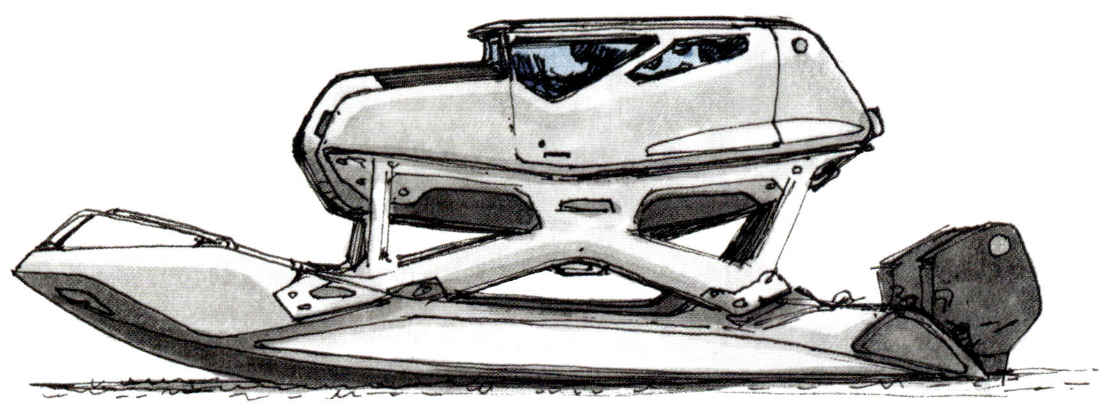
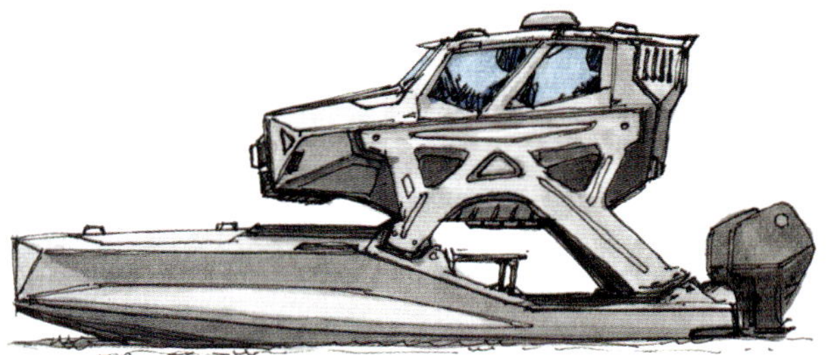

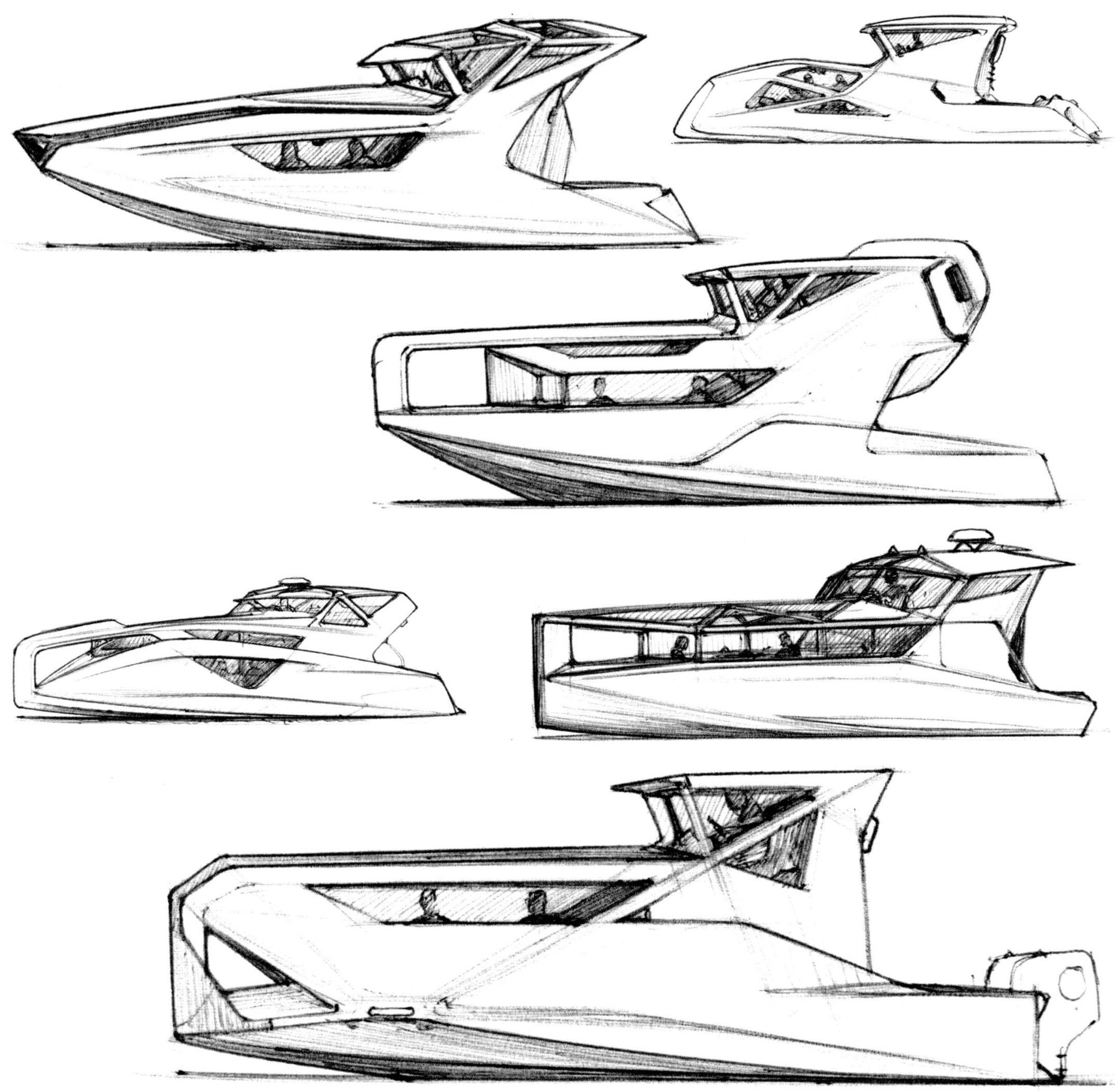

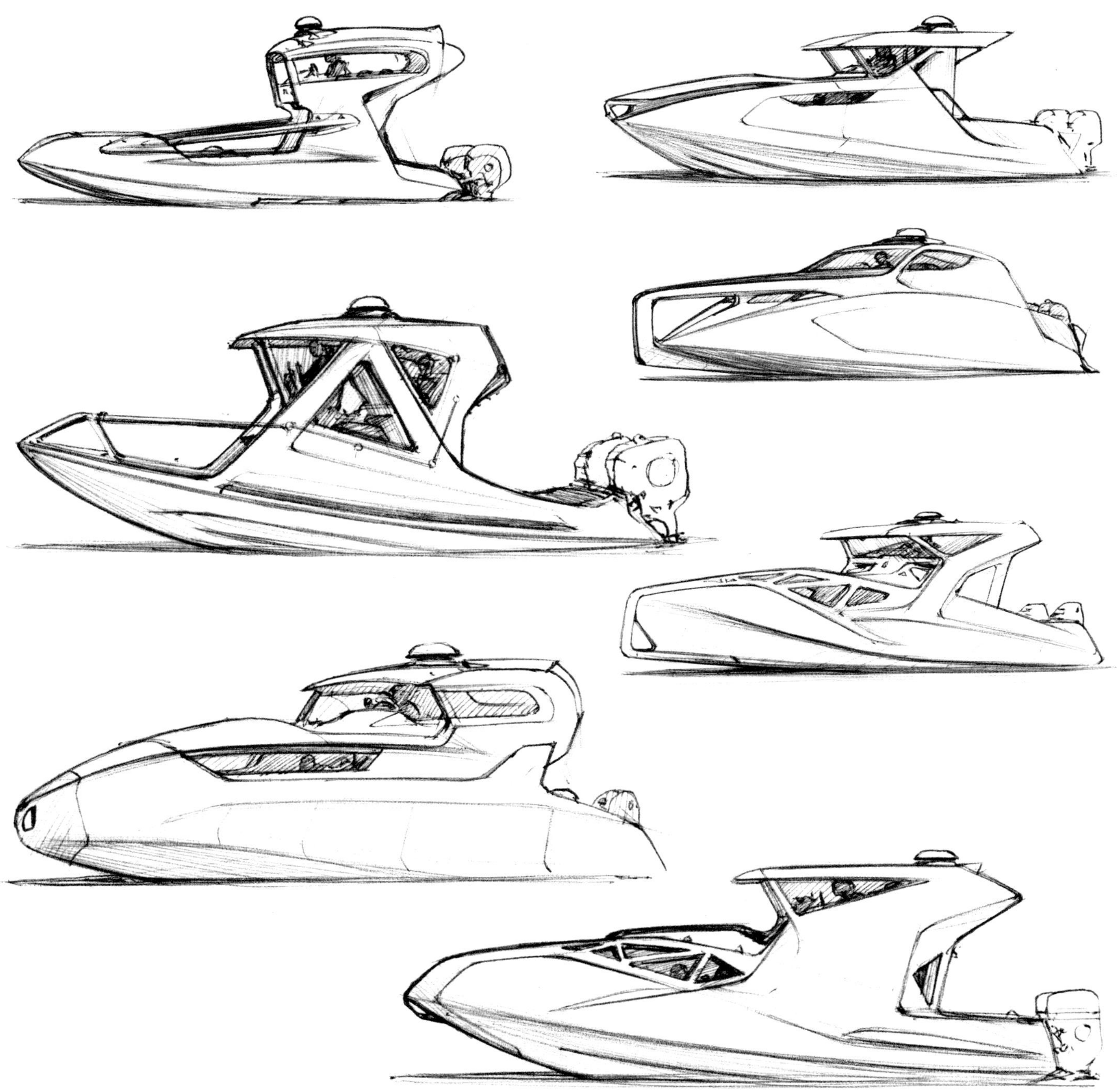

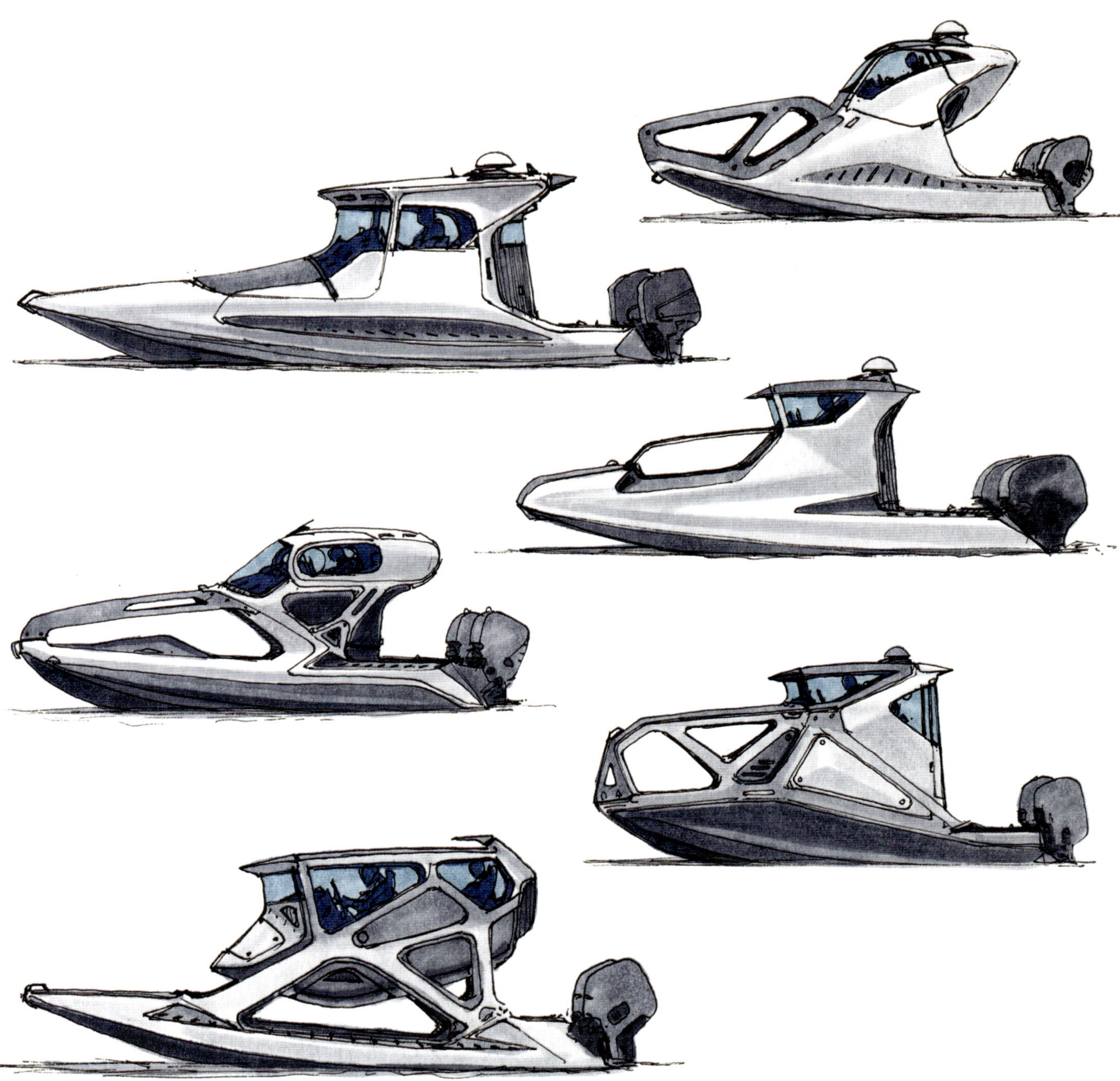

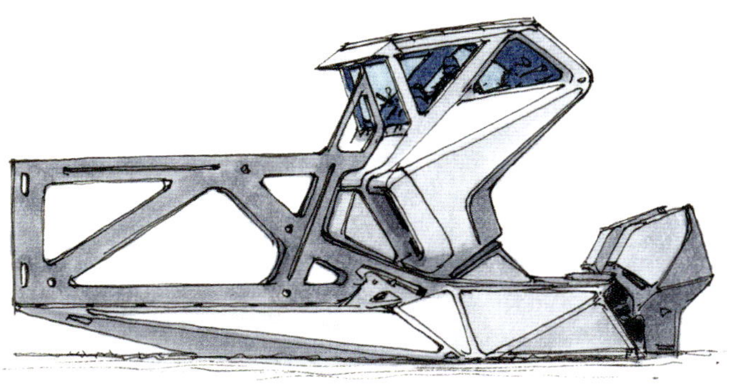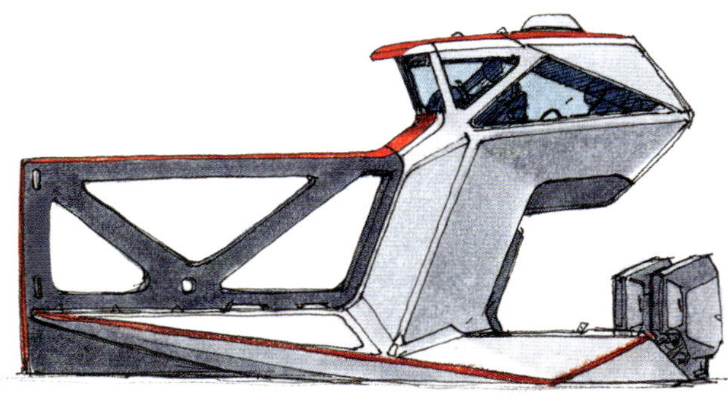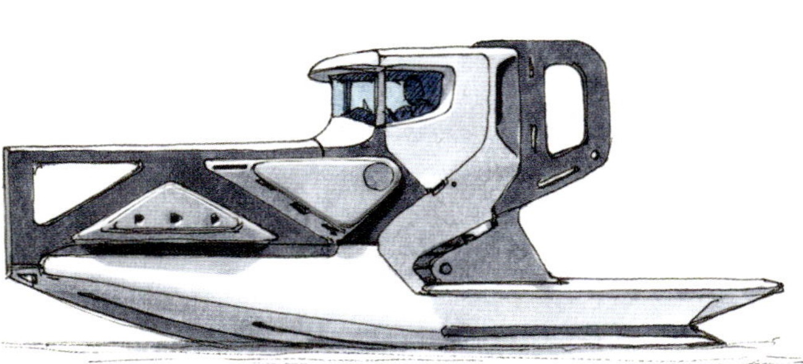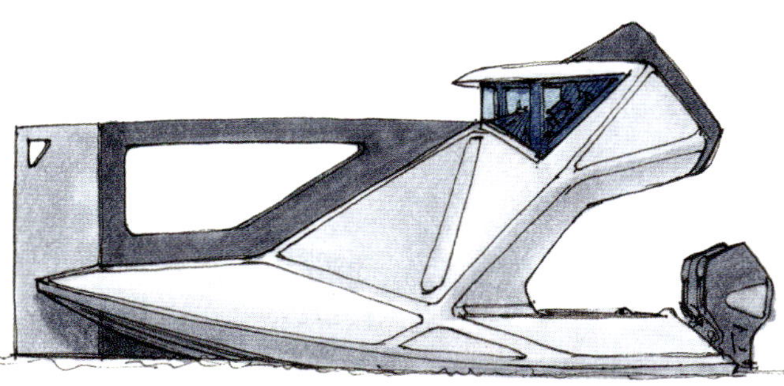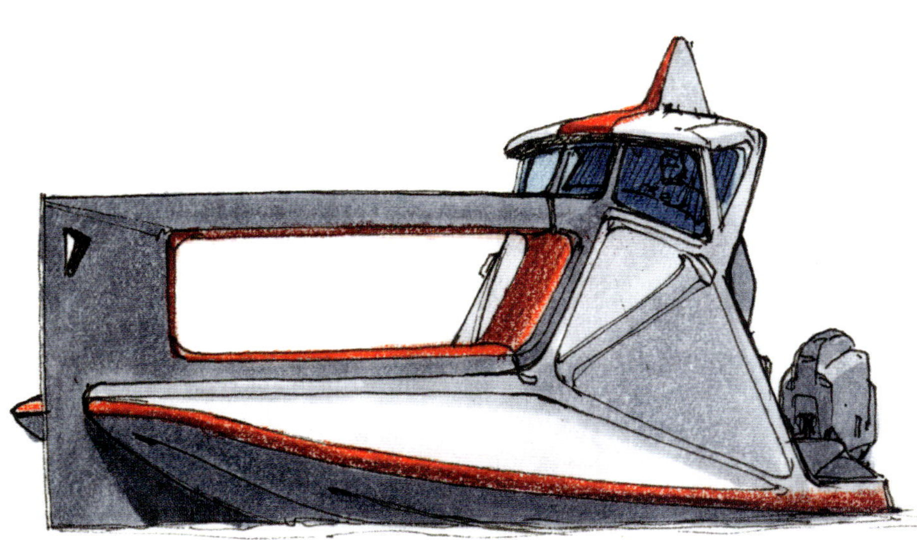

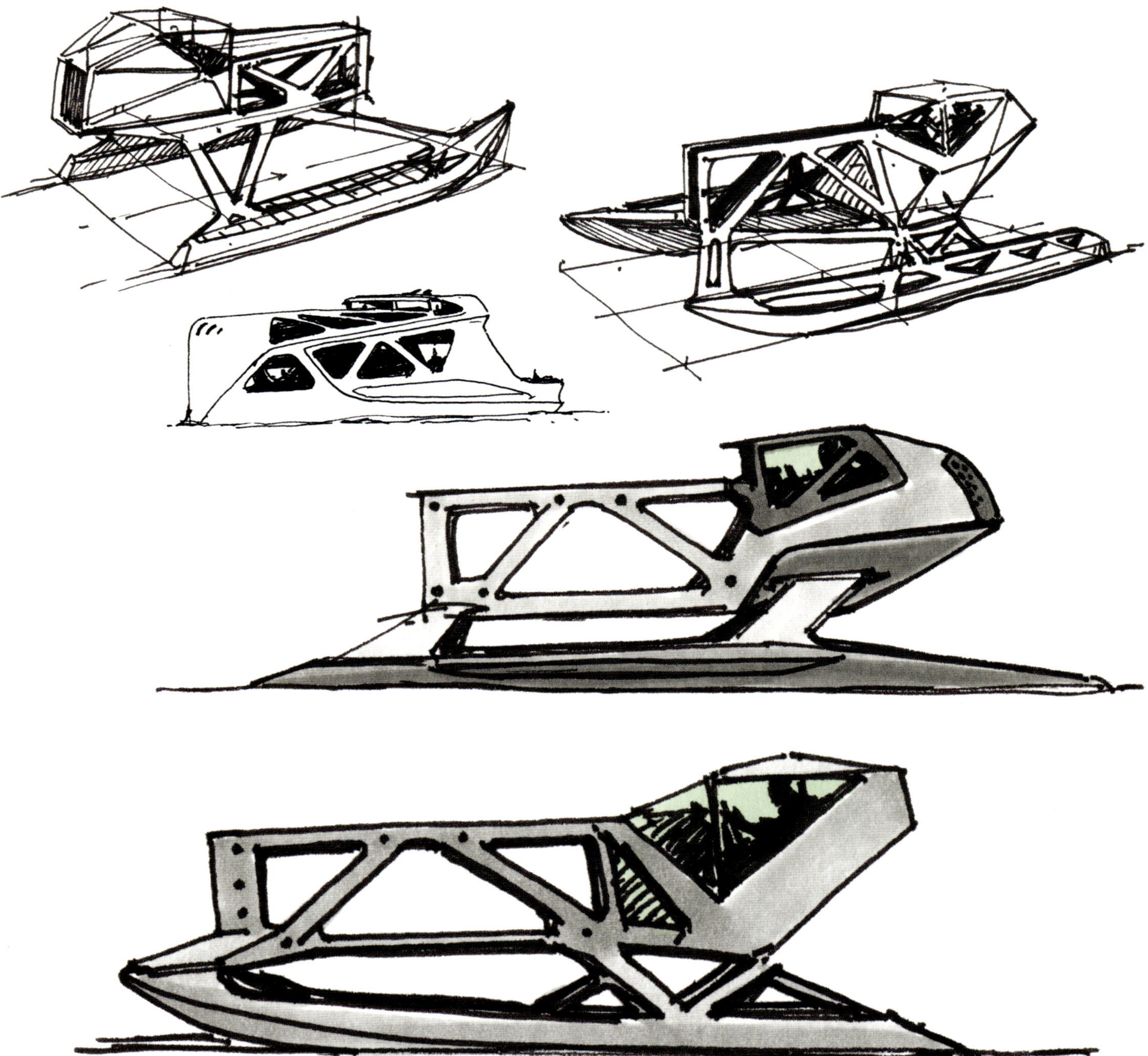

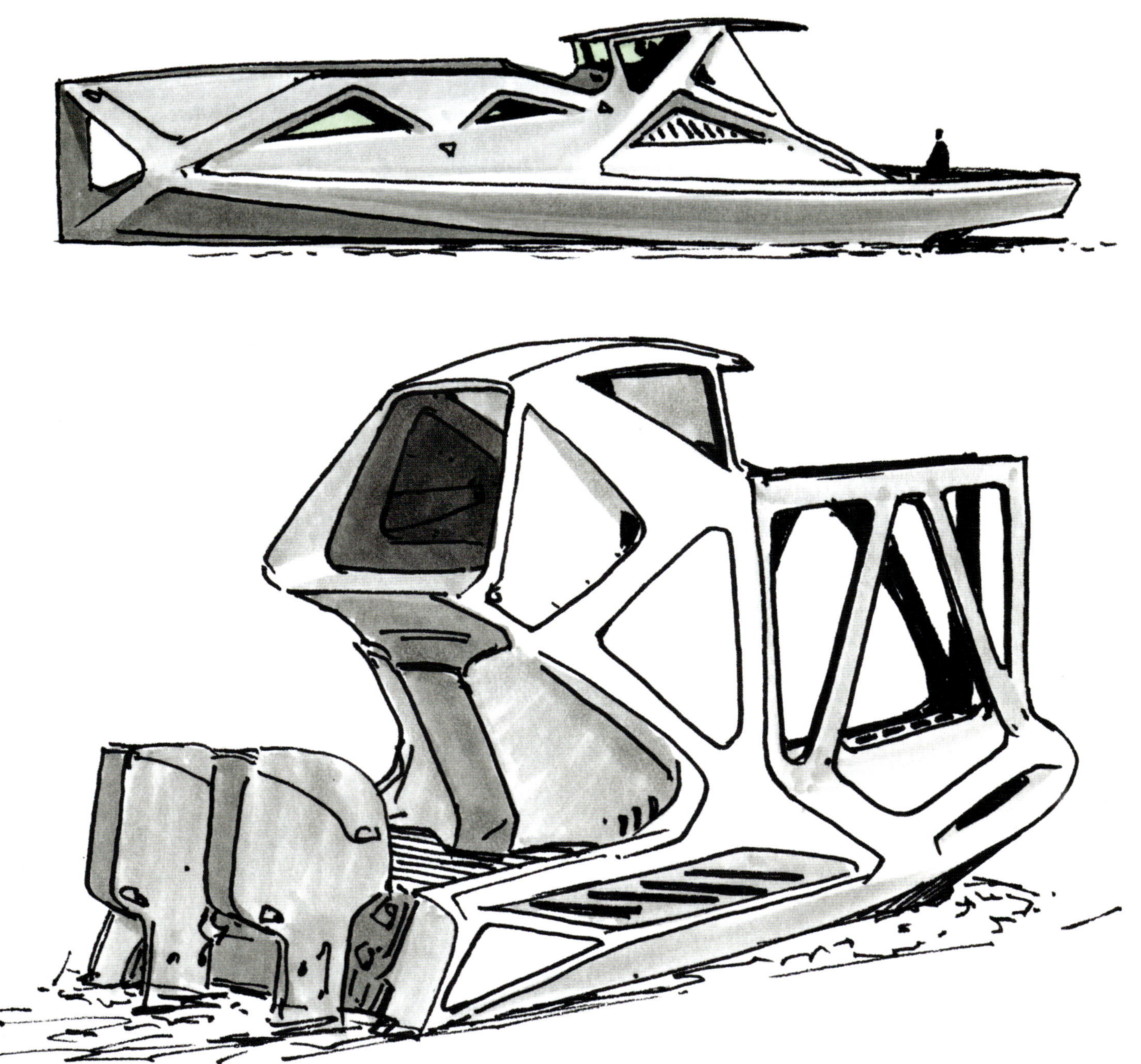

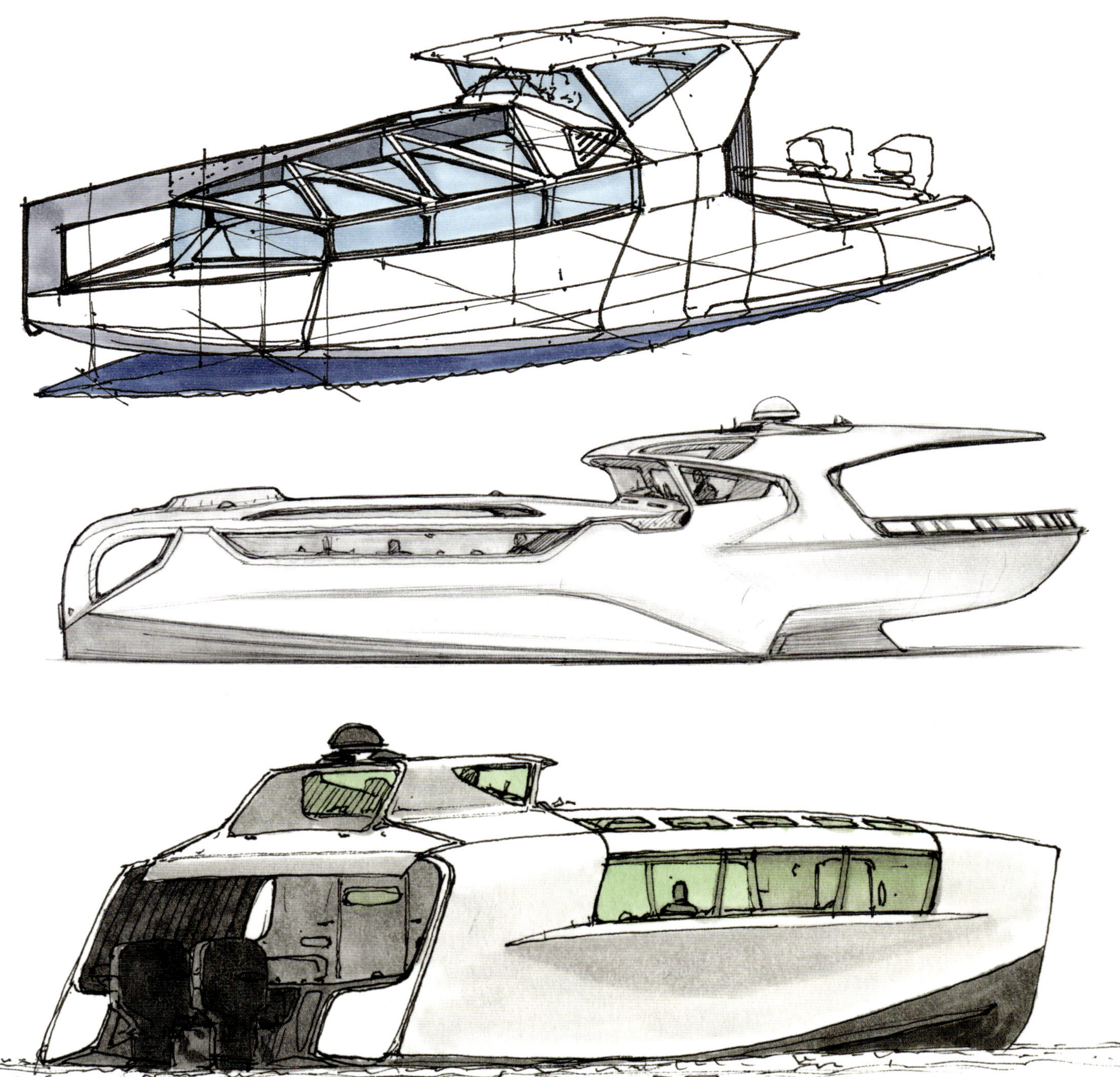

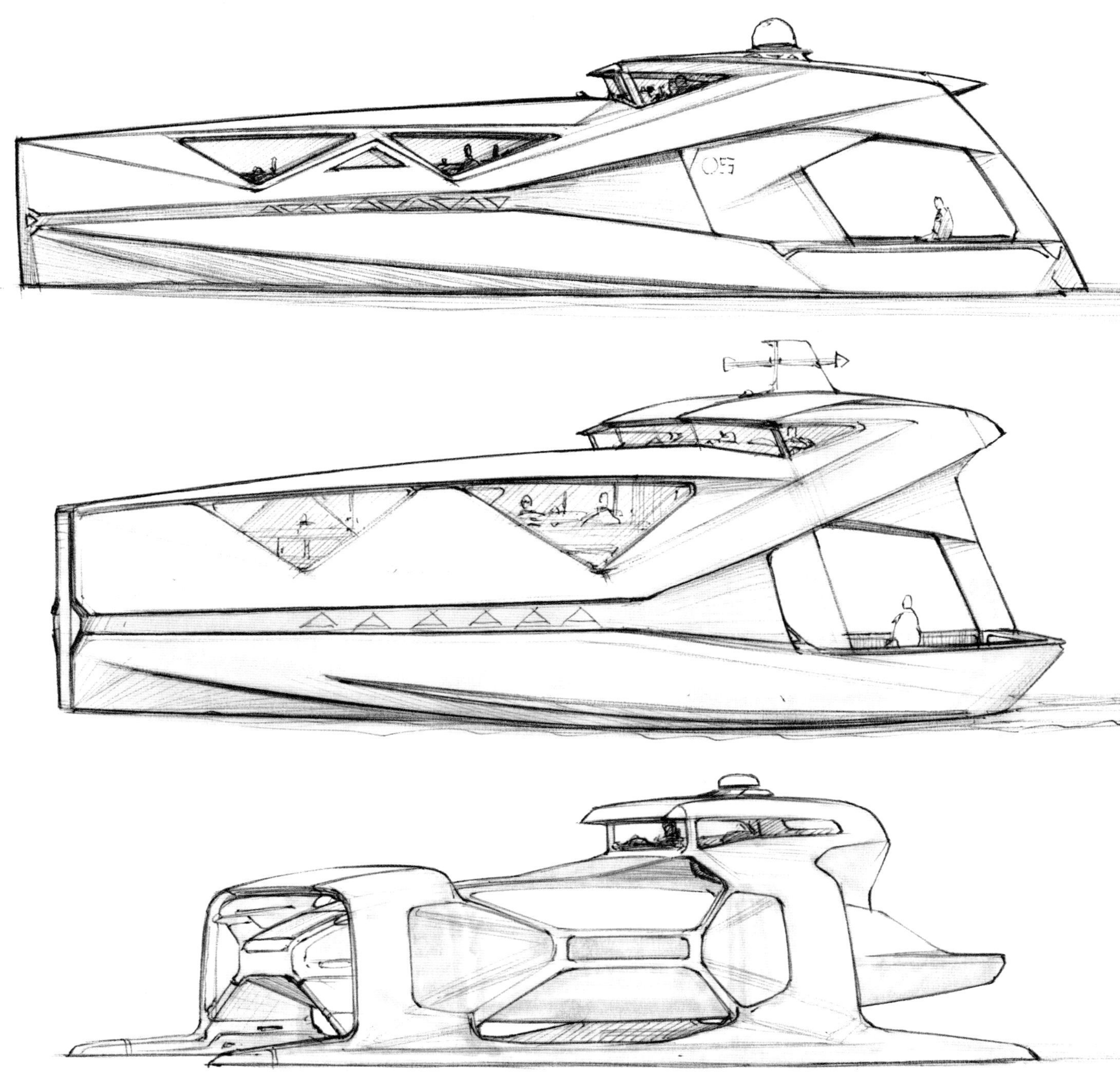

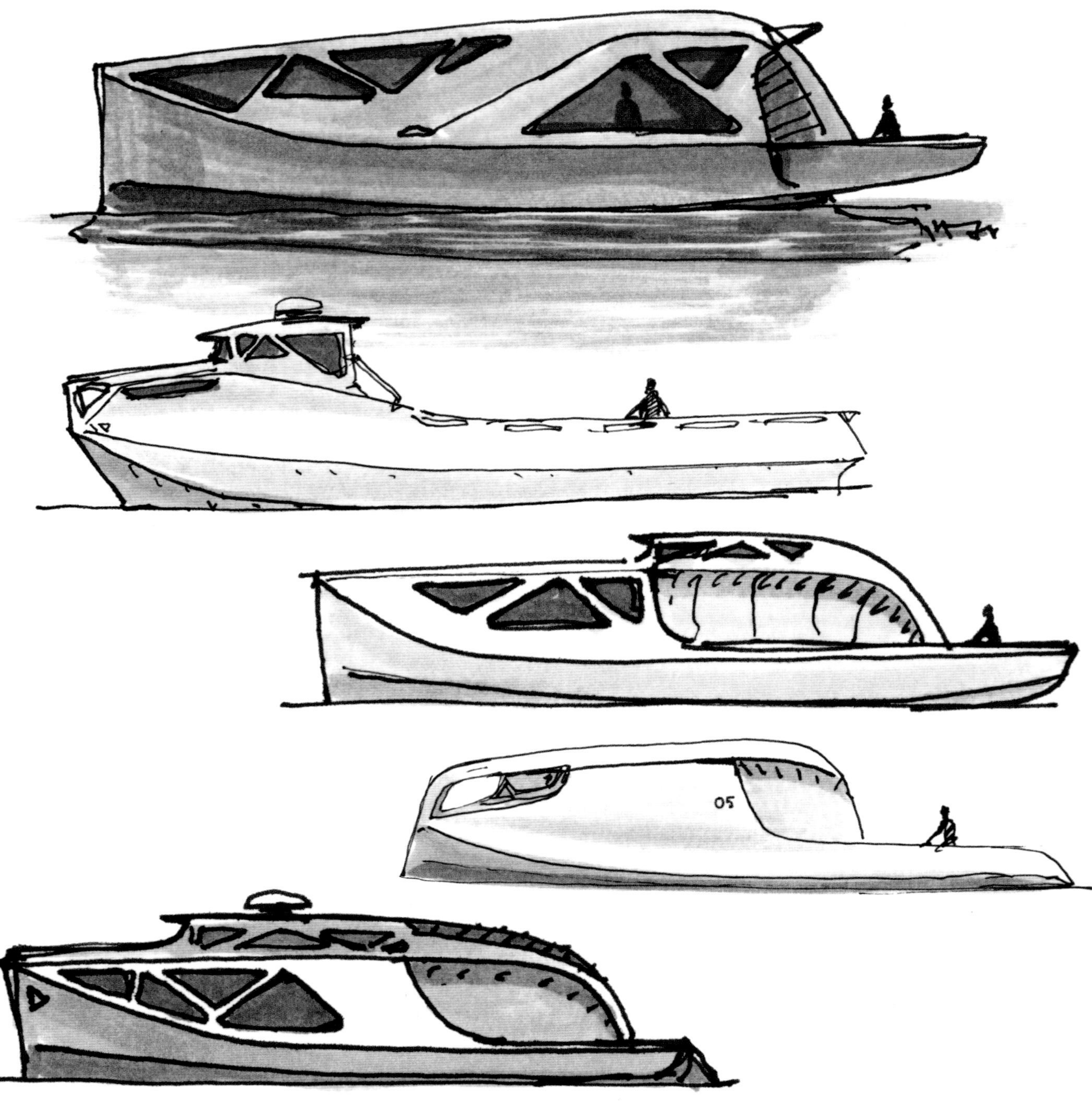

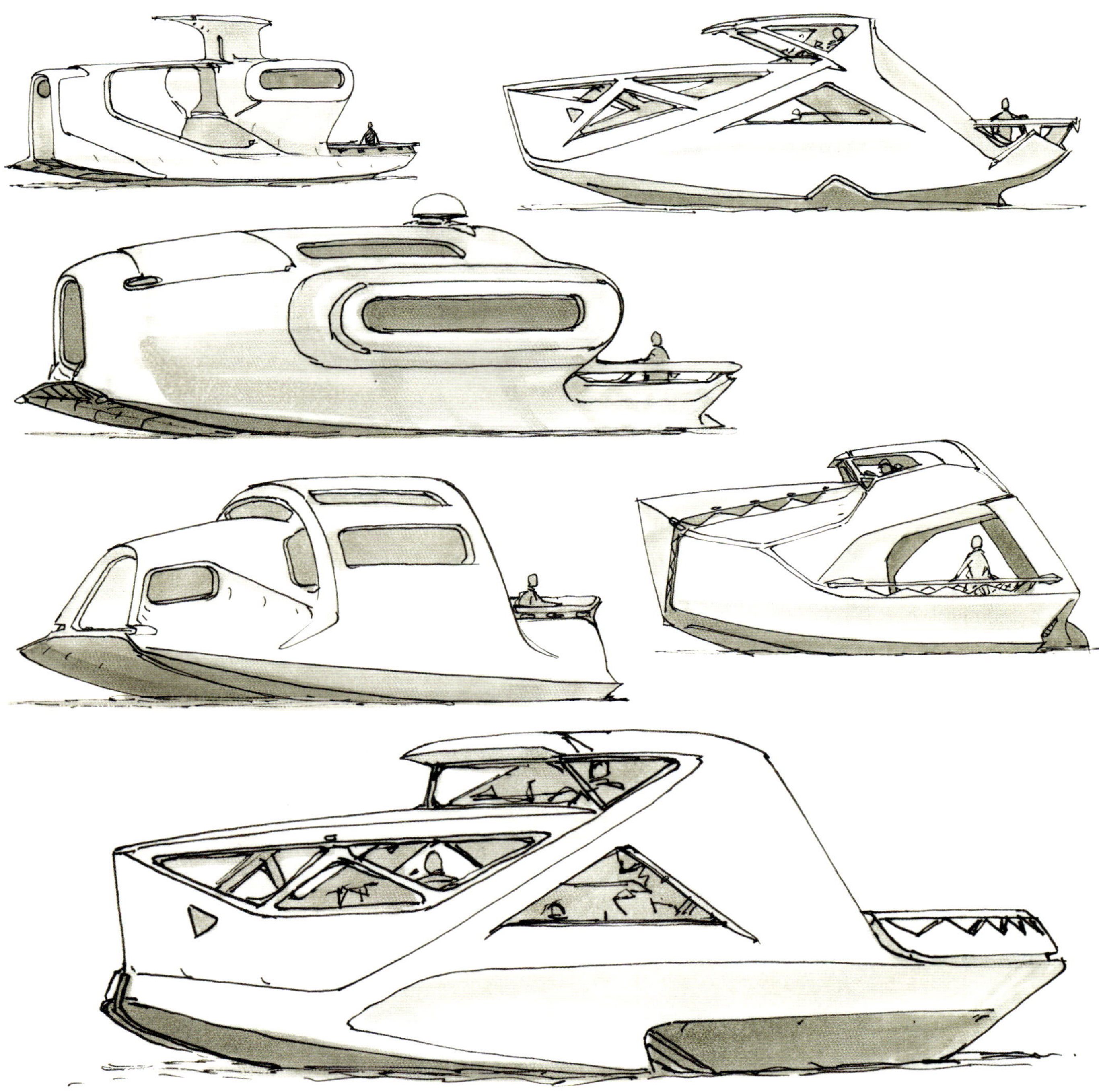

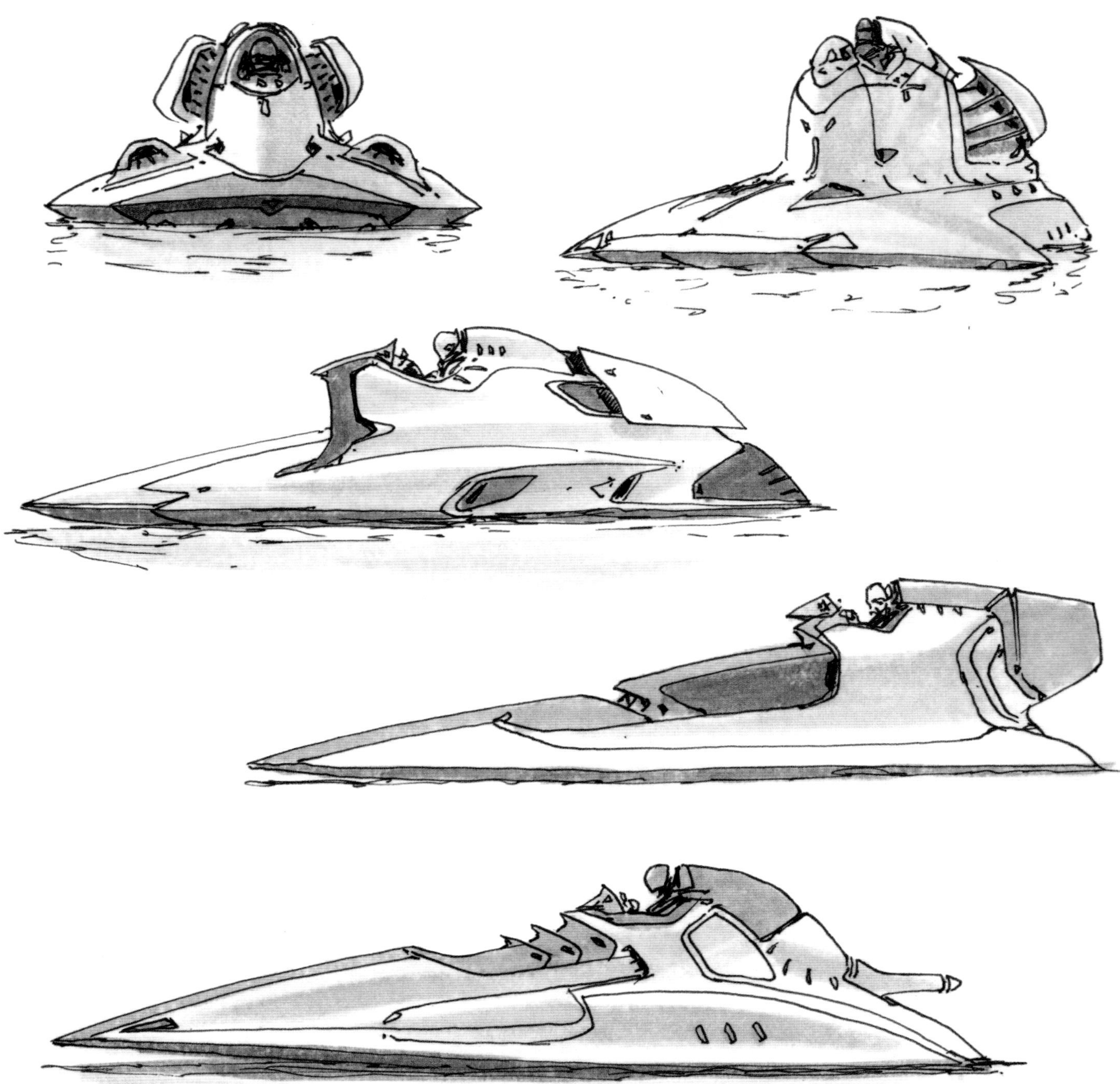

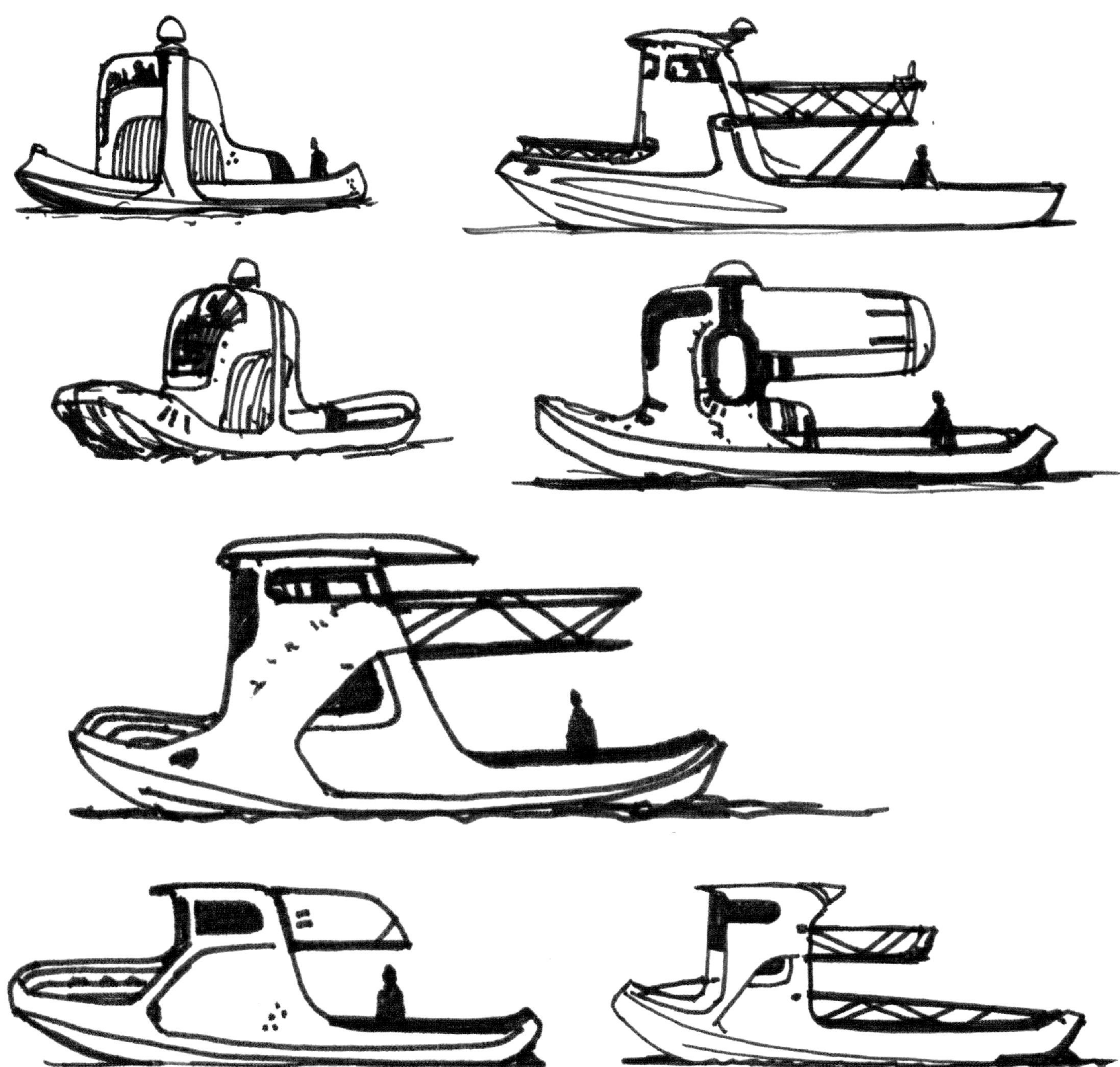

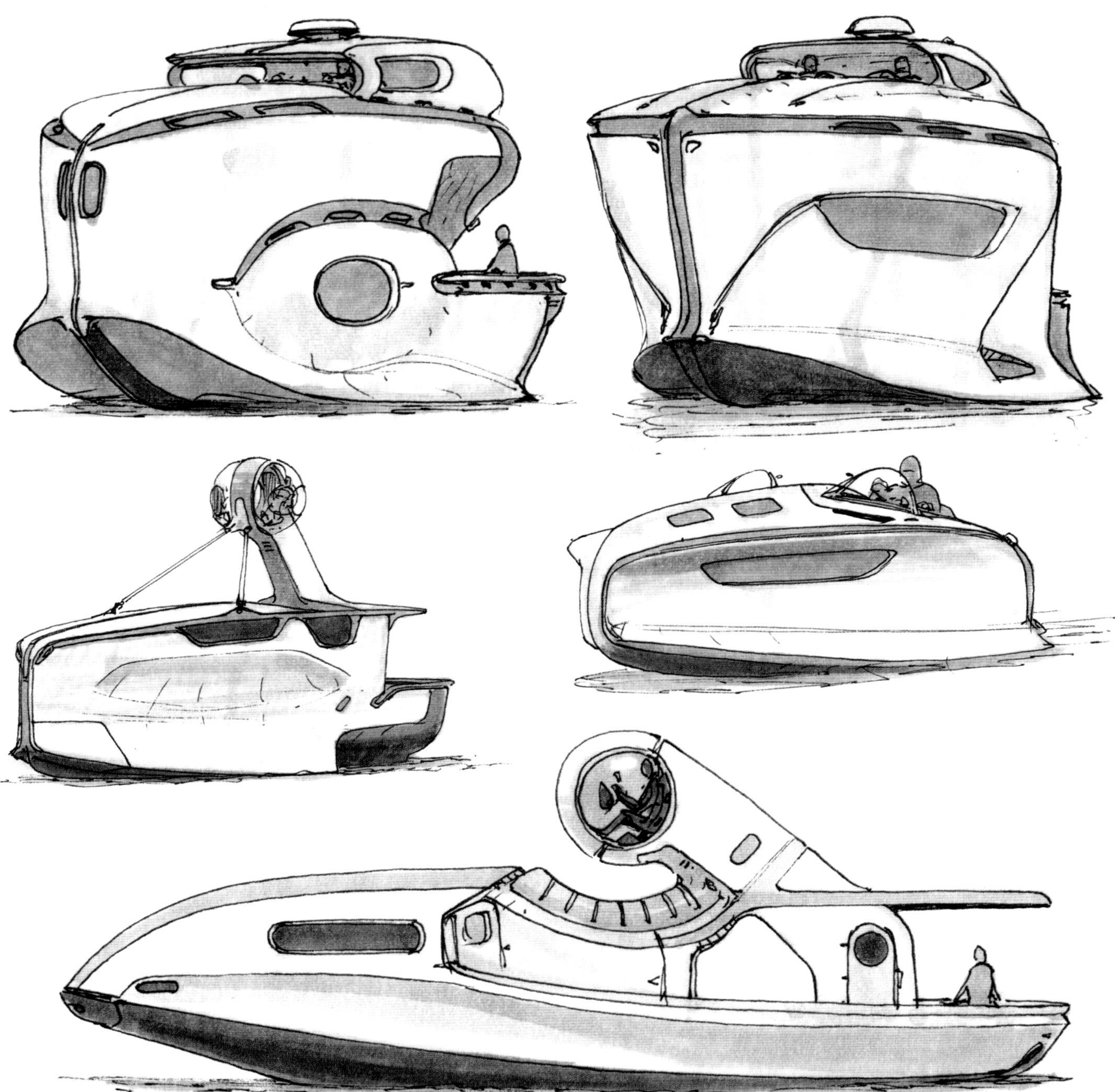

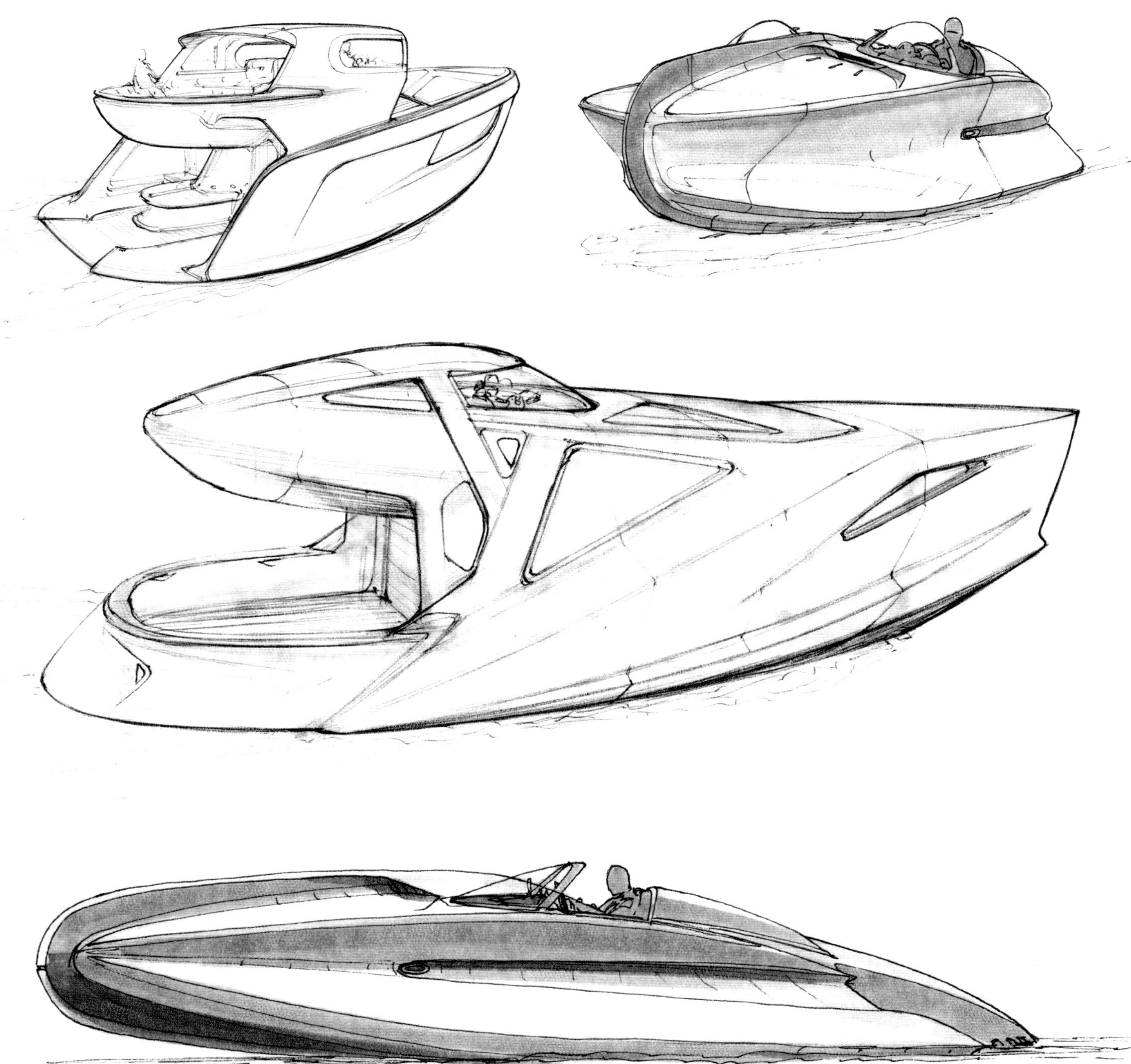

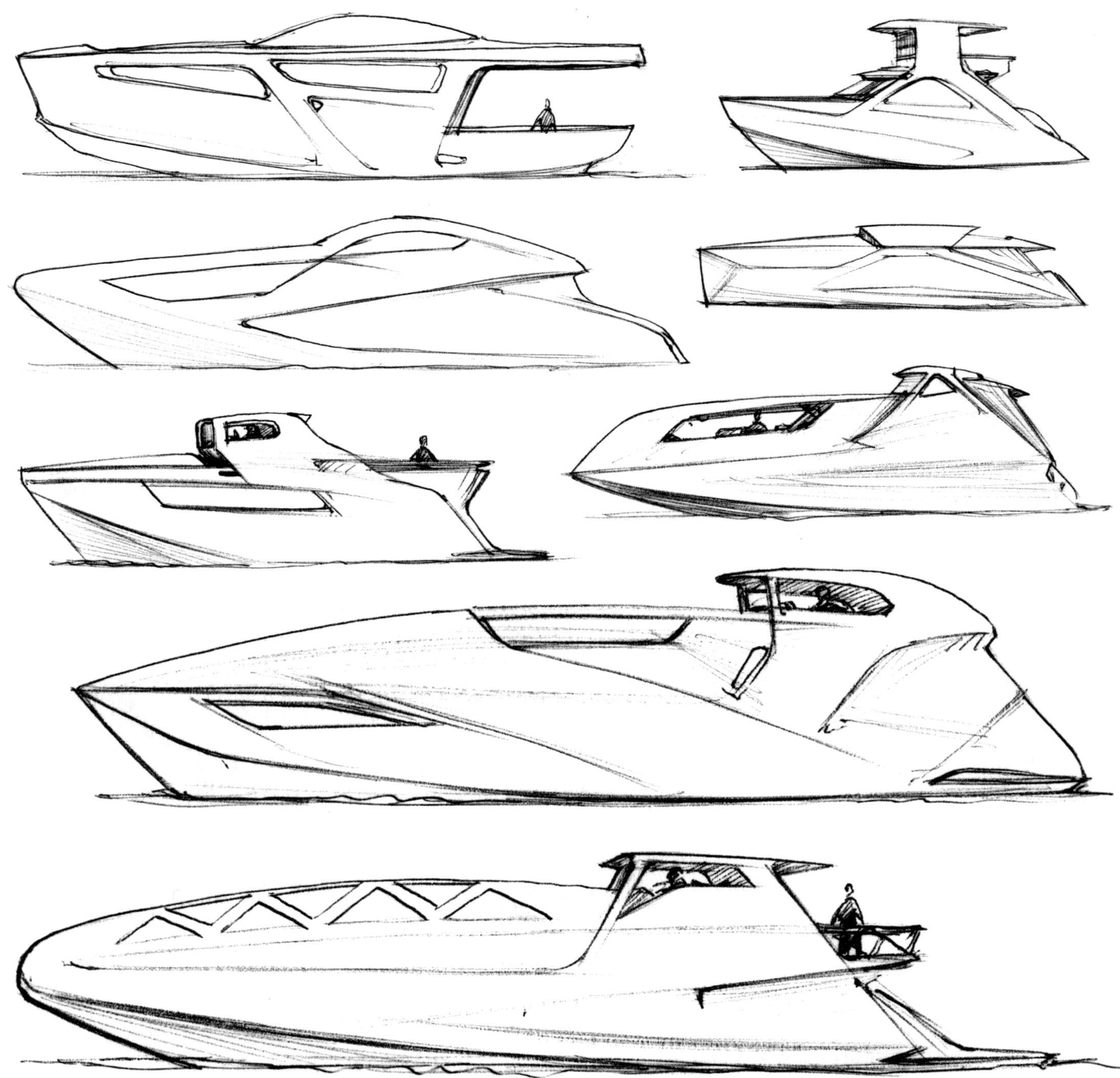

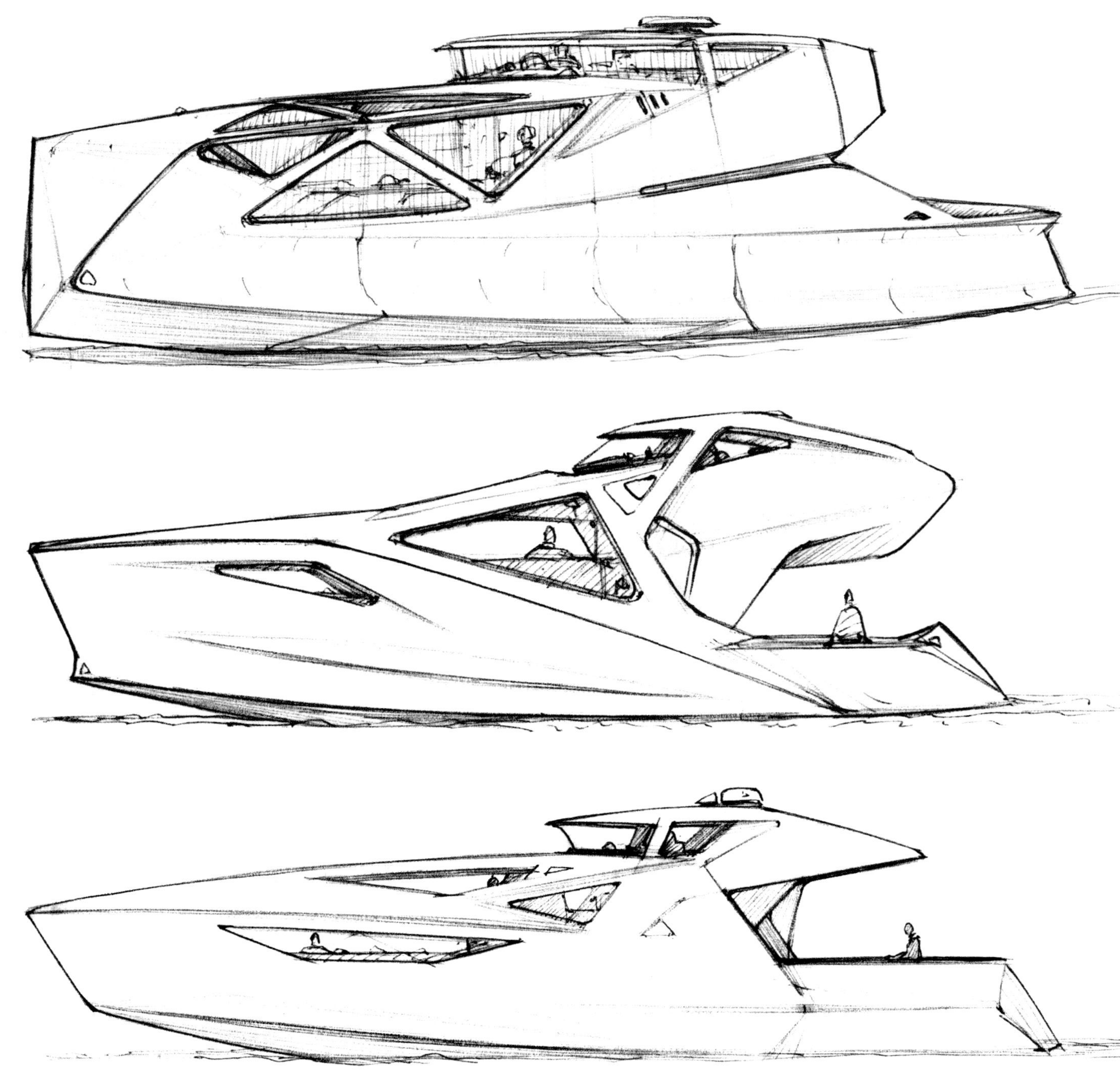

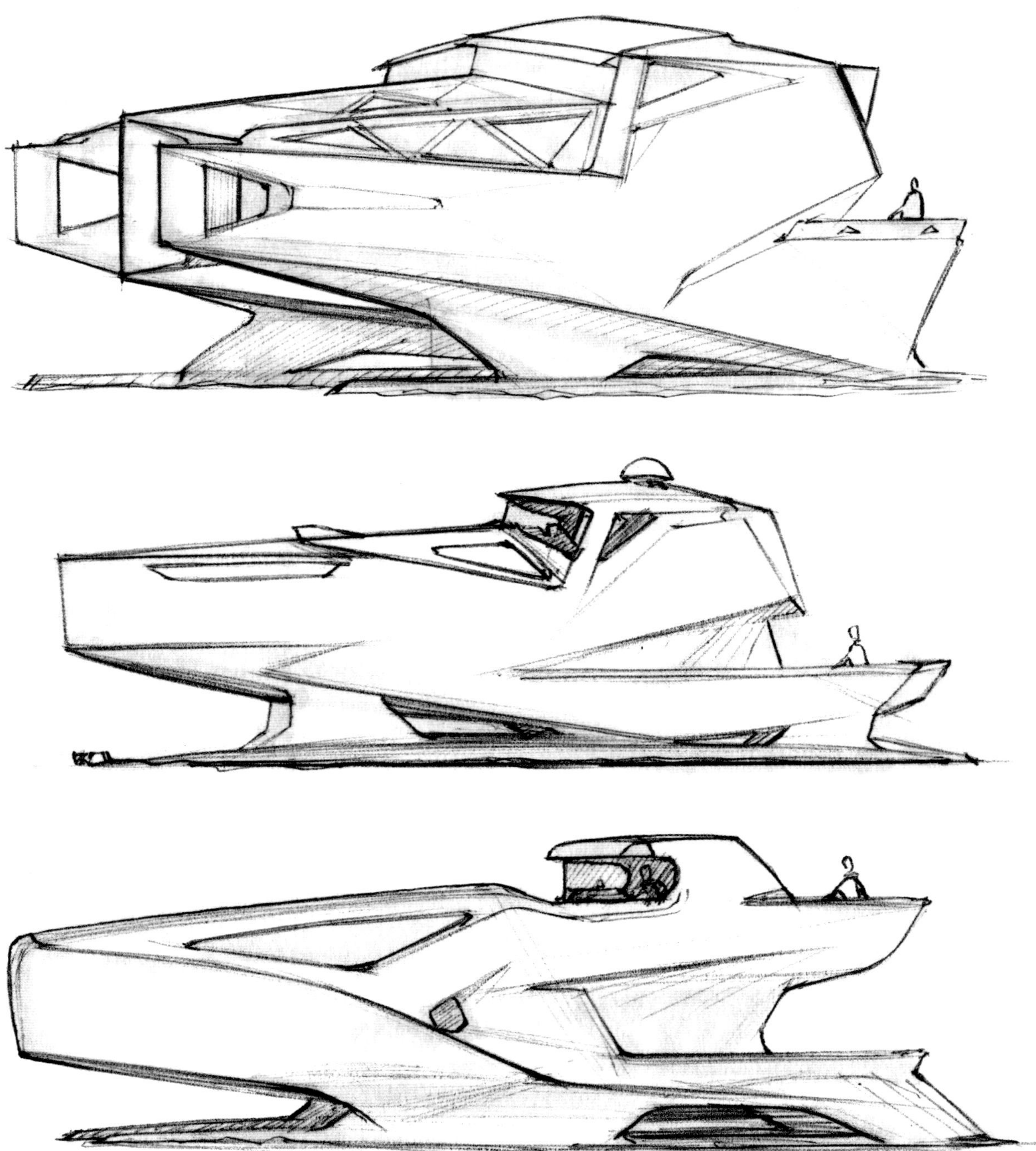

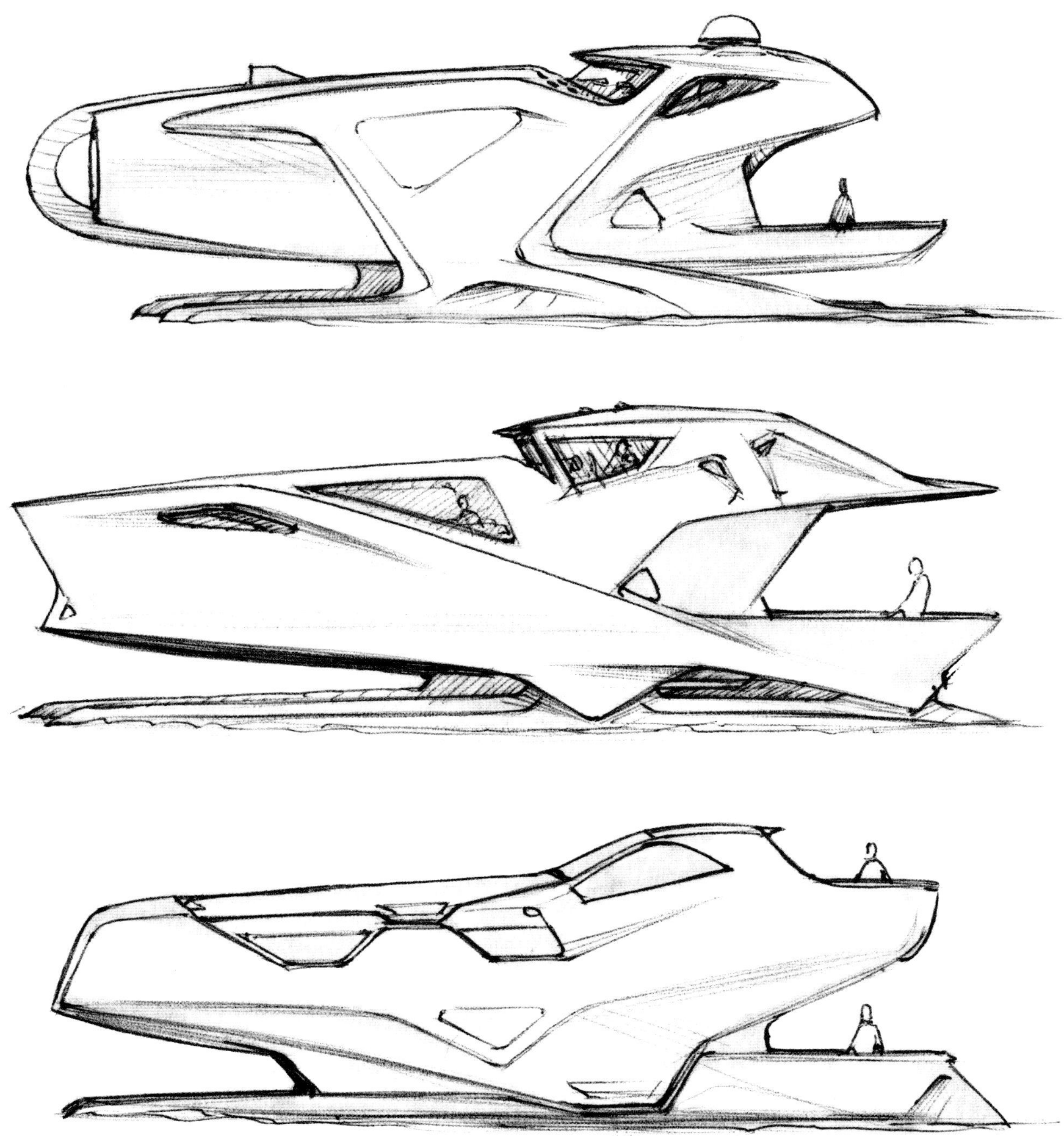

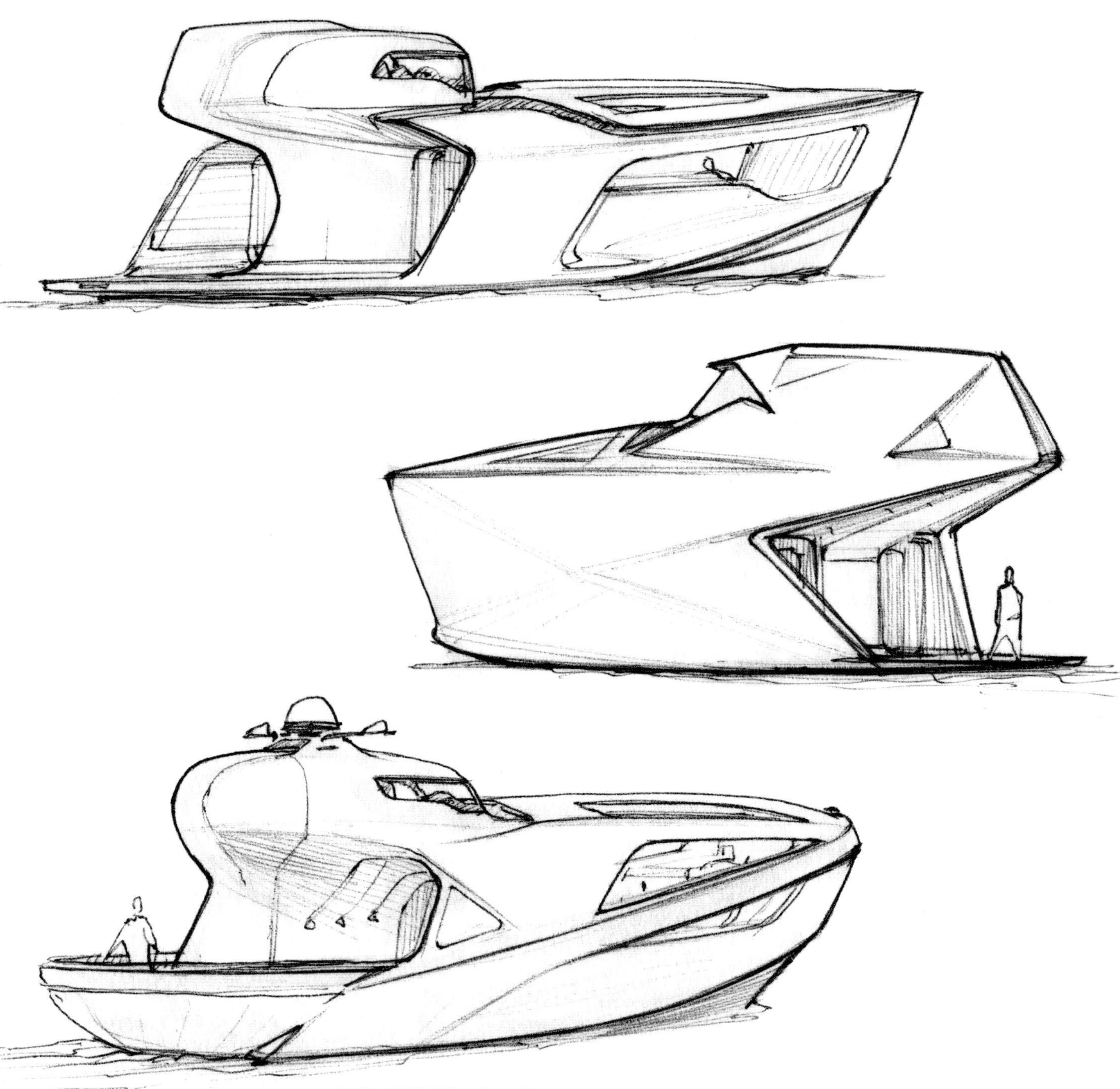

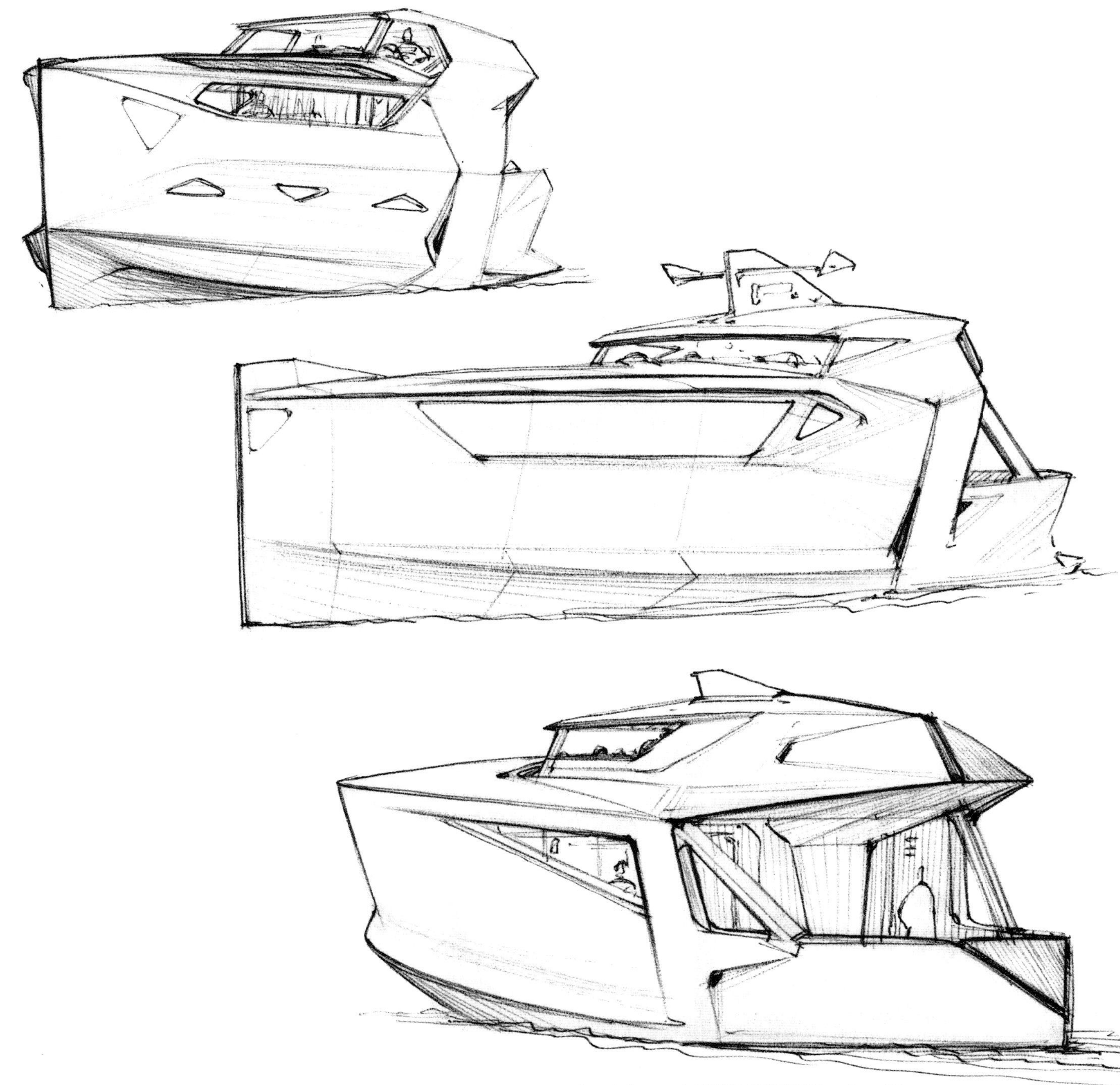

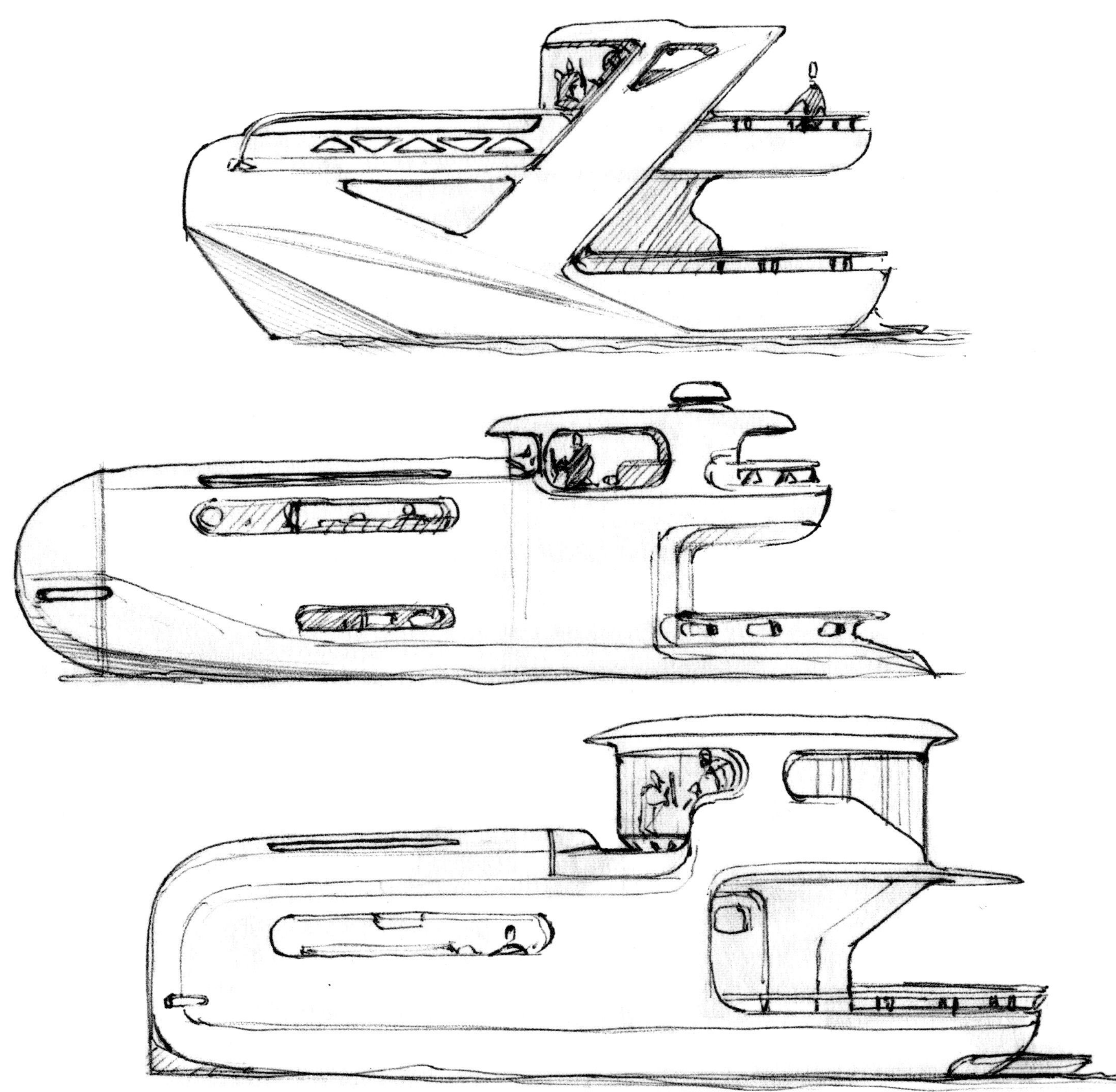

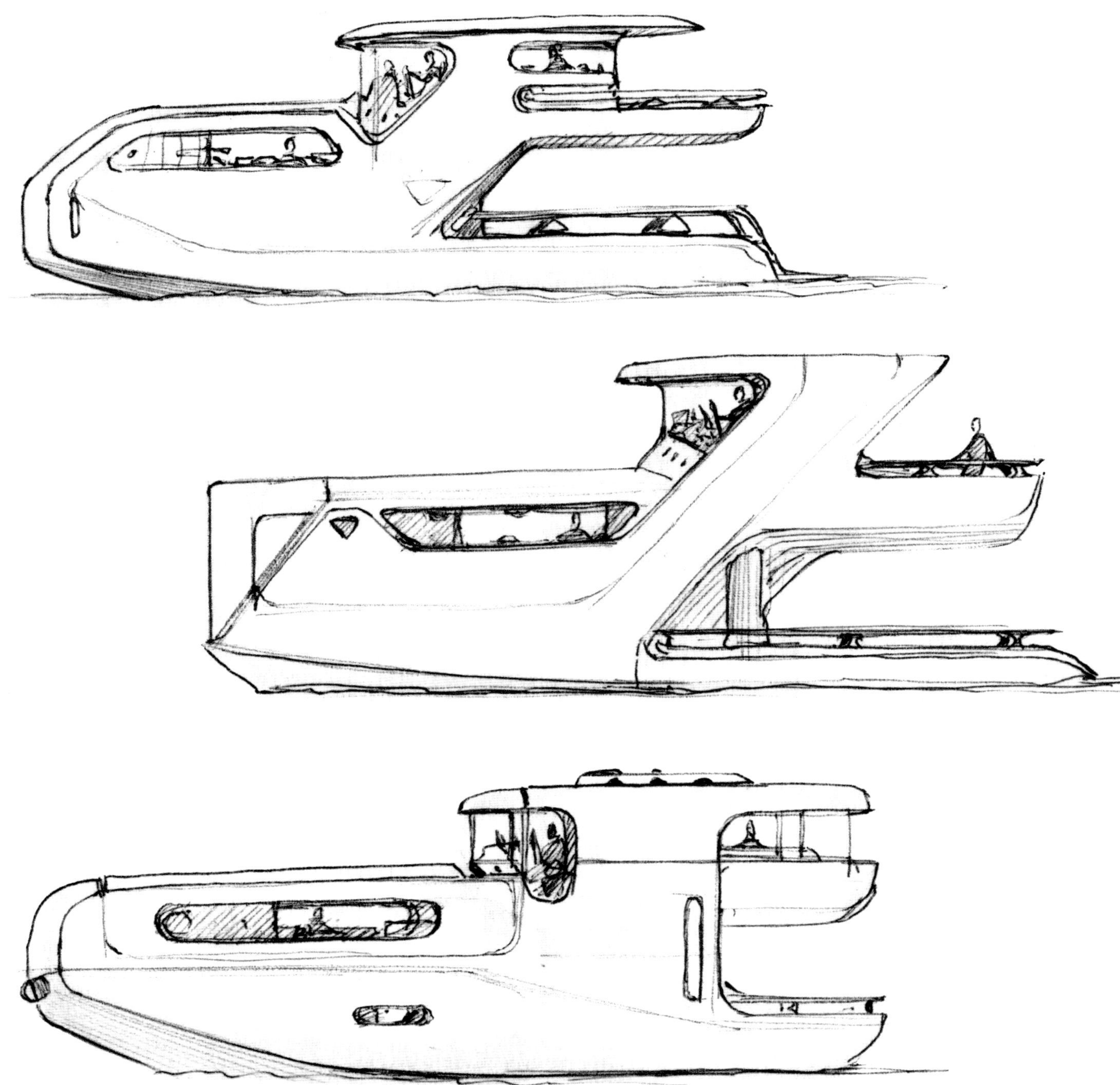

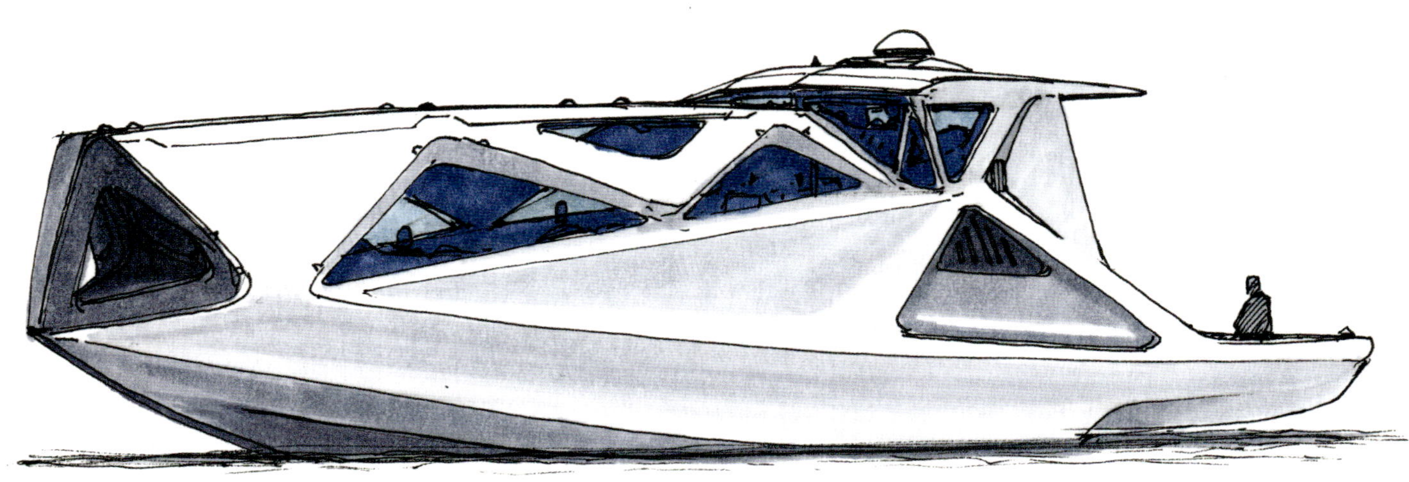

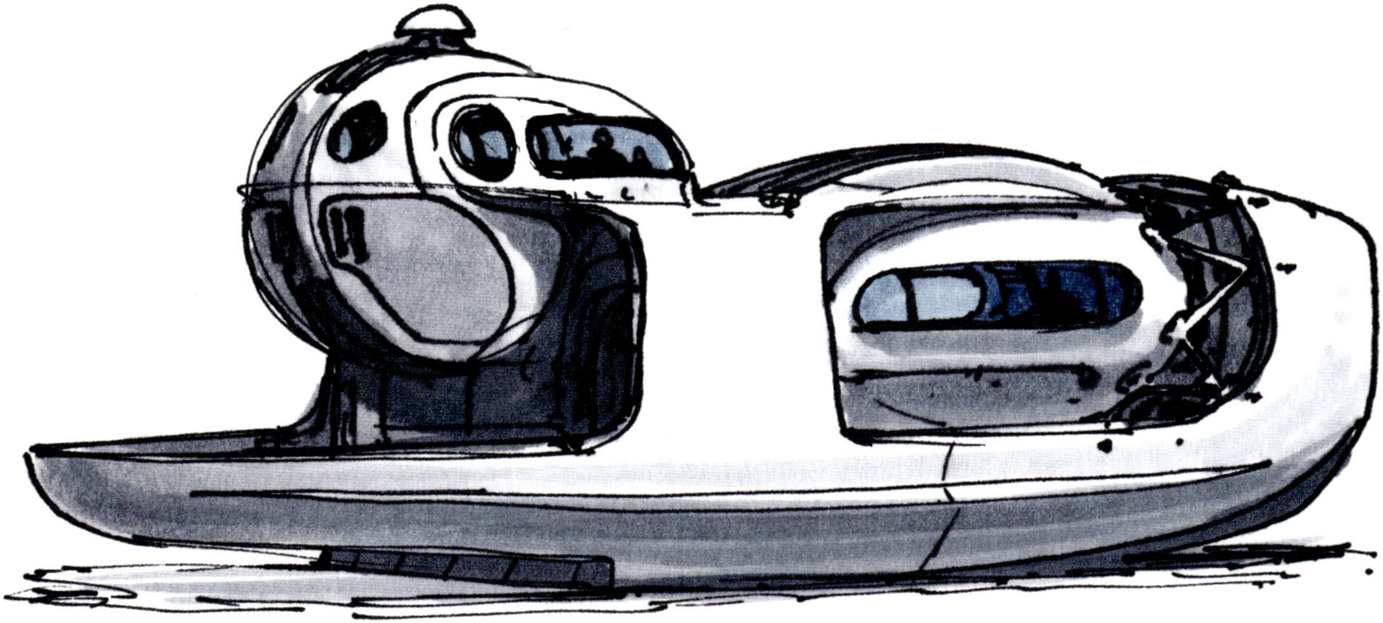

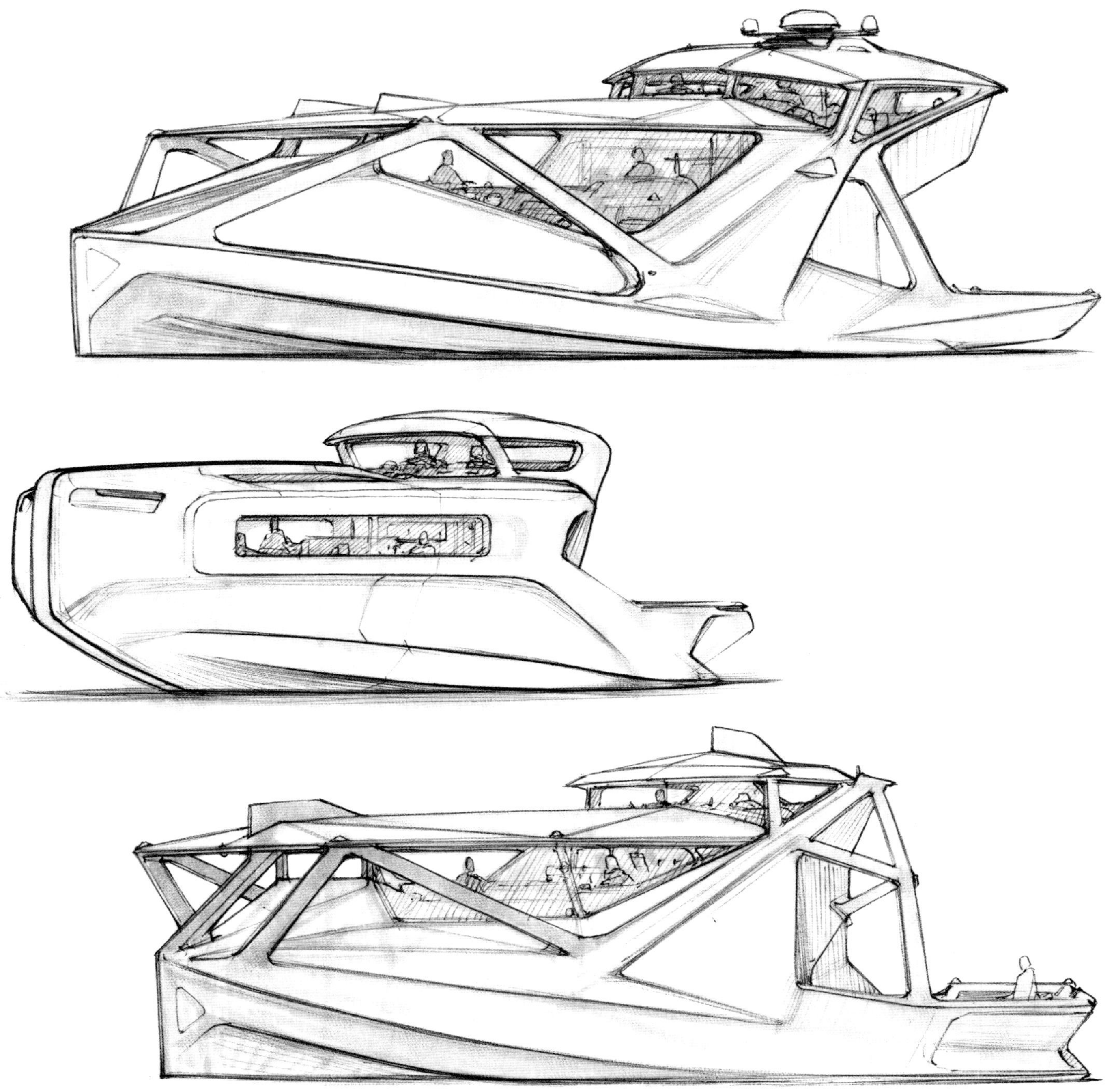

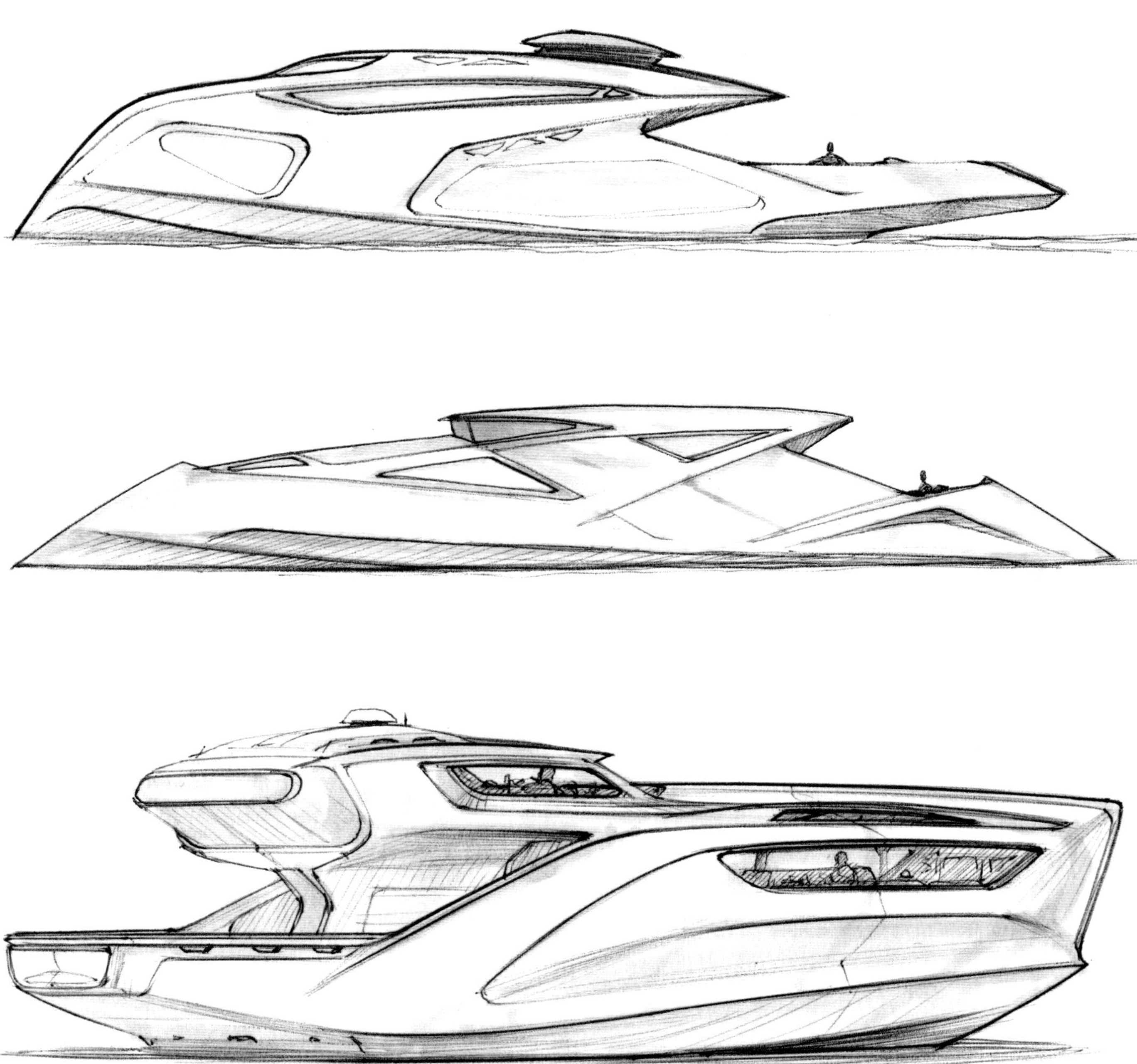

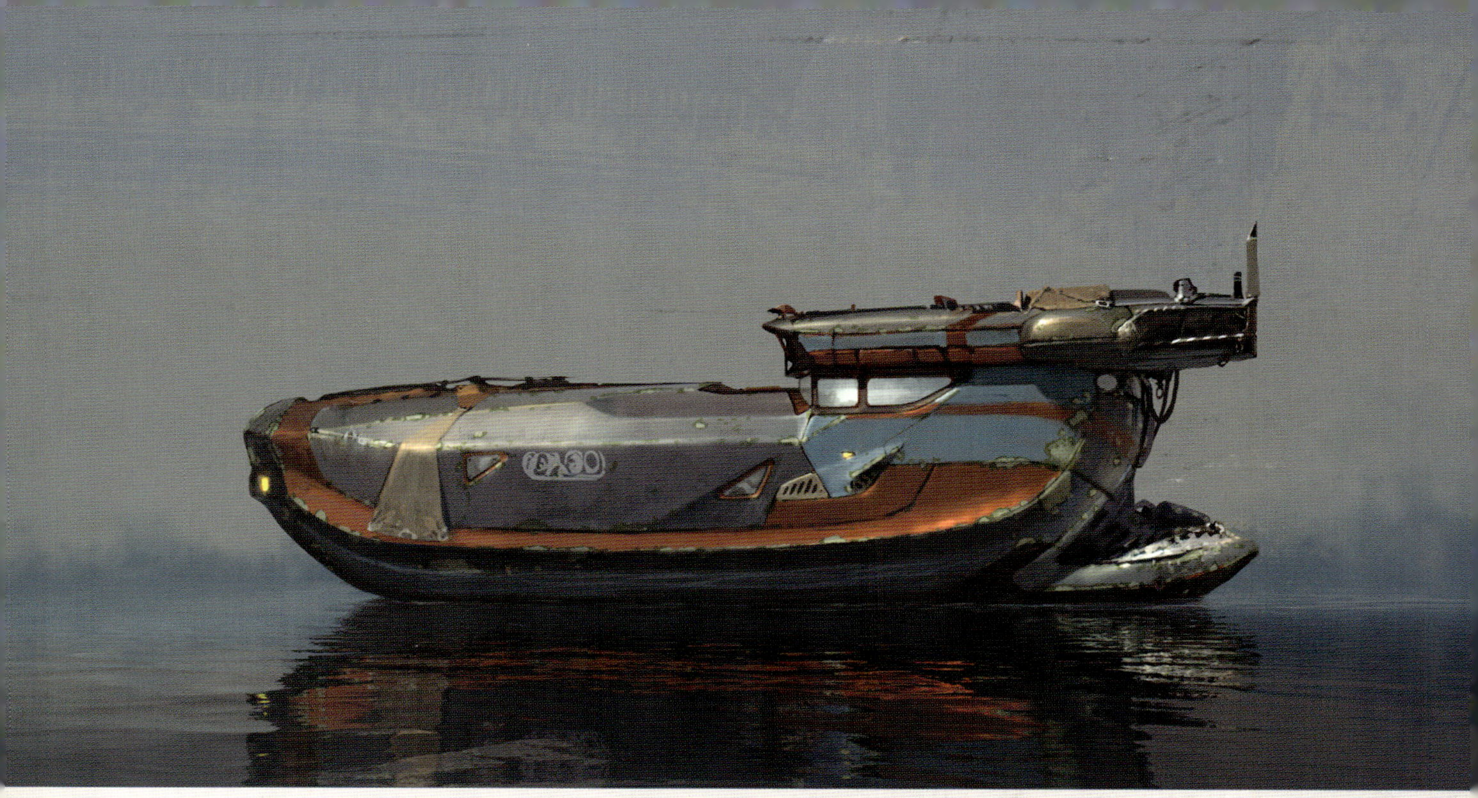

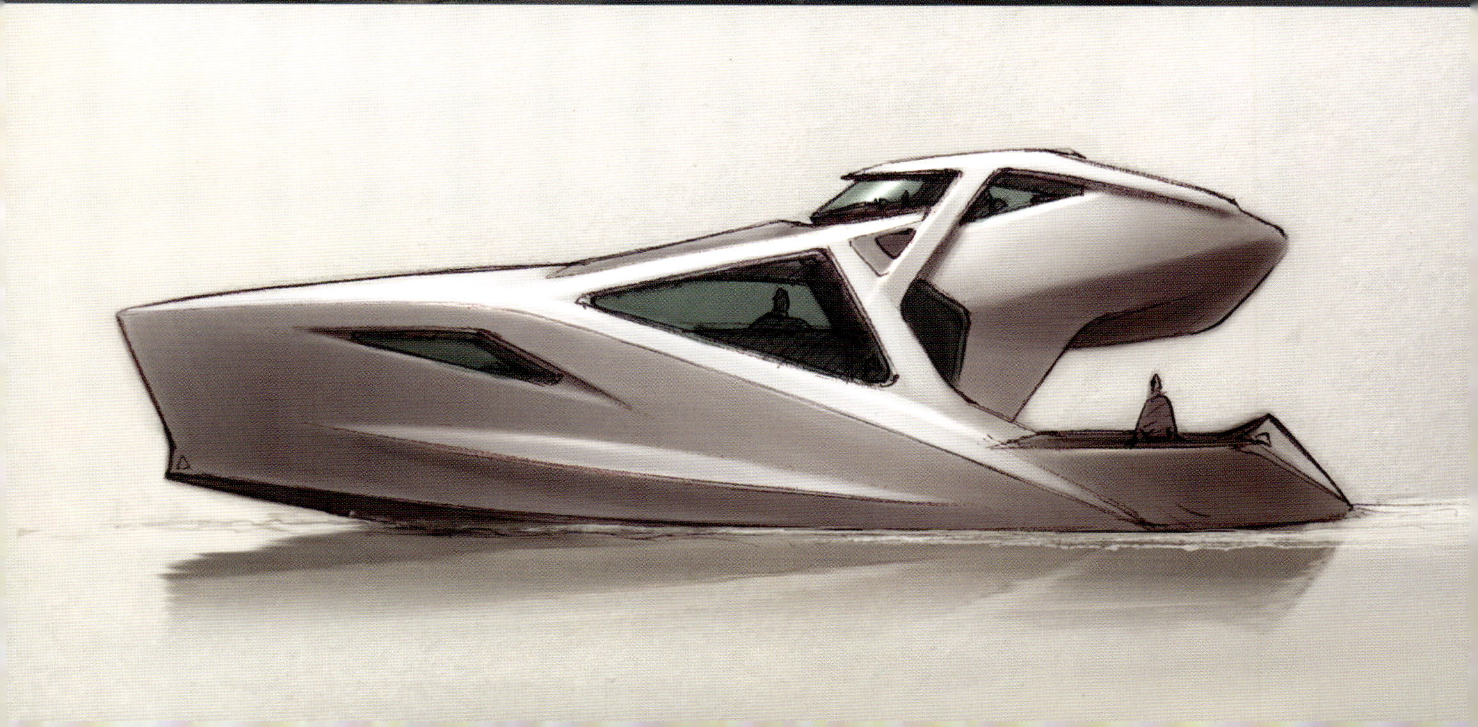

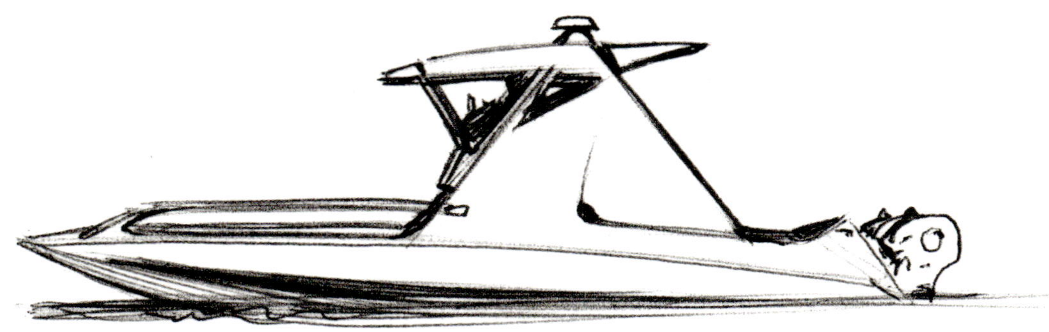

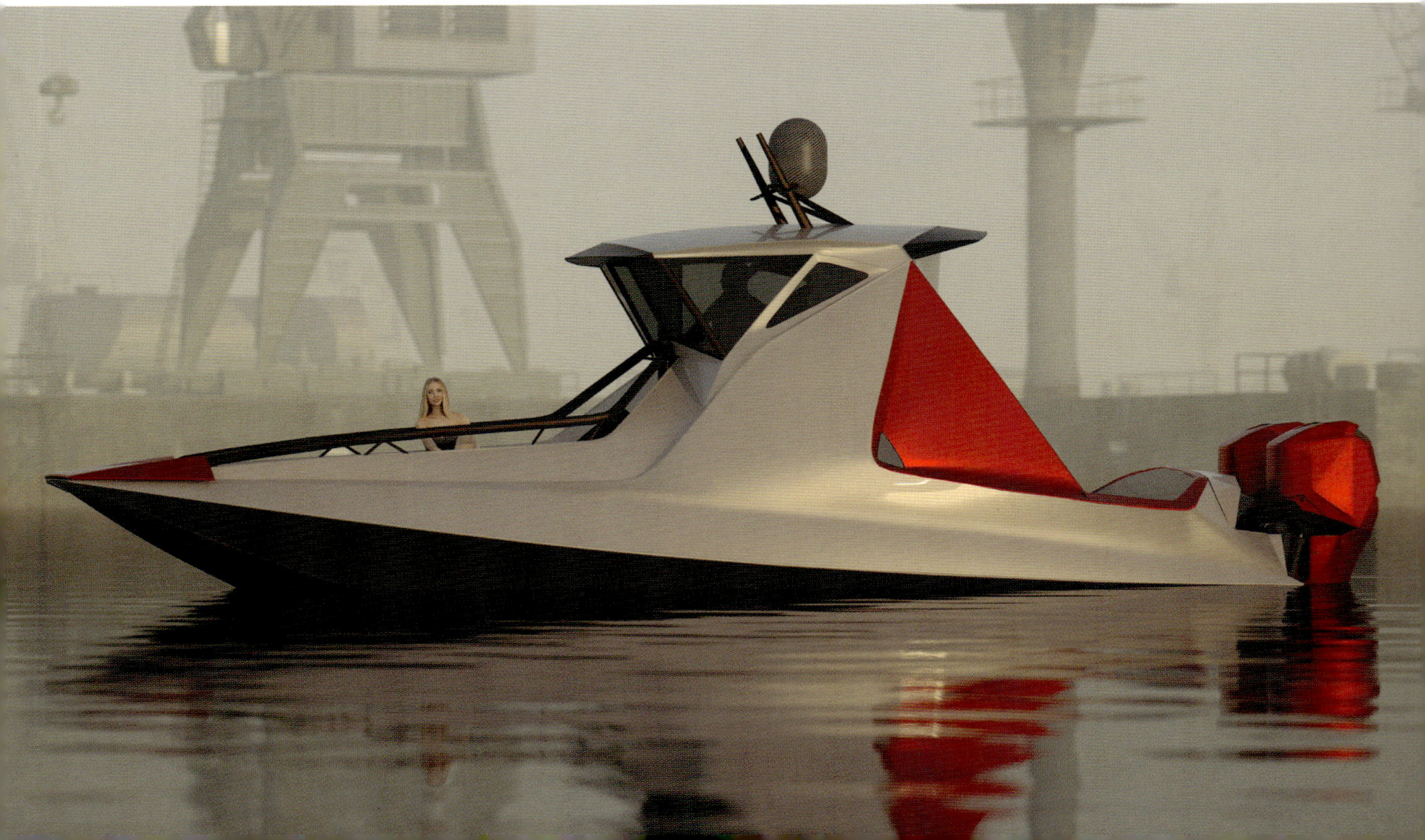

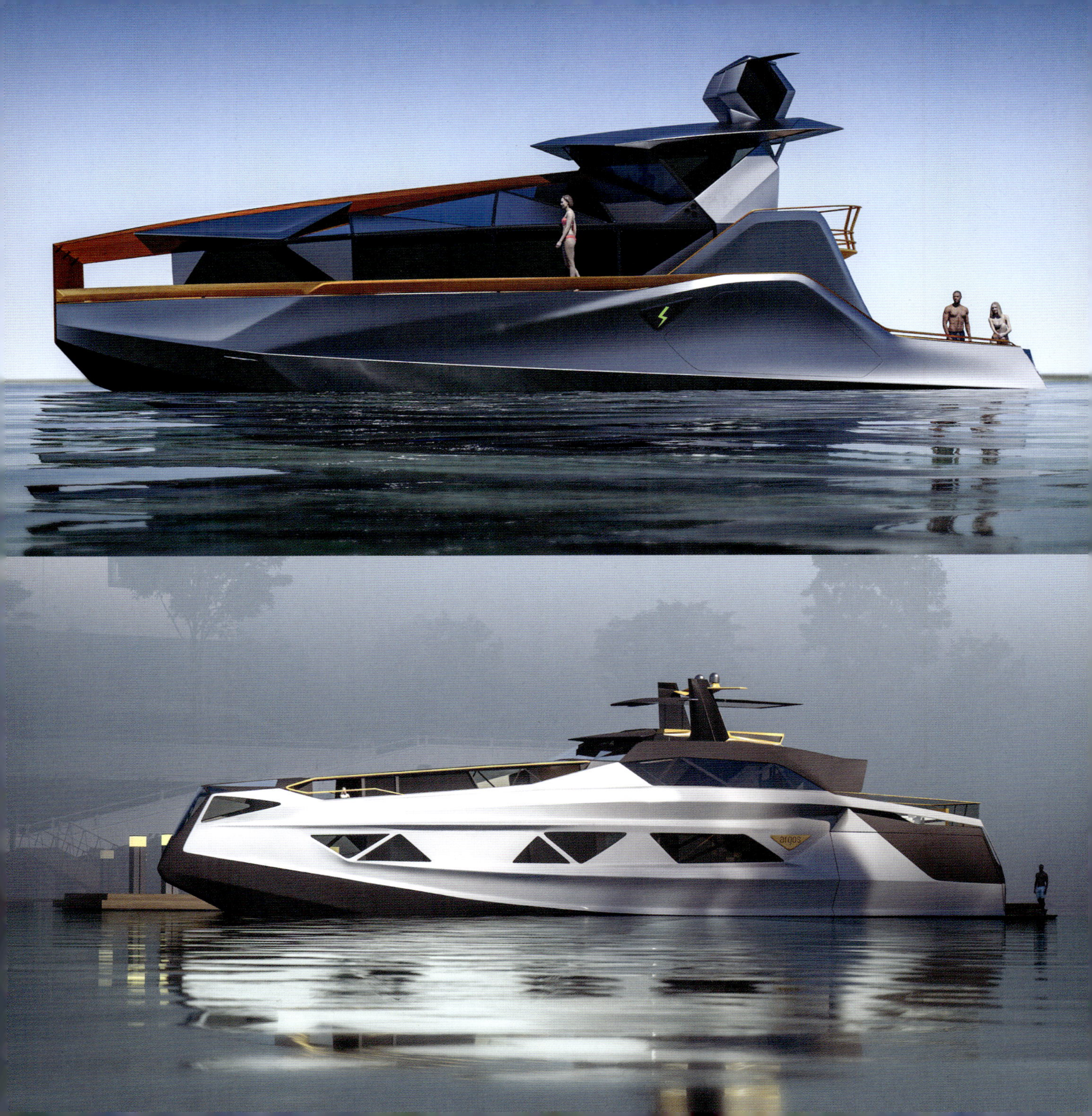

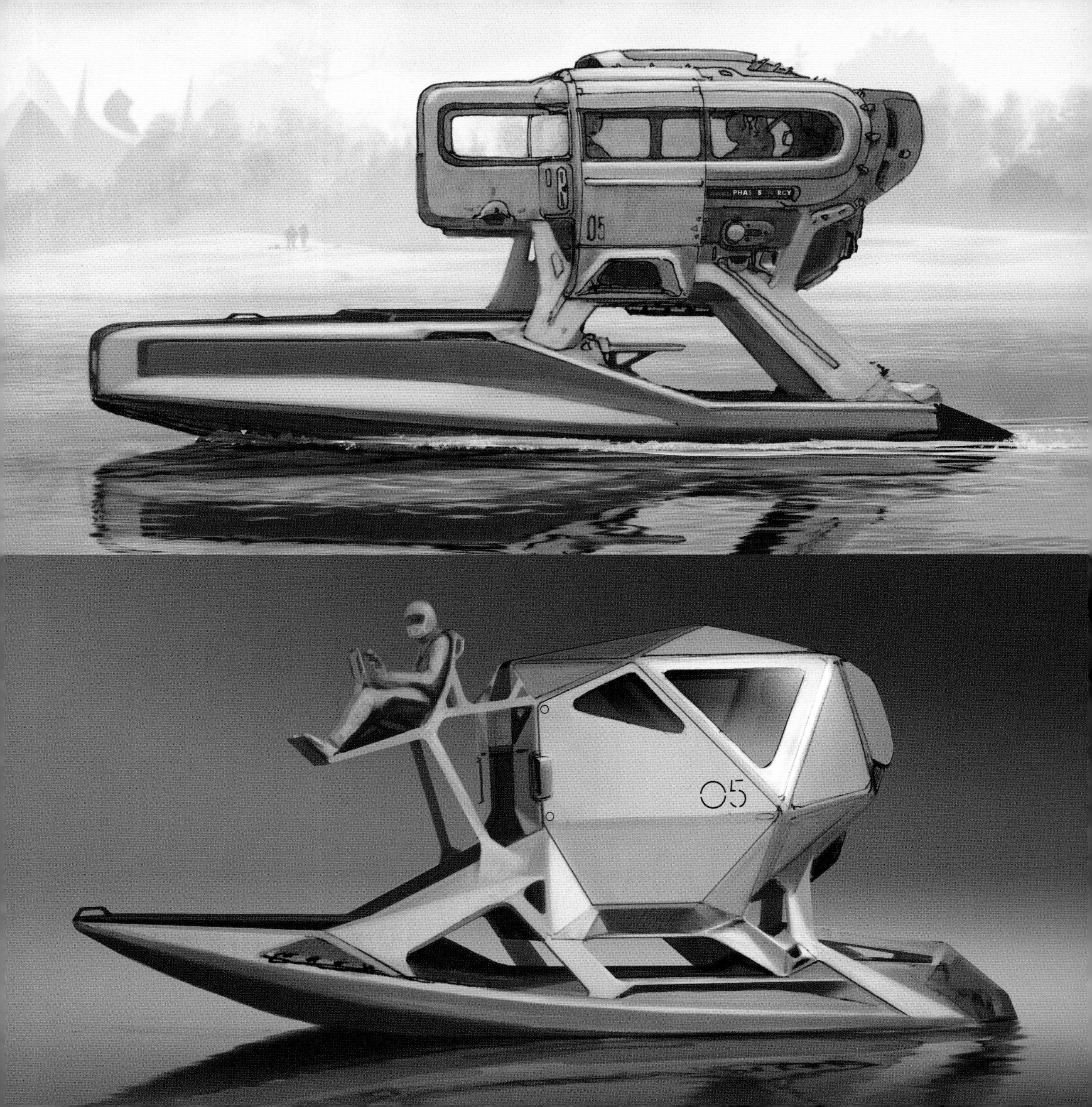
PHAS 5 RGY
05
05

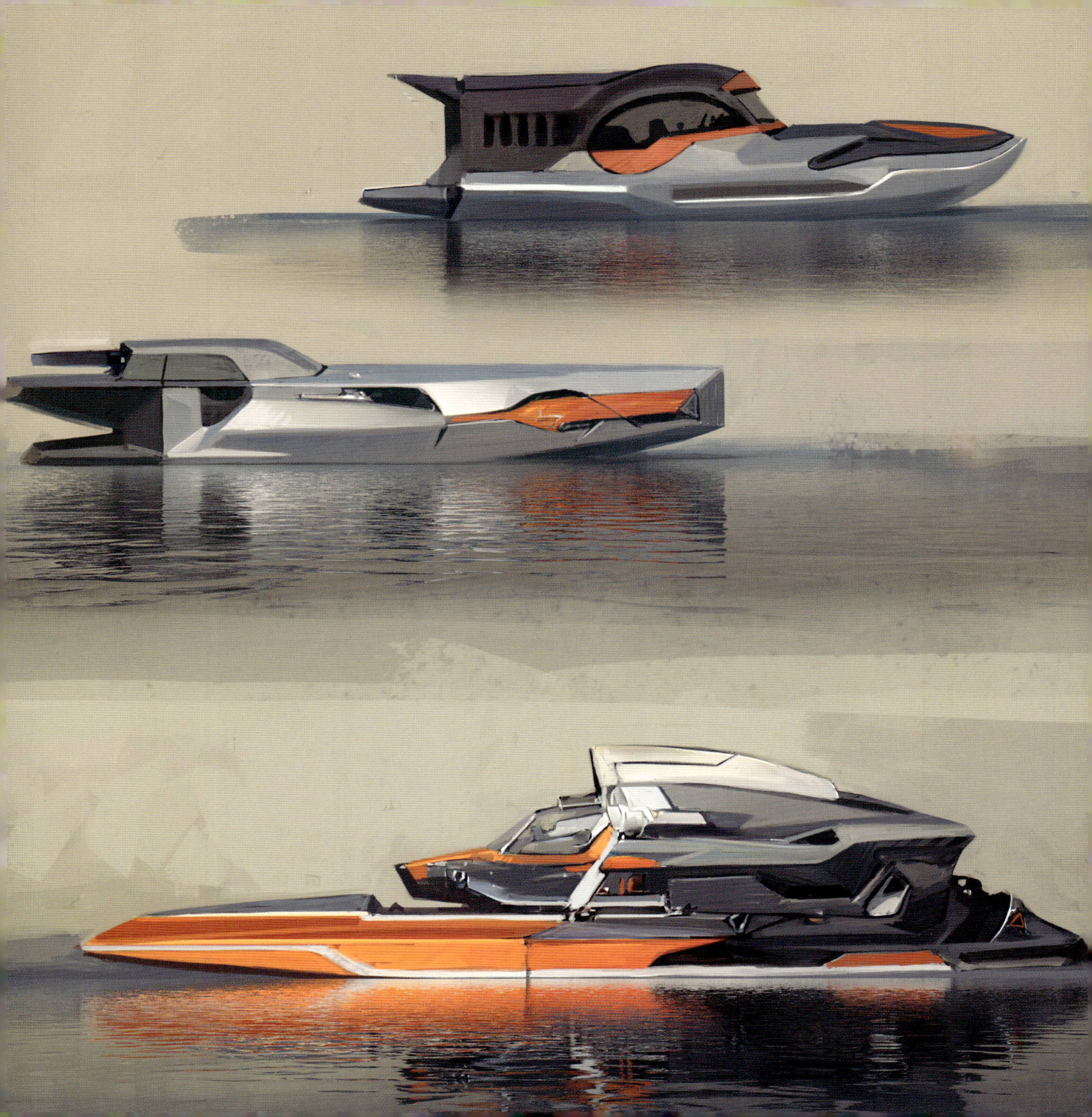

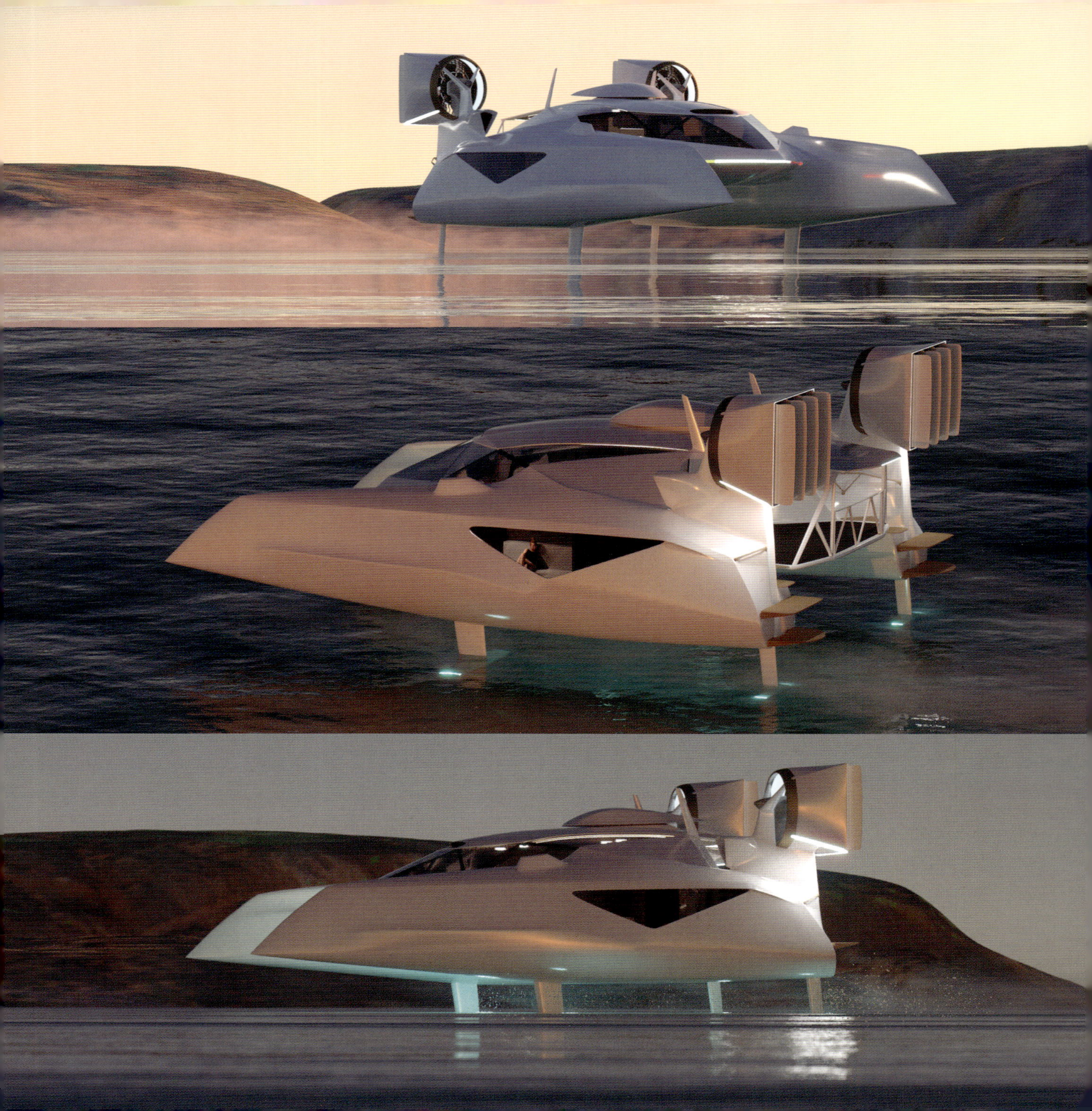

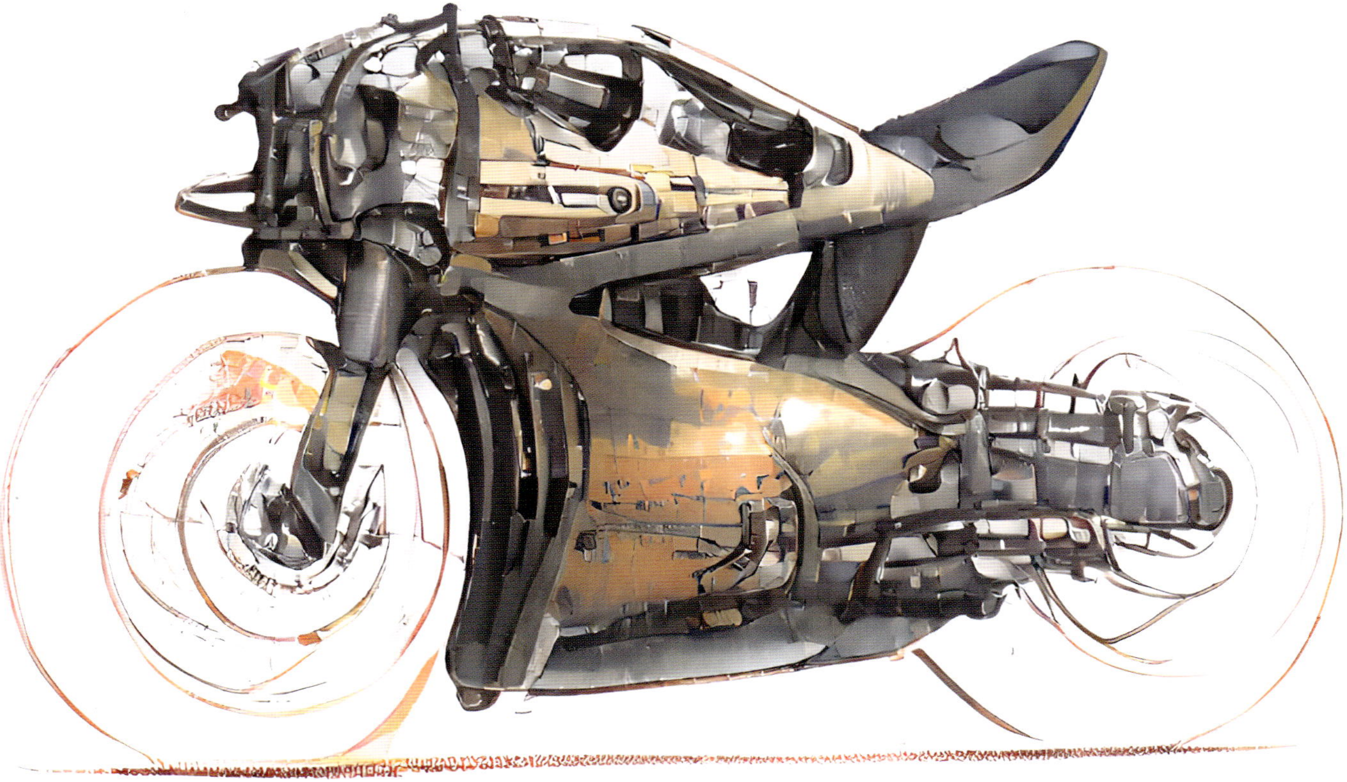

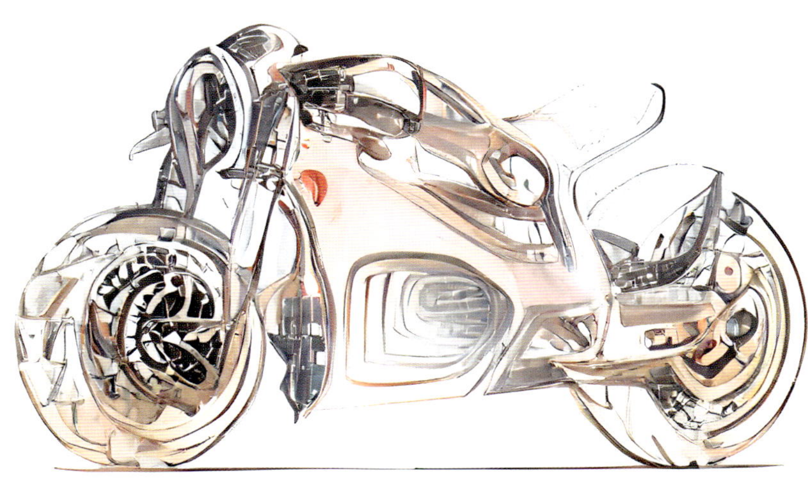

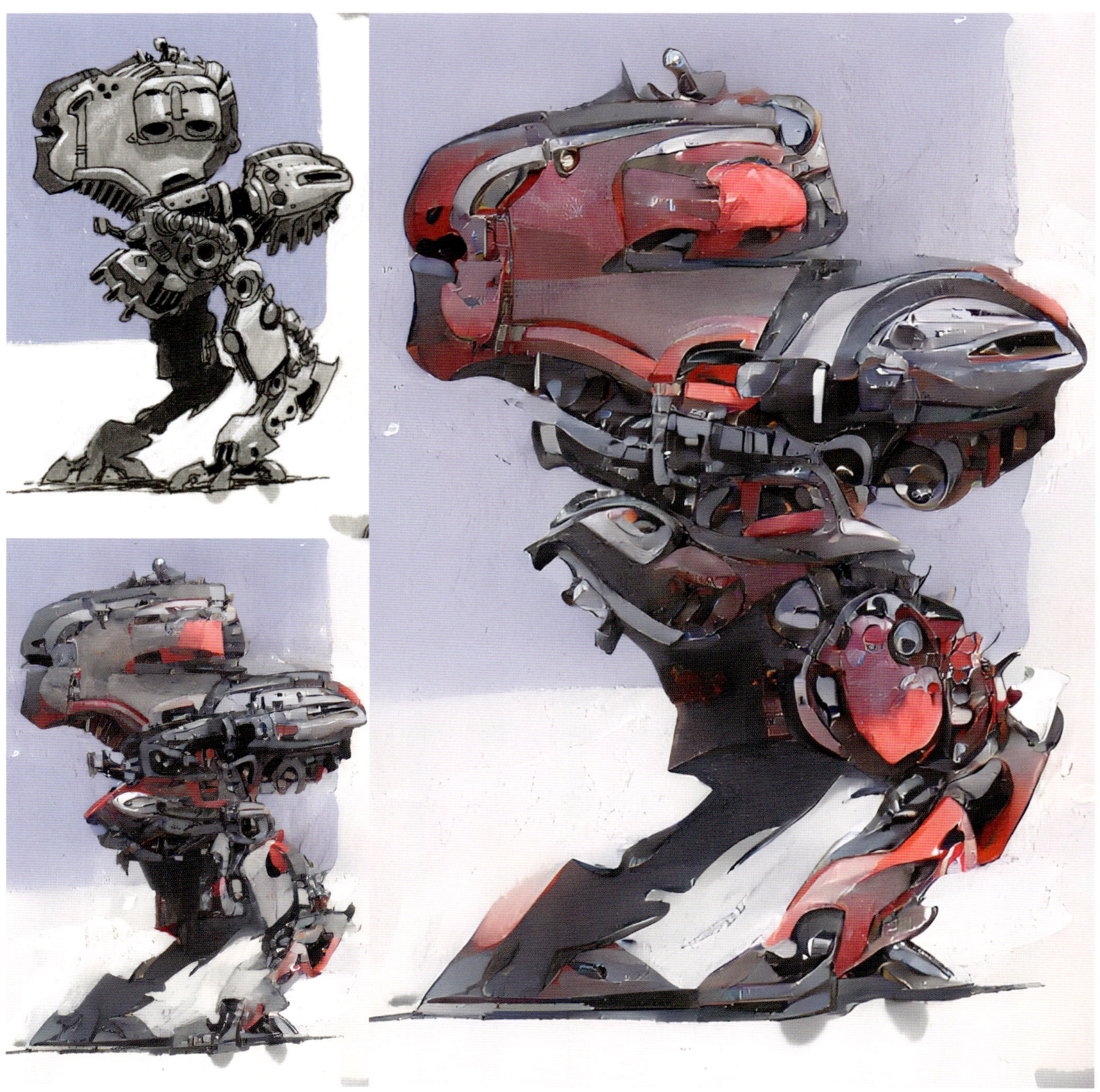

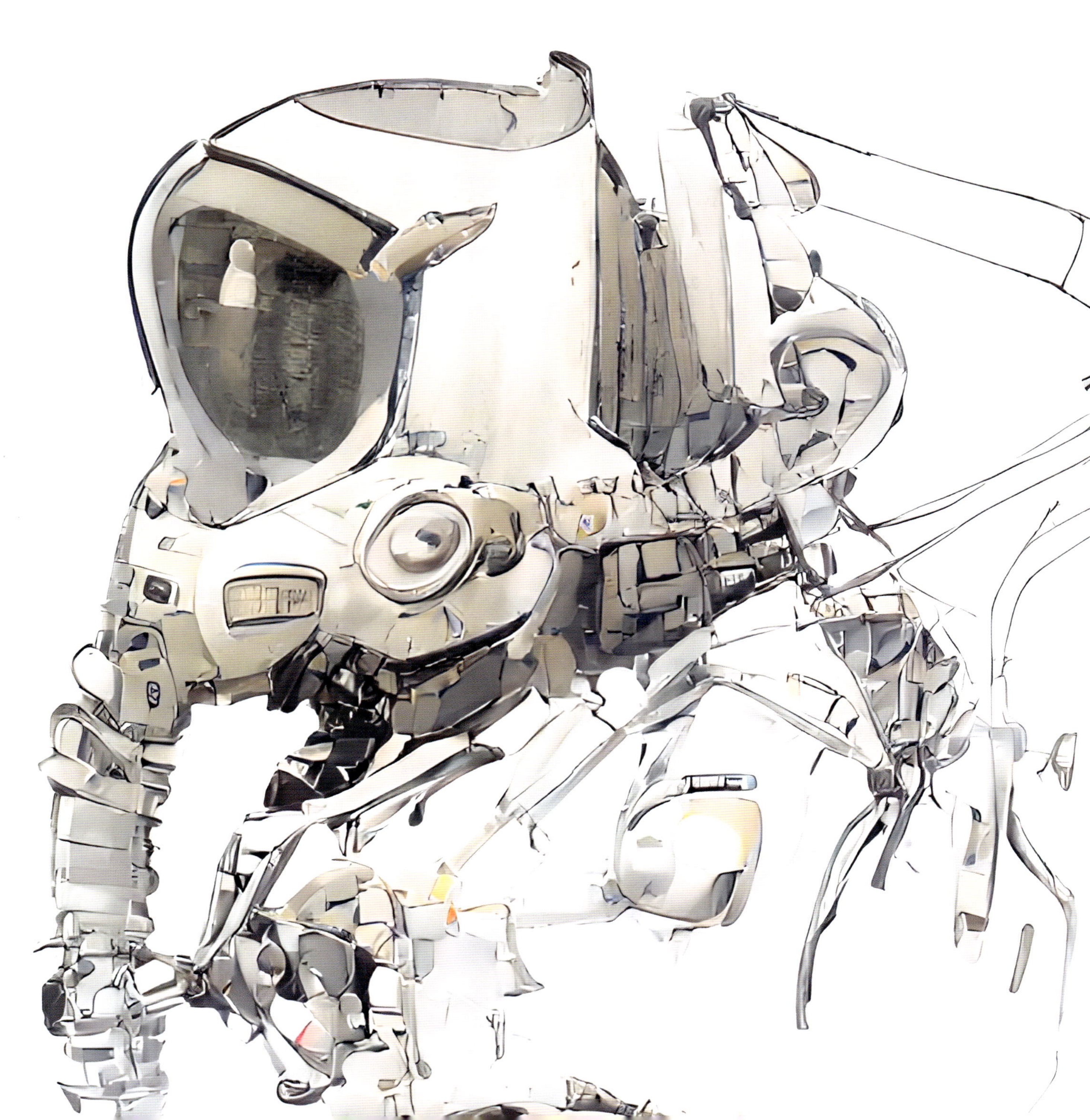

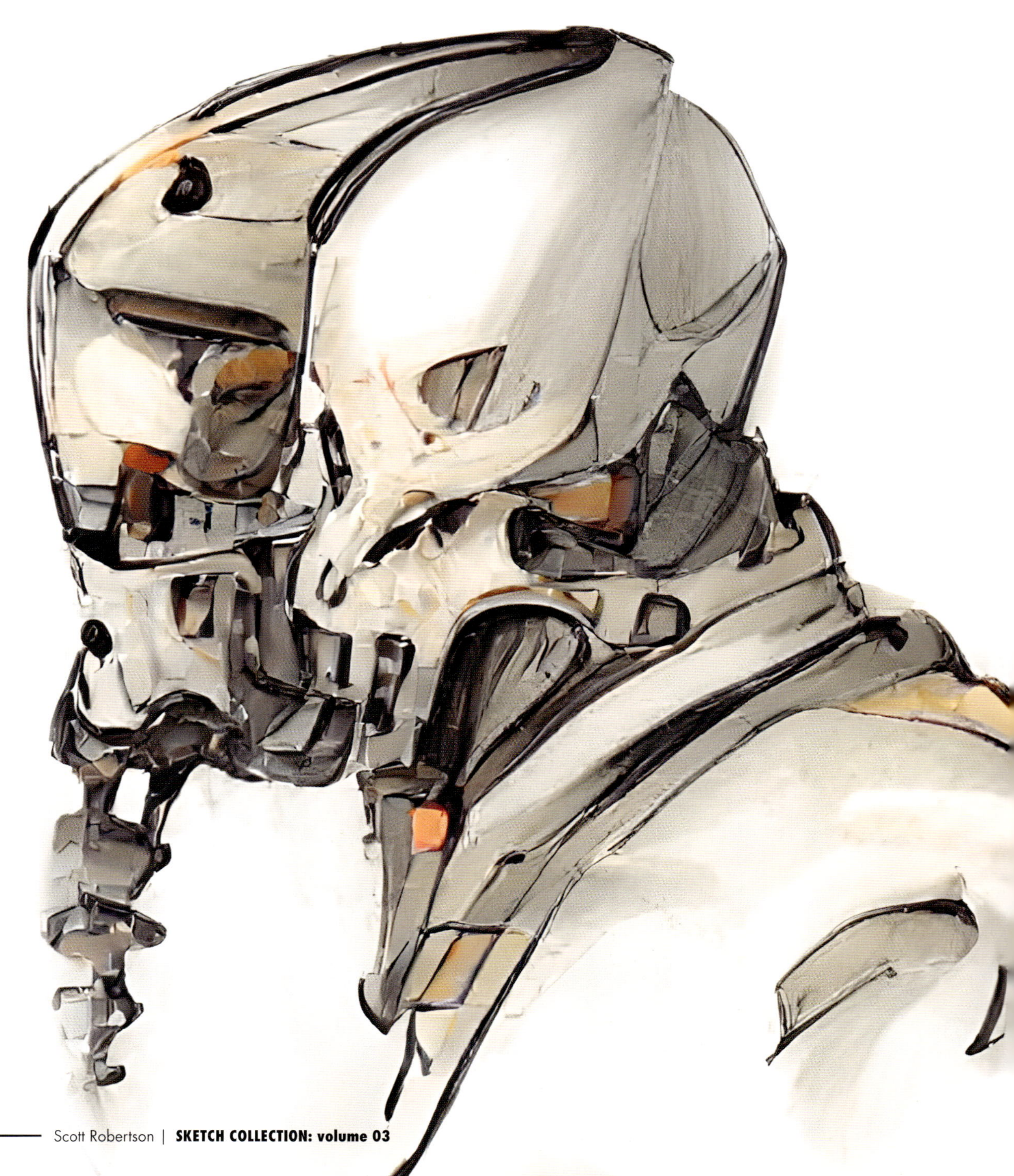

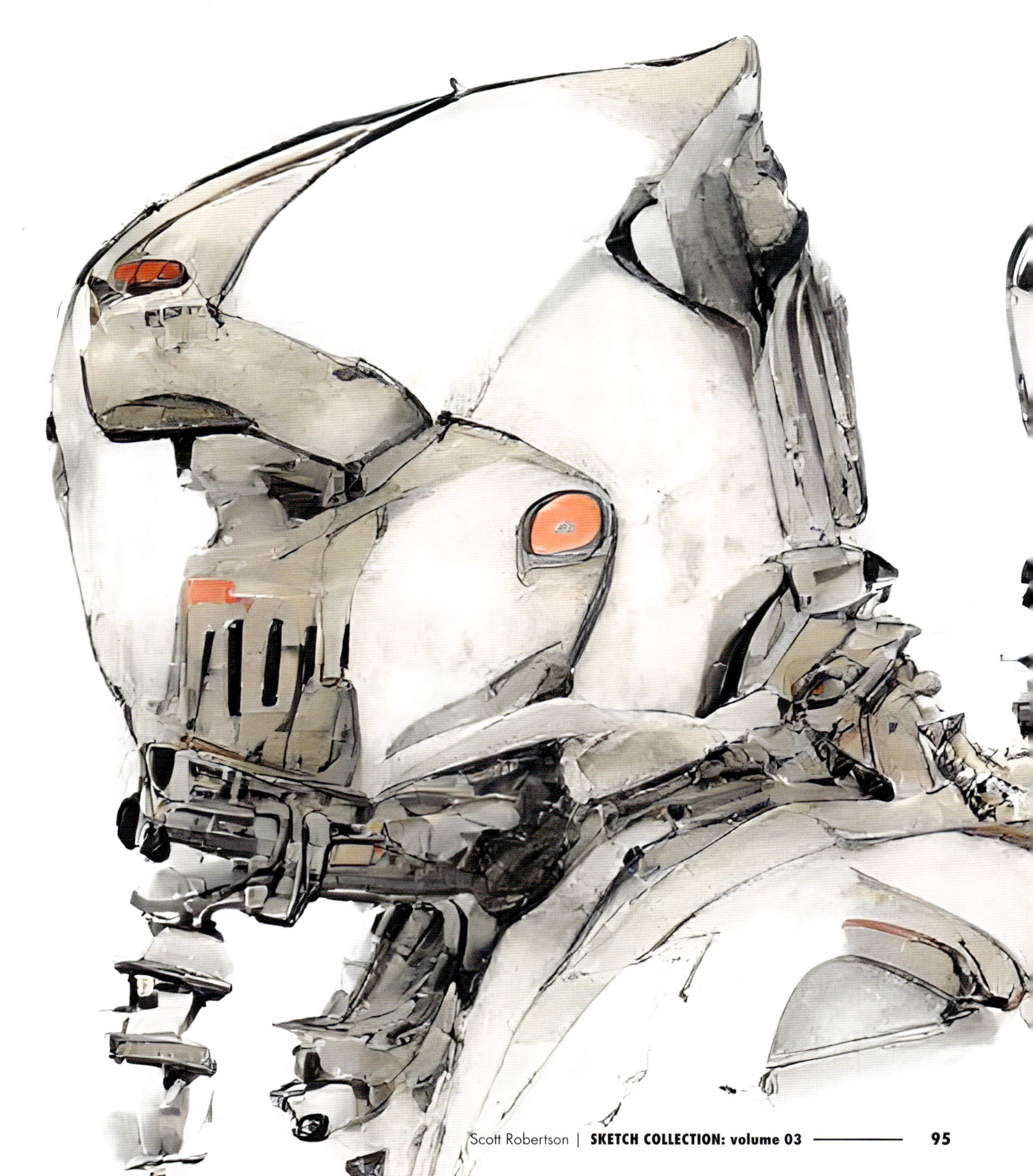

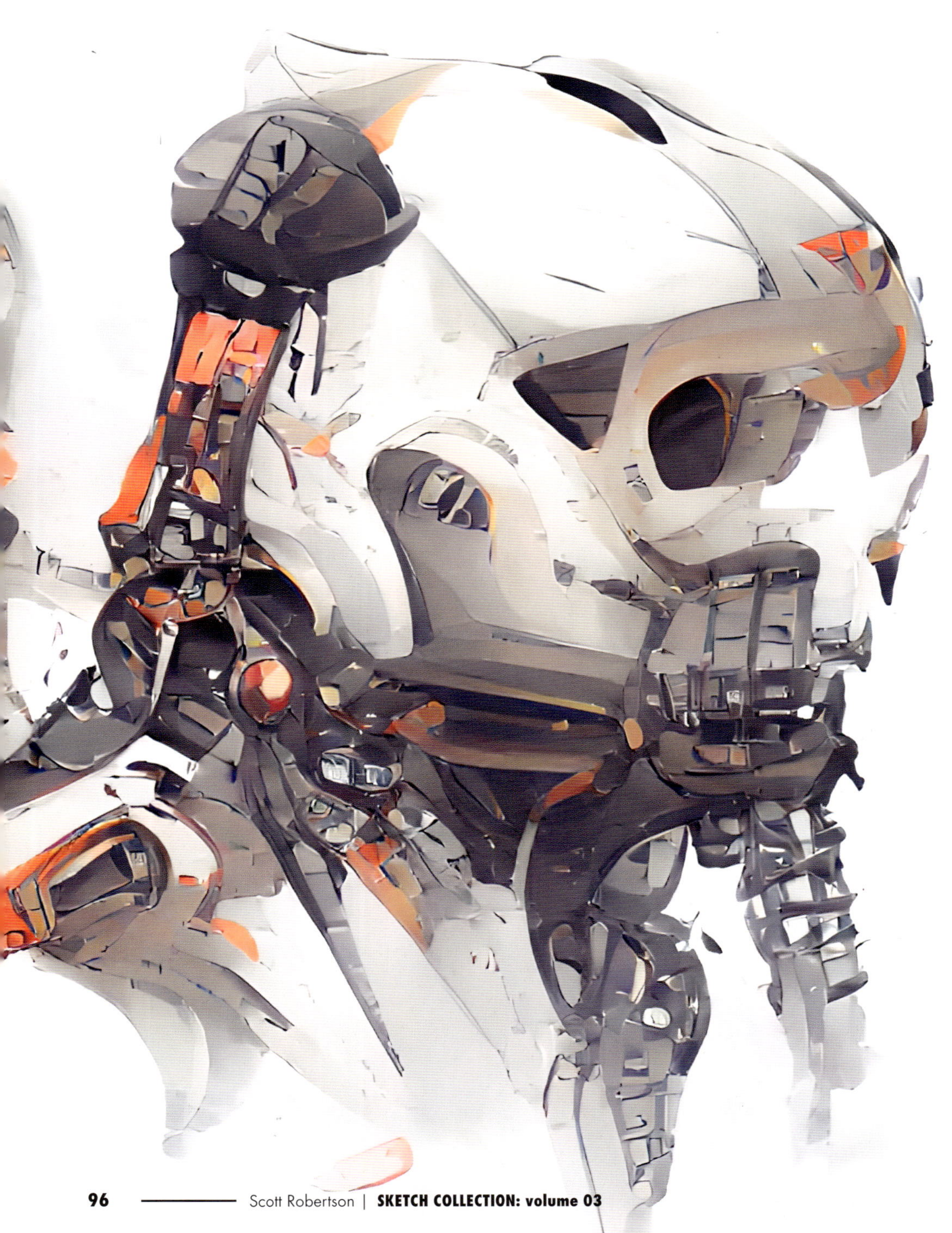

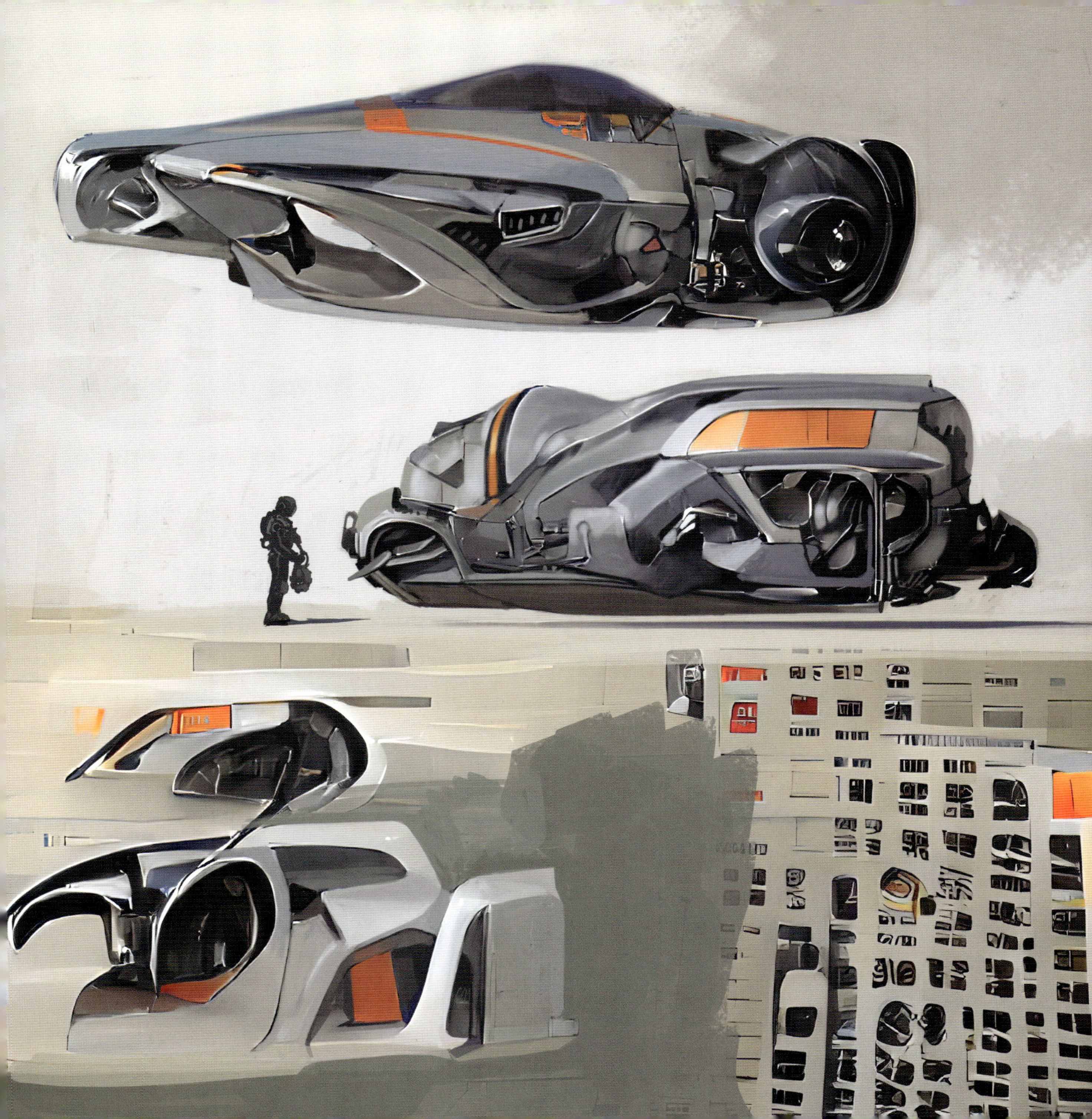

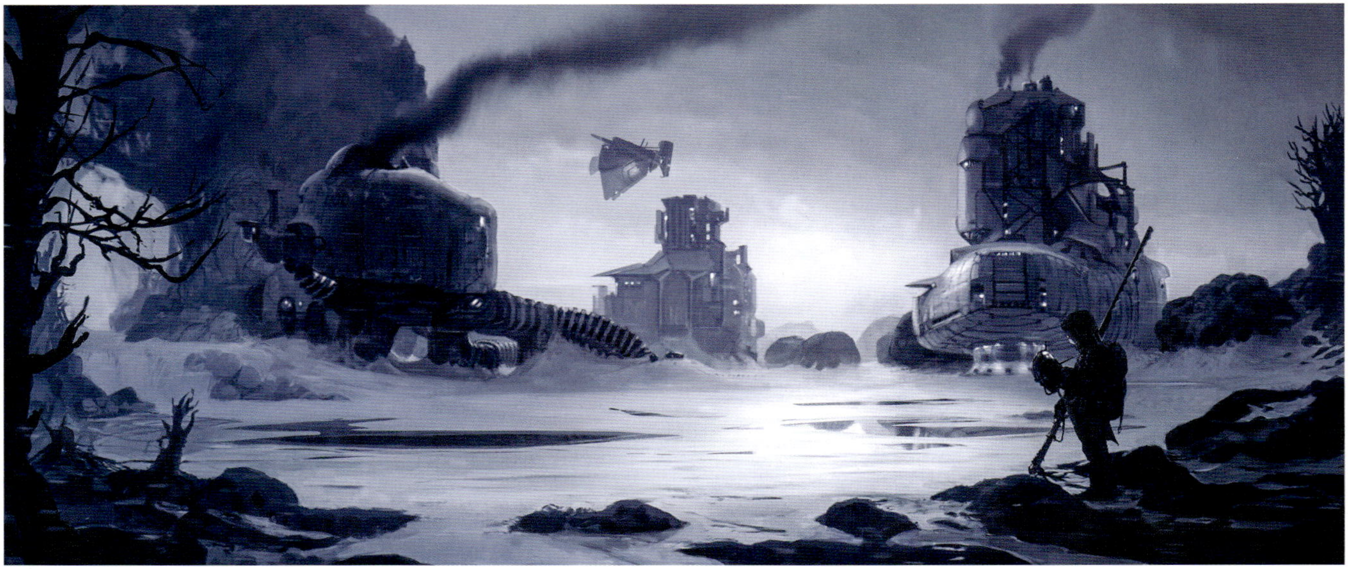

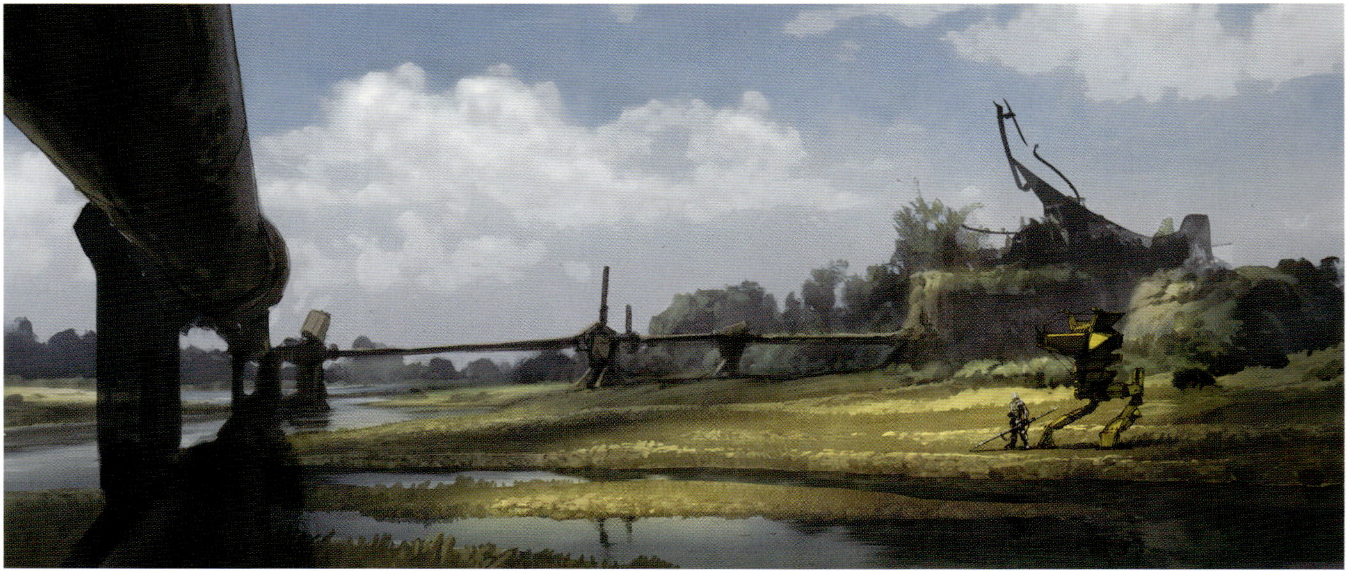

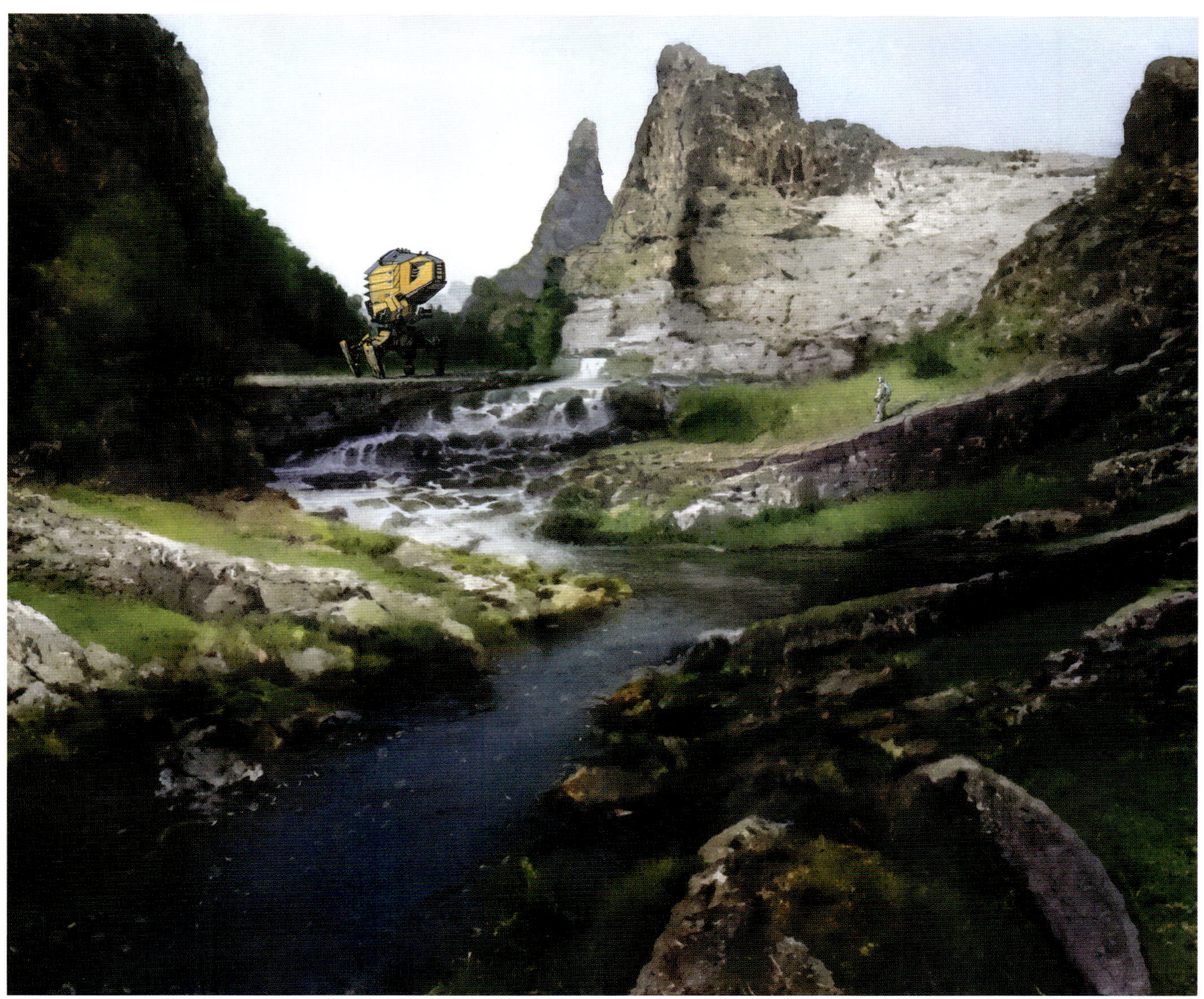

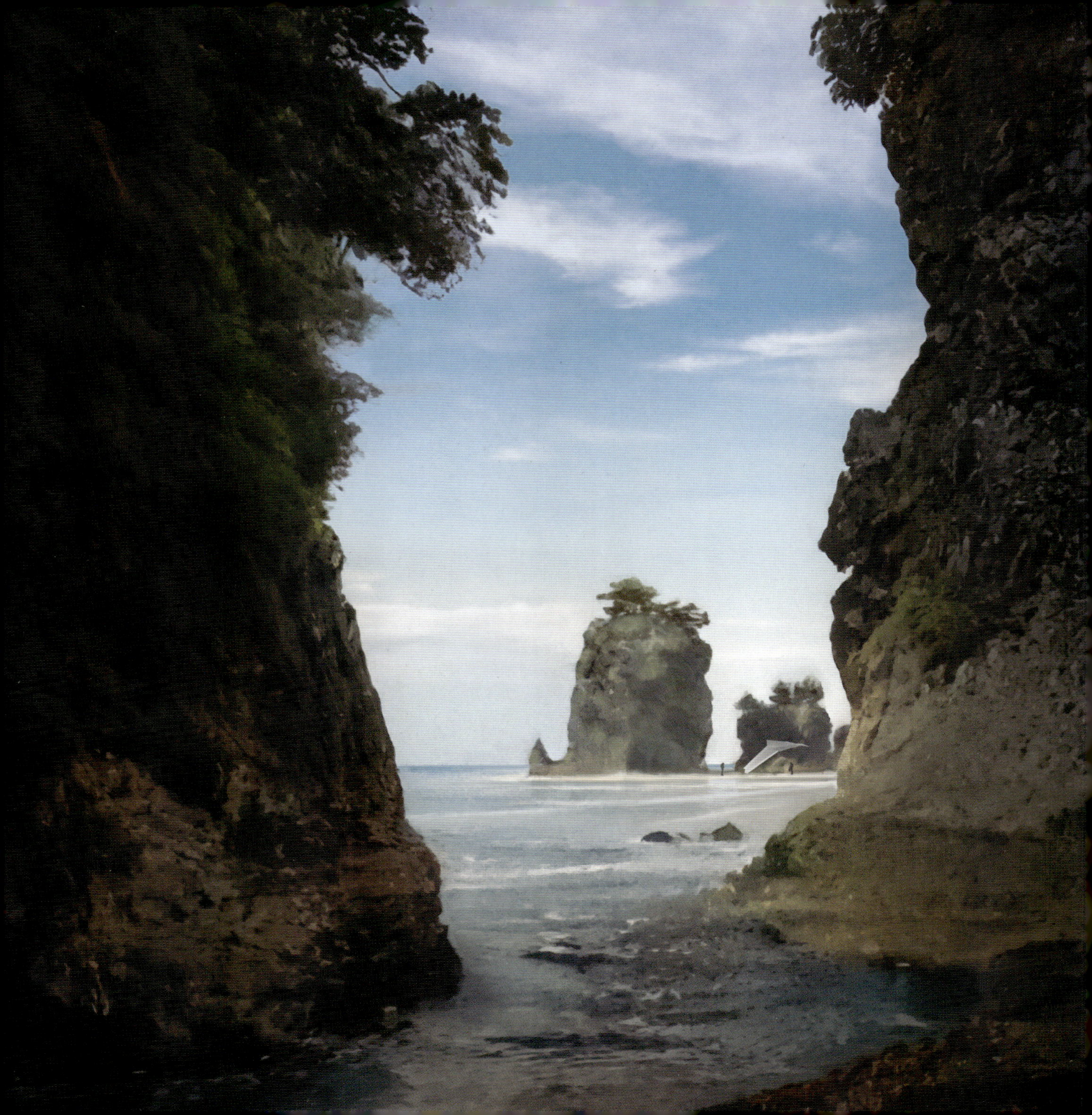

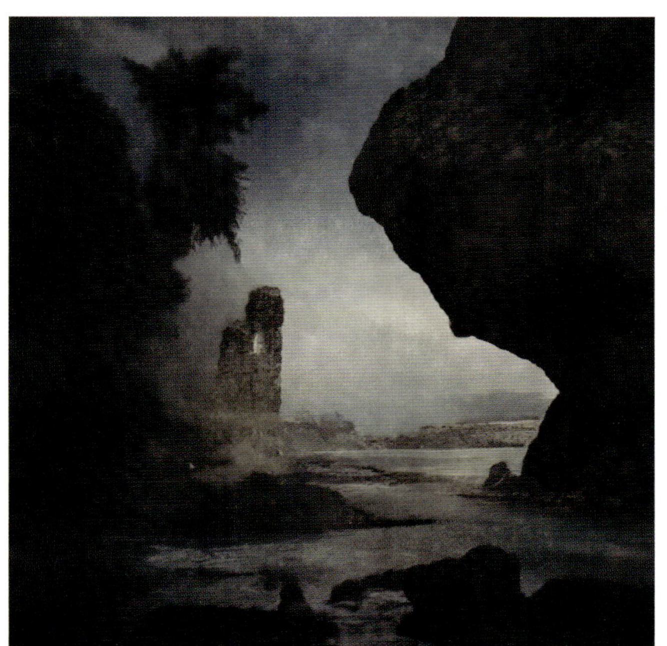

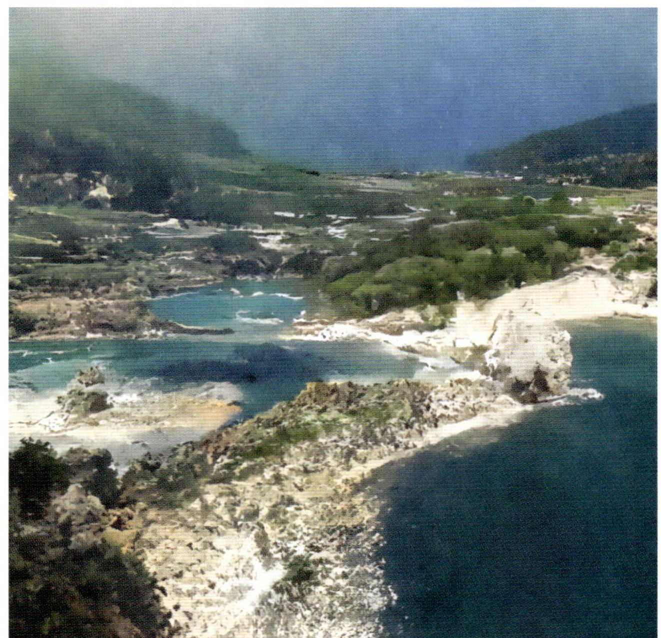

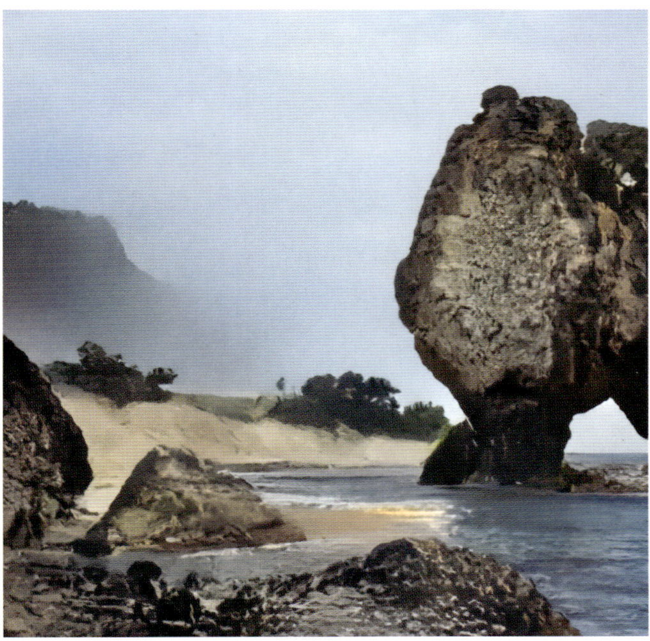

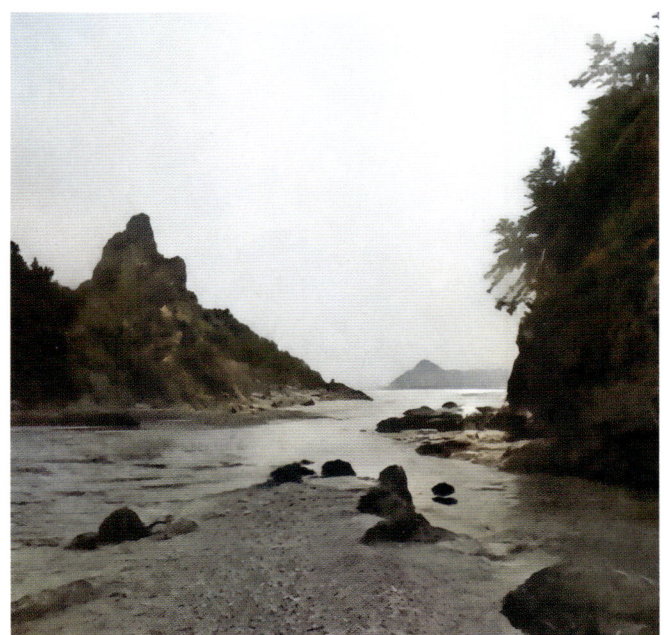

**Scott Robertson**
**Former Chair of Entertainment Design: ArtCenter College of Design**
**Designer / Author / Educator / Co-Producer**

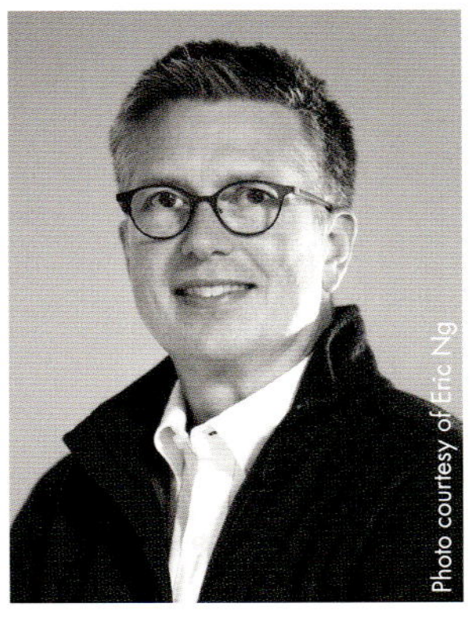

Scott Robertson is a world-renowned designer, author, and educator. After receiving a Bachelor of Science in Transportation Design from ArtCenter College of Design in 1990, his clients included Kestrel, Giro Sport Design, Nissan, Volvo, Yamaha, BMW subsidiary Design-works USA, Bell Sports, Mattel, Hasbro, Patagonia, Nike, Sony, Microsoft, Universal Studios, and Apple.

In 2002, Robertson founded Design Studio Press, a publishing company dedicated to art, design, and education, now with more than 100 titles released, including 13 he authored or co-authored.

Robertson taught industrial design at ArtCenter College of Design for 15 years, eventually creating their Entertainment Design department and serving as its chair. He frequently lectures around the world for various corporations.

Currently, Robertson is co-founder and CCO of AlphaCor Ltd., specializing in advanced motors, turbines, pumps, compressors, and clean energy systems for deployment in the energy, aerospace, nautical, agriculture, manufacturing, and transportation sectors.

Scott can also be followed or contacted online at:
**Facebook: www.facebook.com/scott.robertson.005**
**Instagram: @scoro5**

**X: @scoro5**
**contact email: scott@drawthrough.com**

---

## OTHER TITLES FROM SCOTT ROBERTSON

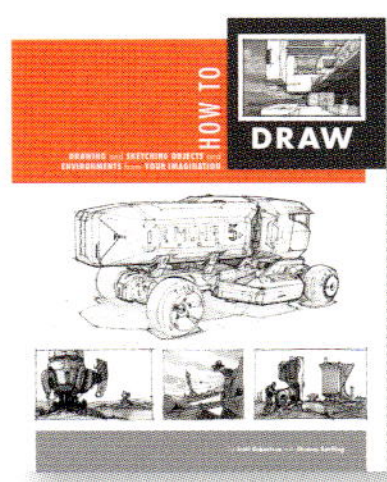

**HOW TO DRAW**
Paperback ISBN 978-1-933492-73-5
Hardcover ISBN 978-1-933492-75-9

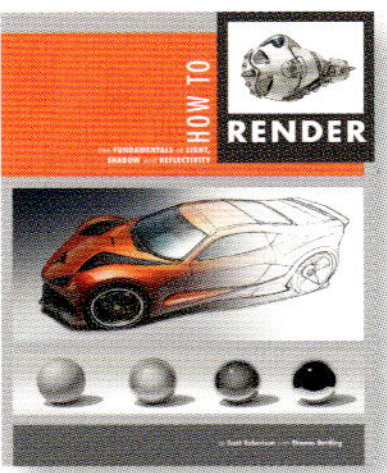

**HOW TO RENDER**
Paperback ISBN 978-1-933492-96-4
Hardcover ISBN 978-1-933492-83-4

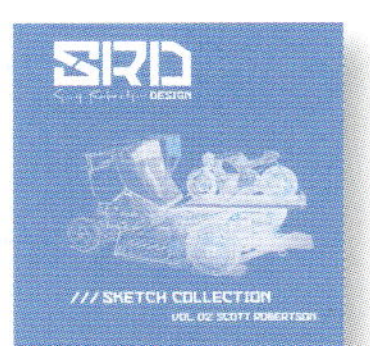

**SRD SKETCH COLLECTION VOL. 02**
Hardcover ISBN 978-1-624650-37-6

## SCOTT ROBERTSON DESIGN: YOUTUBE CHANNEL

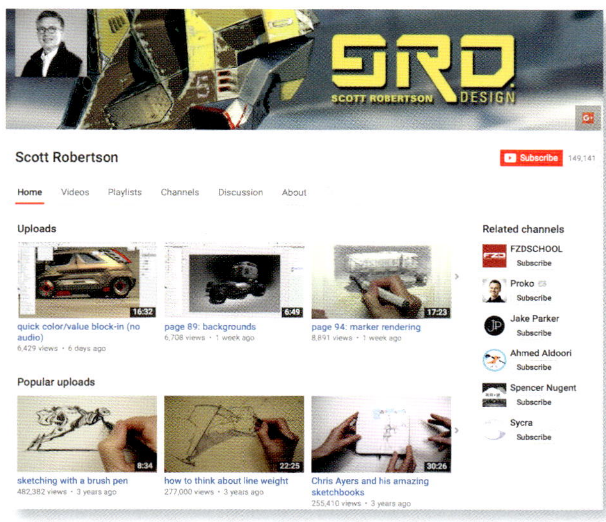

A great FREE educational resource is Scott's YouTube channel,
www.youtube.com/scottrobertsondesign

## SCOTT ROBERTSON DESIGN: GUMROAD

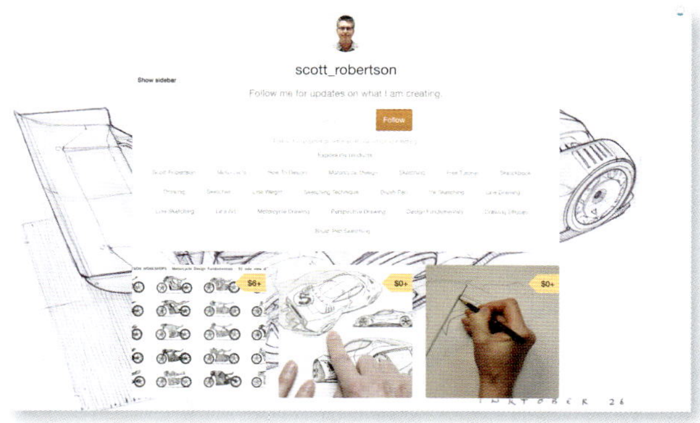

www.gumroad.com/scott_robertson

Published by Design Studio Press.



10 9 8 7 6 5 4 3 2 1

Printed in China
First edition, October 2024
ISBN: 978-1-624650-97-0
Library of Congress Control Number: 2024937186

To order additional copies of this book and to view other books
we offer, please visit: www.designstudiopress.com

For volume purchases and resale inquiries, please email:
info@designstudiopress.com

To be notified of new releases, special discounts, and events,
please sign up for our mailing list on our website. Follow us on
social media:

 www.instagram.com/designstudiopress

 www.facebook.com/designstudiopress

 www.threads.net/designstudiopress

www.x.com/DStudioPress

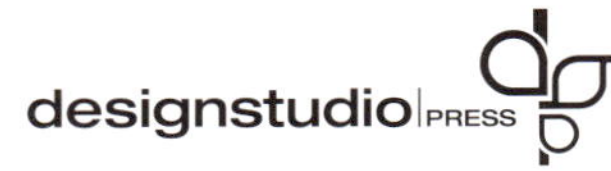

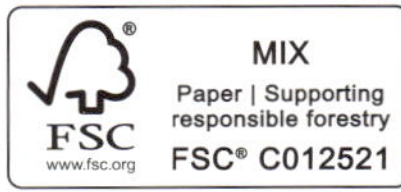